D1000704

Immigration and Education

The Crisis and the Opportunities

David W. Stewart

LEXINGTON BOOKS
An Imprint of Macmillan, Inc.
New York

Maxwell Macmillan Canada
Toronto

Maxwell Macmillan International
New York Oxford Singapore Sydney

Library of Congress Cataloging-in-Publication Data

Stewart, David W.
Immigration and education : the crisis and the opportunities / David W. Stewart.
p. cm.
Includes bibliographical references and index.
ISBN 0-669-24580-1
1. Children of immigrants—Education—United States. 2. Children of immigrants—Education—Social aspects—United States. 3. Intercultural education—United States. 4. Education, Bilingual--United States. I. Title.
LC3746.S74 1993
371.96'75'0973—dc20 92-38157
CIP

Lexington Books
An Imprint of Macmillan, Inc.
866 Third Avenue, New York, N. Y. 10022

Maxwell Macmillan Canada, Inc.
1200 Eglinton Avenue East
Suite 200
Don Mills, Ontario M3C 3N1

Macmillan, Inc. is part of the Maxwell Communication Group of Companies.

Printed in the United States of America

printing number
1 2 3 4 5 6 7 8 9 10

To Billie

Contents

List of Illustrations

Preface

The new and distinctive immigration that the United States has been experiencing since about 1965 is one of the great social forces of our time. Its import and impact are already well understood in places such as Los Angeles, New York, Chicago, Miami, and El Paso. But in Akron, Salt Lake City, Little Rock, Memphis, Bangor, Sioux Falls, and hundreds of other American cities where the new immigrants have yet to make an appearance in large numbers, there is much less awareness of the new world that will also come to them.

American educational and training institutions and agencies are on the front lines of the effort to greet immigrants and to help them productively engage themselves in the life of this country. As an adult educator, I have been cognizant of the need expressed by many of my colleagues to gear themselves to serve this new clientele better. My initial intention was to write a book that would limit its focus to the education and training of immigrant adults; however, it quickly became evident that the real need was for something of wider scope. Others have taken on studies of quite discrete parts of the whole: bilingual education, English as a second language, and refugee education, for example. But a comprehensive view of the education and training of the "new immigrants" did not exist and was needed as the base for understanding of the interrelatedness of the several parts.

My intent in this book is to describe and analyze the educational and training needs of immigrants in the new and distinctive inflow. Described and analyzed, too, are the effects of pressures exerted by the newcomers upon institutions and agencies of education and training that are often quite unprepared for the task that is being presented to them. In some places, difficulties have reached crisis—even explosive—proportions.

But if problems associated with the new immigration are identified in this book, so too are the opportunities. At this crucial time in its history, the United States has openings to capitalize on the vast array of human energy and talent that exists within the pool of new arrivals. The lessons being learned by educators as they serve the new client groups will surely have applications across the board in the nation's educational mainstream. The good health of democracy in our country to a large degree hinges upon the success of these efforts.

Immigration and education are each, in themselves, very intricate and sensitive subjects. An author combines them and tries to make sense of the brew at considerable risk. I received from various sources subtle nudges not to tell all of the truth about some rather touchy matters. I have ignored these sometimes well-meant suggestions; I do not see any other ethical course of action for anyone whose root motivation is that of improving educational opportunities for immigrants. Sensitive subjects are faced head-on—with tact, it is hoped, as well as honesty. Though some may differ with my conclusions, I trust that no group will find that its position has been erroneously described or in any way distorted on these pages.

A vast number of persons, many of whom possess far more experience and expertise than myself in various aspects of this rich story, supplied valuable assistance that has helped me over many hurdles. I wish to acknowledge their contributions. No less than eleven very busy persons read all, or substantial portions, of this manuscript and provided valuable feedback and corrective. They were Bill Bliss, Donald Ranard, David Simcox, Henry Spille, Cordia Strom, Elva Laurél, Carol Mares, Alma Gamez, Denise McKeon, Elizabeth Midgley, and H. Susan Schneider. Not all of them agree with all of my conclusions, and they should not be held accountable for any of them. Errors, if any, are not theirs but mine.

In addition, the publisher sent an early draft of this manuscript to two readers for comment. One returned it with high praise. The other had a different reaction and was quite critical of some aspects of my approach to the task. I would like to thank both of these individuals (whose names I do not know), but especially the critic. She was right, and I have made changes that are generally in line with her constructive commentary.

Assistance of an indispensable sort was provided by those who helped me to find my way through unfamiliar channels in strange cities. Dr. Elva G. Laurél, curriculum director of the Edinburg Consolidated School District, saw to it that I had three very productive days of interviews and visits not only in Edinburg but in much of South Texas. In El Paso, Sue McElligott took me in tow, arranging productive visits and sessions with a number of teachers, administrators, researchers, and business personnel. And I could not have found my way in Los Angeles without the good offices of Alma Gamez and Carol Mares of the Los Angeles Unified School District, who exude passion along with competence in their efforts to provide quality educational services for adult immigrant clients. The world needs more of their kind.

Competent librarians and research assistants are essential if a task such as this is to be performed well. I was fortunate, as always in the past, to receive valuable guidance from many members of the superb staff at the Library of Congress. Staff members of the Gelman Library at The George Washington University were also helpful; for the record, that institution does have materials that the Library of Congress does not. Jill Bogard, librarian at the National Center for Higher Education, took a personal interest in my project, alerted me to a number of good sources, and was never too busy to help. Scott Piroth provided valuable research assistance, saving me many hours of toil.

My editor at Lexington Books, Beth Anderson, is a person of extraordinary competence. Her skills as a professional editor are accented by a sense of tact that served her well in interactions with a tired and sometimes myopic author. If this book is a quality piece of work, she deserves some of the credit. Production supervisor Carol Mayhew and her staff also were most helpful in preparing the manuscript for publication. They saved me from a number of errors and inconsistencies. I am indebted to a large group of people representing community-based organizations and agencies who met with me in Austin, Texas, to discuss their perceptions of the implementation of the Immigration Reform and Control Act amnesty provisions in their state. Their commentary vitally advanced my understanding of both the problems and the opportunities inherent in the amnesty education effort.

The following individuals gave generously by making themselves available for interviews or providing significant information by telephone or letter: Terri Ackerman, Susan Alexander, Sandra Amendola, Norma Plascencia Almanza, Robert Atwell, Ben Avila, Amara Bachu, Emory Biro, Kathryn Susor Bricker, Leonard Britton, Patrick C. Burns, Robert Brzozowski, Ron Cabrera, Noe B. Calvillo, Joyce Campbell, Argelia Carreon, Luis A. Catarineau, John Chapman, Cynthia Coburn, Nydia Cope, JoAnn (Jodi) Crandall, Enrique Cubilos, Mary Clare Walsh Curry, Evelyn Dai, Denise de la Rosa, Jorge H. del Pinal, Phyllis Dorsey, Jamie Draper, E. B. Duarte, J. David Edwards, Richard Estrada, Kim Ferari, Viktor Foerster, Paul Galbraith, Dennis Gallagher, Safar Gerabagi, Dale Goff, Debbie Good, Eugenio Gutierrez, Carl Hampe, Christine M. Hanson, Wilbur Harper, Willie Harris, Roderick Harrison, Andy Herrera, Julia Grimaldo-Herrera, Sharon Hershey, Mike Hoefer, Marguerite Riviera Houze, Eric Huelsman, Eva Hughes, Bertha Ilizastigui, Sharon Jindrick, Karen E. Johnson, Karen M. Kennelly, Nick Kremer, Susan Lapham, Van Le, Margaret Lee, José Lo, Jean Lowe, Jim Lyons, Edith MacArthur, Raphael J. Magallan, Mary Mahoney, Inaam Mansoor, Consuelo Marcelino, Luis E. Marquez, Brooke Martic, Jana Mason, Eliza May, Allan Mazerov, Jack McGrath, Ursula Mehrländer, Doris Meissner, Richard (Mike) Miller, Cecelia Muñoz, David North, Terry O'Donnell, Richard A. Orem, Richard Okun, Lydia Fernanez-Palmer, Robert M. Paral, Jeffrey S. Passel, Marie Pees, John Perez, Margo Pfleger, Luis F. B. Plascencia, Ron Pugsley, Bogdan Pukszta, Mark Ross, Nazy Roudi, Pavlos X. Roussos, Leonard Rowland, Harpreet Sandhu, Jorge G. Sanchez, Mary Lou Schmidt, Lila Silvern, David Smith, Richard Smith, Martha Spencer, Dan Stein, Dennis Terdy, Carmel Thompson, Norm Thompson, Humberto J. Tijerina, George Tryfiates, Don Vickers, Robert Warren, Denise Wilson, and Linda J. Wong. Several other individuals were interviewed but prefer that their names not be acknowledged. Their assistance is nonetheless appreciated.

My wife, Billie, to whom this book is dedicated, has been inspiring and supportive, as always, as I worked at this task. I also thank my mother-in-law, Mattie Stephens of Burnet, Texas, and her kin for providing the bed and board that greatly facilitated my research in their home state. This includes Sue McElligott in El Paso, T. M and Vonne Jarvis in Corpus Christi, Grace and Ervin Gabbert in McAllen,

Harold and Rose Stephens in Edinburg, and Norman and Mary Carolyn Stephens in Mission.

I am greatly indebted to Bill Kroger for giving me the idea for this book. I owe an equal debt to James Murray for his assistance in locating and approaching a publisher. Finally, I thank those members of Congress who were responsible for passage of the Freedom of Information Act. Some of the information that appears in this book would not be here without it.

David W. Stewart
Washington, D.C.

1

Through (or Around) the Golden Doors: A History in Brief

The world's people are on the move in one of the most massive population shifts in history. The implications for both sending and receiving nations are very significant, though they are not generally well understood.

Measured as a proportion of population growth, immigration to the United States is at the highest level since the decades between 1900 and 1910, when it accounted for 27.8 percent of growth in the number of U.S. residents. More than one-third of the nation's population growth in the decade of the 1980s was the result of immigration.[1] Currently, the United States admits nearly as many legal immigrants and refugees as the rest of the world combined.[2]

The U.S. Census Bureau projects that between nine and twelve million immigrants, a record number, will enter the United States in the 1990s. Urban Institute researchers Barry Edmonston and Jeffrey Passel estimate 1990 immigration from all sources at about 1,070,000 and project increases to 1,125,000 by the year 2005.[3] The larger numbers will in part result from a substantial increase in legal admissions authorized by the immigration law passed by Congress in 1990. The balance will come from refugee admissions, as well as a swelling tide of illegal immigration.

Moreover, the source countries of the influx have changed significantly during the twentieth century. Europe, once the chief source of immigration to the United States, has been eclipsed by other source areas since passage of the Immigration Law of 1965. For example, in the 1980–90 period, the proportion of visas issued to immigrants coming from Europe amounted to only 10 percent. At the same time, the share of Asian immigrants rose to 48 percent; Latin Americans accepted for immigration during the same period constituted 35 percent of the total. If illegal or undocumented immigrants are counted, the proportion of Europeans becomes even smaller.[4]

Many of the newcomers to the United States, as in years past, qualify as "tired . . . poor . . . huddled masses . . . wretched refuse of other teeming shores," to borrow some phrases from a well-known American lady. But others, by recent congressional decree, are drawn from the ranks of the skilled, the educated, and even the wealthy of other nations. By any standard, it is a new immigration, and it is a phenomenon that must be accommodated more effectively by educators in the United States.

Assumptions

Two basic assumptions undergird this analysis of education and the new immigration in the United States. First, heavy immigration (in both its legal and illegal manifestations) will continue and even increase in the foreseeable future. World political and population pressures, as well as a U.S. political environment that favors immigration—or at least resists structures of it—will assure this result.

Second, the social and economic health of the United States depends upon greatly improved educational and training opportunities for immigrants. Under present haphazard arrangements, immigrants are not receiving the educational opportunities they deserve and are severely straining the resources of institutions and agencies that are ill prepared to receive them. The costs of improvements to the system will be substantial. These expenditures are paltry, however, when compared to the far greater and very damaging economic and social costs of inaction.

The First Arrivals

The new challenges that face the United States need to be related to our history of immigration and education. Over the more than two centuries of the nation's existence, immigration policy has evolved from one of almost total openness during frontier days to the restrictive era of the 1920s, 1930s, and 1940s to the once-again liberal policies that began in 1965. George Washington set the tone of the early days in proclaiming that the "bosom of the America is open to receive not only the opulent and respectable stranger, but the oppressed and persecuted of all nations and religions, whom we shall welcome to a participation of all our rights and privileges." And so they came, in such numbers and with such impact that by 1819 the U.S. government began to count immigrants.[5]

In colonial America and during the early federal period, almost all voluntary immigrants to what is now the United States were from the British Isles and northern or western Europe. Some 95 percent of all immigrants between 1820 and 1860 were from this region.[6]

Of course, many thousands of Africans were transported involuntarily during most of these same years. The first slave ship, a Dutch vessel, brought its human cargo to Virginia in 1619. By the last decade of the same century, a substantial share of the population in the southern states were slaves of African ancestry.[7]

The Boom Years

In the nineteenth century, immigration to the United States rapidly picked up speed. Furthermore, its composition changed dramatically. By the late nineteenth century, the "old" wave of largely Protestant western or northern Europeans (except for the Irish Catholics of the 1840s) had been largely replaced by something new altogether. These newcomers were more often from southern and eastern Europe; many were Catholic or Jewish.[8] They came in very large numbers. Between 1900 and 1910, more than 8 million immigrants (including some 1.3 million in the peak year of 1907) were admitted to the United States. This new surge lasted through the first two decades of the twentieth century.[9]

Social tensions were an inevitable accompaniment to the massive and largely unsupervised inflow, and it was not long before Congress began responding to public pressure for more controls. The first restrictions had appeared in 1875, when prostitutes and convicts were barred from admission.[10] There was good reason for this law; some European countries, using a tactic that would later be employed by

Fidel Castro, had found it convenient to empty their prisons and almshouses in filling immigrant ships bound for America.

A less defensible restriction came in 1882 when Congress, in an overtly racist action, curbed Chinese immigration. The nation also began screening out what the law called "lunatics, idiots and persons likely to become public charges." In addition, a head tax was placed on each immigrant.[11] The nation got serious about systematizing the process of immigration in 1891 when a position as superintendent of immigration was created within the Treasury Department, and the Ellis Island facility was opened in New York harbor.[12]

Little attention was given to the educational attainments of immigrants until 1887, when an attempt was made to prohibit immigration by male adults who could not read or write in their own language.[13] The first widely supported legislation to this effect, a product of intensive lobbying by the Immigration Restriction League, was passed by Congress in 1897. As is usual in immigration legislation, the pro–literacy test coalition was an eccentric one. A strong nativist element led by Massachusetts's conservative Senator Henry Cabot Lodge was joined by American Federation of Labor President Samuel Gompers, whose union members feared the competition of immigrant labor.[14]

A veto by President Grover Cleveland, who called illiteracy a pretext for exclusion, derailed this effort.[15] The same action by Presidents William Howard Taft and Woodrow Wilson stopped similar legislation during their administrations.[16] But the literacy test was not to die. In the war year of 1917, during President Wilson's second administration, another literacy test bill passed conference and became law when Congress overrode Wilson's veto.[17] This was a weak law, however, requiring only a simple reading test at a time when the rate of literacy in Europe, the chief source of immigrants, was steadily rising.[18]

In 1907, Congress established the Joint Commission on Immigration, headed by Senator William Dillingham. In their subsequent report, the commissioners concluded that the new immigrants from southern and eastern Europe were racially inferior, resistant to assimilation, "inclined toward violent crime," and "drove old-stock citizens out of some lines of work."[19] Their work resulted in an increased head tax on immigrants and an expansion of exclusions. In addition, a "gentlemen's agreement" with Japan virtually eliminated all immigration from that country, and the Naturalization Act of 1906 included a provision making knowledge of English a requirement for citizenship.[20]

The Trickle Years

Very significant changes in U.S. immigration law occurred in 1921. In that year, faced with an increasing mood of hostility toward the large numbers of immigrants who had entered the country from southern and eastern Europe, Congress established a quota system limiting the number of immigrants of each nationality that would be permitted to enter the country. Permissible immigration was cut across the board, but the total quota for northern and western Europe nations was lowered by only 29 percent, whereas immigration from southern and eastern Europe was cut by 87 percent. Further changes incorporated in the Johnson-Reed Act of 1924 forced even more drastic cuts, with southern and eastern Europe allowed only 14 percent of the total.[21]

An era of large-scale immigration to the United States ended. President Calvin Coolidge, the man who solemnly proclaimed that "the business of America is business," announced with equal solemnity in his first annual message to Congress that "America must be kept American."[22] These essentially racist immigration laws remained largely unchanged during the 1930s, but in the wartime year of 1942, bilateral agreements were concluded with Mexico, British Honduras, Barbados, and Jamaica under which temporary workers could enter the country under the so-called bracero program. Ultimately, the bracero program would bring in 4.8 million temporary Mexican workers between 1942 and 1964, when it was terminated.[23] Also, in a gesture to China, a wartime ally, the infamous Chinese exclusion law was repealed in 1943.[24]

After World War II came immigration pressures that had not existed before, and Congress gladly responded by passing the War Brides Act, which allowed the entry also of the husbands and children of armed forces personnel. The refugee era began in 1948 when Congress passed the Displaced Persons Act to facilitate the entry of 400,000 refugees, most of them victims of the dictatorial regimes of Adolf Hitler or Joseph Stalin.[25]

Major revisions to immigration law came in 1952 with the Immigration and Nationality Act. Generally known as the McCarran-

Walter Act, this legislation reaffirmed the national origins system giving each nation a quota equal to its proportion of the U.S. population in 1920. It also limited immigration from the Eastern Hemisphere to about 150,000 persons annually; unrestricted immigration from the Western Hemisphere was permitted. Preferences were established for skilled workers and relatives of U.S. citizens. Reflecting a concern about communist infiltration, security measures were tightened, as were screening standards and procedures.[26]

In action that was to have long-term implications, Congress also included the so-called Texas Proviso which explicitly exempted employers from fines or imprisonment on grounds of "harboring" illegal aliens, in the McCarran-Walter Act. Reflecting the desire of Texas agricultural interests for cheap Mexican labor, this loophole was not closed until 1986. In the meantime, it facilitated the illegal entry to (or continued residence in) the United States of several millions of Mexican laborers, most of them poorly educated. This inward flow persists.[27]

In the first major measure stretching immigration limits, the Refugee Relief Act, passed in 1953, enabled more than 200,000 refugees to be admitted outside existing quotas. In response to the exodus resulting from Fidel Castro's revolution, the Cuban Refugee Program was established in 1960.[28] Schools were among the first of the nation's institutions to feel the impact of the resulting immigration of hundreds of thousands of Cubans.

The New Immigration Begins

The Immigration and Nationality Act of 1965 represented a marked shift of policy. It did away with the national origins system, replacing it with selection criteria focusing on family reunification and desired occupational skills. The nation regained its conscience as immigrants from the Eastern Hemisphere were for the first time allowed to enter the United States without regard to national or racial origin.[29]

The effects of the 1965 legislation were as dramatic as they were unexpected. Immigration from Europe declined precipitously. At the same time, huge increases were recorded in immigration not only from Asia but from Latin America—to the point where more than 80 percent of all immigration to the United States in the early 1990s comes from these two continents.[30] Although immigration from

Africa more than doubled, the numbers arriving from that continent remained relatively small.[31] The pie charts in figure 1–1 show the dramatic changes in sources of immigration to the United States between the 1901–1920 and 1980–90.

Close relatives of adult citizens (parents, spouses, and children) were enabled to enter the United States with no necessity to qualify under the numerical limits, and by the early 1980s some 30 percent of all immigrants were entering under this provision. Also, the new preference system assured that at least 80 percent of the 290,000 limited-issue visas would be given to more distant relatives of U.S. citizens or residents. In all, more than 70 percent of all immigration to the United States in the early 1980s was that of persons related to someone already admitted to this country.[32] This had the effect of severely limiting the number of persons admitted on the basis of their job skills. It also resulted in a fairly high proportion of immigrants with lower educational attainment.

How did it happen that immigrants from Asia and Latin America eventually began to dominate the immigrant stream following passage of the Immigration Act of 1965? Certainly this outcome was not expected at the time the law was enacted. Then-Attorney General Robert Kennedy was something less than prescient when he responded, when asked how many Asians would immigrate under the new law, that "5,000 [Asian] immigrants would come in the first year, but we do not expect that there would be any great influx after that."[33] There were five basic reasons for the lopsided numbers: (1) decreasing interest in immigrating among Europeans, (2) large families and strong family ties in Asian and Latin American nations, (3) assertive use of tourist and other nonimmigrant visas as a means of facilitating subsequent adjustment to immigrant status, (4) technical intricacies in the new immigration law that unexpectedly benefitted some national groups more than others, and (5) disproportionately high illegal immigration from Latin America.

When the United States liberalized its immigration laws in 1965, most of western Europe was democratic and newly prosperous. Its citizens had little incentive to look elsewhere for a better life. Eastern Europe, an earlier source of immigration in this century, was under communist lock and key, which effectively prevented the escape of all the most fearless and determined of its citizens. Immigrants in the pre-1970s waves, most of whom were European, thus were relatively few in number. Moreover, by the time they became eligible under the

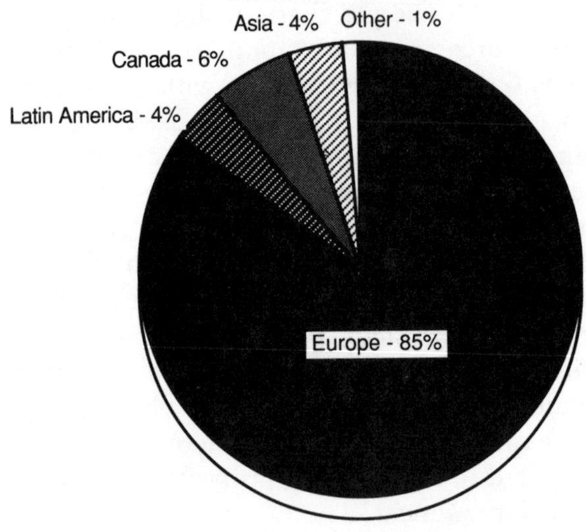

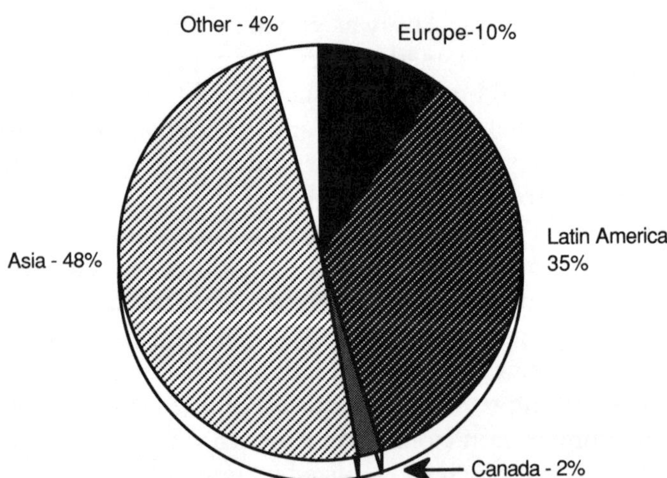

Figure 1–1. Contrast in Sources of Legal Immigrant Admissions to the United States

Sources: INS Statistical Yearbooks, 1980–87 and "Immigration to the U.S., the Unfinished Story," *Population Bulletin* 41, No. 4 (Washington, D.C.: Population Reference Bureau, Inc., 1986) p. 16. Technical Note: Latin America includes Mexico and the Caribbean.

new family reunification provisions, they tended not to have children, parents, or even younger brothers and sisters who were interested in leaving their homelands. The new Asians and Latins, on the other hand, were both young and from large families with many members eager to leave their poor or war-torn countries. As the relatives came in, they, too, were quick to augment their own families by bringing still more relatives to the United States.

Tourist, student, and other nonimmigrant visas to the United States paved the way for a large number of Asians and Latin Americans. Once inside the country, many of them were successful in petitions to have their status adjusted to that of permanent resident alien. Marriage to a citizen of the United States qualified many such persons for entry; so did gainful employment in skilled or semiskilled occupations where U.S. citizen applicants were in short supply.[34]

In addition, Asians in particular took advantage of a transition arrangement between the old (1952) and new (1965) laws that facilitated a fast start on family reunification.

Illegal immigration took a sharp jump upward in the early 1970s and continues at high levels to this day. The bulk of this flow is from Mexico, Central America, and the Caribbean. The United States had admitted persons qualifying as refugees prior to 1980, but the Refugee Act of that year systematized the process. The president was empowered to determine the number of refugees to be admitted each year after consultations were held with Congress. The president was also given authority to respond to "unforeseen emergency" refugee situations.[35]

In 1986, the nation addressed the increasing problem of illegal immigration for the first time when Congress enacted and the president signed the Immigration Reform and Control Act (IRCA). Over the bitter opposition of certain employer and Hispanic immigrant advocacy groups, the federal government for the first time acquired the right to impose sanctions on employers who knowingly hired illegal aliens.

In 1990, Congress substantially revised the immigration laws, increasing the number of legal entrants permitted by 40 percent. New emphasis was placed on job and occupational skills as a criterion for admission. Immigrants entering on the basis of family relationships were not, however, disadvantaged as a result of the 1990 immigration law. These types of admissions were in fact increased, by 20 percent for the first three years and 10 percent thereafter. The new law also

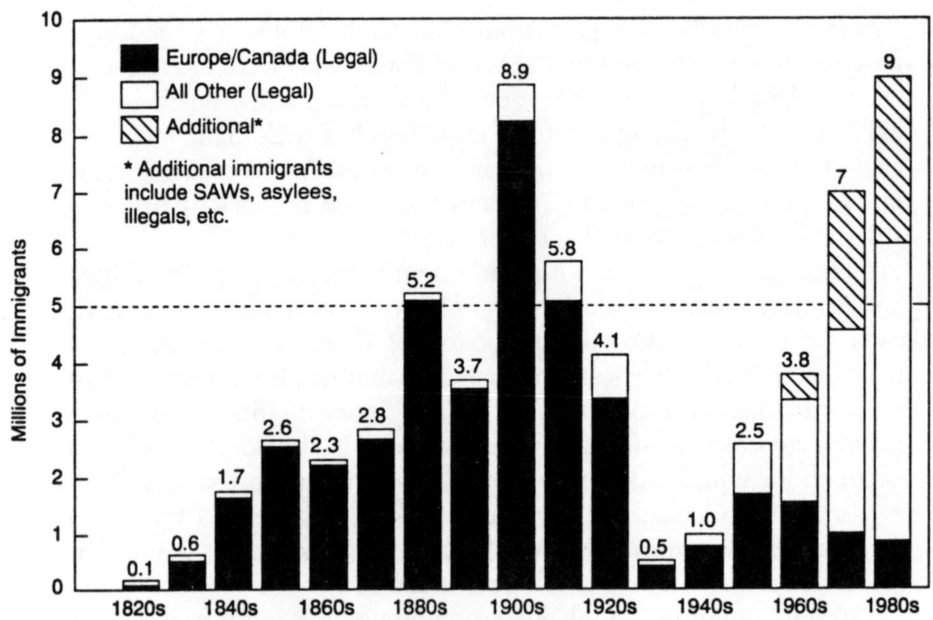

Figure 1–2. Immigration to the United States by Decade: 1821–30 through 1981–90

Source: The Urban Institute, Washington, D.C.

retained relatively large allocations of visas for the brothers and sisters of American citizens—an important factor in the continuing high level of Asian immigration.[36]

Several categories of temporary "diversity" visas were also authorized to facilitate immigration from "traditional sending nations," most of them in Europe, whose nationals had experienced difficulty in arranging immigration under the law. Figure 1–2 shows the patterns of legal and illegal immigration to the United States, both numerical and by source nation, for each decade since 1820.

Immigrant Education in Historical Perspective

Not until 1968, when it enacted the Bilingual Education Act, did Congress allocate significant funds for an educational program primarily serving immigrants. The Emergency Immigrant Education Act of 1984 was developed to help alleviate the financial crisis facing school districts with large numbers of immigrant children. The Immigration Reform and Control Act of 1986 provided funds for the education of previously illegal immigrants given amnesty under its provisions. These pieces of enabling legislation need to be seen in light of immigrant education controversies rooted in the past.

Two basic issues frame the history of immigrant education in the United States. The controversies center on approaches to cultural assimilation and to the primacy assigned to English language instruction. So-called Americanization in education or instruction, aimed at socializing immigrants to the norms of the existing culture, can be traced back to the colonial period. Anxious to maintain their ideals, the early Puritans did not shrink from attempts to impose them on newcomers. The objective then and in the early years of the federal period was that of indoctrination—achieving unity through homogeneity.[37]

In the last years of the nineteenth century, a somewhat more benign approach appeared. Social settlement workers Jane Addams, Ellen Gates Starr, and Robert Woods, among others, to some extent encouraged the preservation of immigrant cultures. Still, their major effort was that of enabling the newcomers to think and act more like native-born residents. At Hull House, the Chicago settlement house founded by Addams and Starr, residents of the surrounding poor immigrant neighborhood were introduced to the prevailing habits of social interaction, eating, dress, health care, and personal hygiene.[38]

The push to Americanize was driven in part by fear that the mainstream culture could not accommodate the incoming rush, but a strong altruistic motivation was also present.[39] A genuine concern for the welfare of immigrants was a characteristic of one of Americanization's most notable proponents, Frances A. Kellor. Supported by the North American Civic League for Immigrants, she encouraged a variety of approaches to the education of immigrants. Aided by wealthy donors, she was even successful in getting the federal government to establish a Division of Immigrant Education as part of the Bureau of Education.[40] During its five-year life, this entity assisted schools in establishing Americanization programs.[41]

As the flow of immigration peaked in the early twentieth century, schools were at the forefront of efforts to accommodate the great crowds of newcomers. Given the widely divergent backgrounds of the youngsters, it was not an easy task. The U.S. Senate Immigration Commission, in a 1908 survey of 36 cities, discovered that 60 different nationalities were represented in the schools. Furthermore, some 58 percent of all students in the population surveyed had fathers born outside the United States. The students, however, were virtually all of European extraction.[42]

Strongly influenced by the educational philosopher Ellwood Cubberly, the nation's schools generally took a very hard line in the years during and immediately following World War I in seeking the assimilation of the new immigrants from southern and eastern Europe. In Cubberly's view, these newcomers were "largely illiterate, docile, often lacking in initiative, and, almost wholly without the Anglo-Saxon conceptions of righteousness, liberty, law, order, public decency, and government"; their coming had "served to dilute tremendously our national stock and to weaken and corrupt our political life." Given this crass definition of the problem, a kind of ruthless assimilation was prescribed so as to preserve "our national character."[43] Employers and even YMCAs and other community agencies followed suit. It was called "citizenship education." It was actually an attempt to indoctrinate Anglo-Saxon and Protestant values.[44]

Not everyone shared an enthusiasm for this approach. The philosopher John Dewey noted that "many of us feel like blushing every time we hear the term 'Americanization,' because to such an extent the idea has been seized upon by certain groups as a means of forcing their own conceptions of American life upon other people."[45] Frank V. Thompson, in a now-classic 1920 book on the schooling of immigrants, favored persuasion rather than compulsion in the pursuit of Americanization. He suggested incentives—"furnishing convenient means in the way of free instruction, and perhaps . . . granting privileges which may be withheld from the non-citizen." A democratic method would permit the immigrant to "Americanize himself."[46]

With the advent of greatly restricted immigration following enactment of the new immigration law in 1924, the debate over Americanization and other immigration-related issues eventually subsided. In the present era, the tainted term *Americanization* is no longer used. But the incarnate issues are being replayed in somewhat different form. Diane Ravitch concludes, in her respected history of the New York City schools, that each of the system's "great school wars" or major reorganizations coincided with a "huge wave of new immigration" to the city. It is the public school where the fears of the native population and the hopes of the immigrants meet and collide.[47] This same phenomenon, she believes, is evident in the crisis that the New York schools now face as they struggle with new waves and new varieties of newcomers.[48]

I would extend this perspective to include all sectors of education in the United States. Wherever immigrants meet the native-born in educational settings, new issues emerge. Should the public schools actively assist immigrants in maintaining their native language and cultures? To what degree should curricula in schools and in colleges be multicultural? Are resources that would otherwise be applied to meet the needs of disadvantaged native-born adults being diverted to meet equally deserving immigrants? These questions, among others, are being examined and debated by a new generation of citizens and newcomers.

2
The Dynamics of Immigration

The village of Napízaro in the Mexican state of Michoacán is like many in impoverished rural Mexico in exporting its people to the United States. Researchers Peri Fletcher and J. Edward Taylor reported in 1990 that nineteen of every twenty families in this little hamlet sent migrants to the United States in the previous year. Almost half of the people born in Napízaro had moved to the state of California, most to North Hollywood, Pacoima, and nearby communities in the San Fernando Valley.[1]

Population pressures in places like Napízaro have been, and will continue to be, a major stimulus for legal and illegal immigration to the United States. Mexico, its extreme poverty fueled by overpopulation, is filled with desperate would-be immigrants. The same conditions exist in Haiti and in many other poor nations in Central and South America, Asia, and Africa. Jobs for the rapidly increasing numbers of young people in these nations are in very short supply—a serious problem given their rapid rates of population expansion. Dr. Antonio Golini, a demographer at Rome's Institute of Population Research, estimates that the eligible labor force in less developed countries will grow by 733 million in the next twenty years, fifteen times more than in developed countries.[2]

Unrest stemming from political, ethnic, or religious strife is the second major immigration trigger. Many persons have arrived as refugees from such war-wracked nations as Vietnam, Afghanistan, and Ethiopia. Still others are fleeing the ethnic and religious hatreds of the Middle East and eastern Europe. An estimated 25 percent of the entire population of the war-torn and desperately poor Central American nation of El Salvador has immigrated to the United States, Canada, Mexico, or other Central American countries.[3] Haitians by the thousands are attempting to leave their impoverished land. Many are seeking to enter the United States illegally, generally in flimsy boats that are unsafe for the sea voyage involved in such a desperate effort. In 1992, a U.S. Embassy official in Port-au-Prince estimated that some 80 to 88 percent of all Haitians would immigrate to the United States if possible.[4]

In the absence of restrictive immigration policies that are enforced, massive immigration flows are inevitable to the wealthy United States from countries where poverty levels are very high. Once the flow begins from almost any nation, it is sure to increase as first-comers establish themselves and family reunification provisions of current immigration law take effect.

Four states—California, Arizona, New Mexico, and Texas—line the U.S.-Mexican border. Some idea of the force of immigration pressures from Mexico can be sensed from the disproportionate increases in population in these states beginning as early as the 1970s. Between the 1970 and 1980 census reports, population growth in these border states was 23 percent, more than twice the national average during the same period. The concurrent 40 percent increase in the population of the 25 border counties was almost four times the national rate. Immigration was a substantial contributor to this surge, according to a U.S. Department of Labor study issued in 1989.[5]

It is survival on decent terms and the well-being of their families, not U.S. immigration law, that occupies the minds of those moving northward. Given this stark fact, it is small wonder that the costs of transportation, payments to "coyotes" (those who smuggle undocumented immigrants across the border), and related costs are seen as relatively low barriers. These immigrants, often motivated by imported television programs showing a way of life that they perceive will never be possible in their homeland, seek economic opportunity in the United States. If they tend to enter life at the bottom in the United States, even this is generally superior to what they left behind. The economy in Southern California, for example, produces wages that are five to ten times what can be expected almost anywhere below the Rio Grande.[6]

China is much farther away than Mexico, but the pressures are building there also. Grinding poverty is the norm in the world's most populous nation, and many Chinese have acquired a taste for something other than totalitarian government. Aided by smugglers charging as much as $50,000 and employing a sophisticated array of fraudulent documents, tens of thousands of Chinese are joining the already heavy flow of illegal immigration.[7] As one young Chinese worker said in a conversation with a reporter, "There are two kinds of people in China these days. First, there are those who simply want to go to the United States. And second, there are those who are already well along in their preparations to depart." Another student put it this way: "I'm optimistic about my own future, because I plan to go abroad, but I'm pessimistic about China. Anyone with talent is trying to leave. Absolutely everyone I know is looking for an exit."[8]

Many residents of Hong Kong, fearful at the prospect of the takeover of that British crown colony by China in 1997, also are planning to leave. While most people in the nation are unaware of the impending immigration pressures from Hong Kong, the existing Chinese community in the United States is alert and intends to be prepared. Some years ago the superintendent of schools in Miami was surprised to receive a request from the local Chinese community, most of whom are not native speakers of Chinese, for Saturday classes in the Chinese language. He learned that the reason for this request was that the local community wants to be ready for the expected influx when Hong Kong reverts from British to mainland Chinese control.

Kenya, which has the world's highest birthrate, pumps about 150,000 young people a year into its job market. Yet this nation, with a corrupt government and stagnant economy, creates only 3,000 new jobs a year.[9] Comparable conditions exist in Nigeria, which holds one-fifth of Africa's rapidly expanding population. The Immigration Law of 1990, which encourages greater immigration from Africa, will surely result in more immigrants in search of jobs of almost any variety.

Few indications suggest that the future holds anything other than more motivation in the direction of immigration to the United States. The former Soviet Union is being shaken by forces that may signal the forcible uprooting of many persons who will find themselves trapped in hostile environments. Eastern Europe and the Middle East remain tinderboxes. Exploding populations in Latin America, Asia, and

Africa will press further upon the already depleted resource base of those continents.

And it is not just the United States that is feeling the pressure. Western Europe, Canada, Australia, and more recently even Japan, which has very restrictive immigration laws, are finding newcomers at their doors. The movement is from less developed to the more developed countries. "Here is better than my country," was how one twelve-year-old Soviet immigrant put it after living in the United States for some months.[10] The word is being passed along. We are witnessing the overture to a new epoch.

Pressure Indicators

The indicators of immigration pressures are plentiful—intense pressures on Congress for more generous provisions in immigration laws, increased levels of application for immigration visas, and increases in unauthorized border crossings. As of January 1992, nearly 3 million people were on a worldwide waiting list for admission to the United States. The largest backlogs were for citizens of the Philippines, Mexico, India, China, Taiwan, Korea, and Vietnam.[11]

Some idea of the competition for immigration visas to the United States can be gleaned from experience with a temporary visa lottery program conducted for the fiscal years 1990 and 1991. It authorized 10,000 additional visas to be granted to natives of "underrepresented countries." More than 3.2 million people worldwide applied for these visas.[12]

A near stampede erupted in October 1991 at a Fairfax County, Virginia, post office that had been designated as a processing station for another lottery of 50,000 green cards authorized under the 1990 immigration law. Just prior to the event, many hotel managers in the area of neighboring Washington, D.C., were astonished to find their facilities booked to capacity on what would otherwise have been a slow weekend, as illegal immigrants from all over the nation and even would-be immigrants and couriers from abroad converged on the suburban post office.[13] The U.S. State Department had planned for 5 million applications; it received 19 million.[14]

Fidel Castro's Cuba was extorting $1,000 from any of its citizens who applied for nonimmigrant visas to the United States in 1991. Even so, some 32,000 visas were granted through July of that year, when a backlog of 28,000 applications forced processing to be suspended for a time.[15] Under terms of the Cuban Adjustment Act of 1966, any Cuban who manages to remain in the United States for a year may apply for permanent resident status. Experience has indicated that this option is the goal of about 40 percent of Cuban nonimmigrant visa seekers.[16]

The pressures exerted by would-be immigrants to the United States pop out in intriguing places. The GED Testing Service of the American Council on Education develops and maintains examinations that are now used by all states and most Canadian provinces as the basis for awarding high school diplomas to adults. These examinations are also available at overseas locations; the intent was to make them more readily accessible to dependents of members of the military services and to the Canadian military. The examinations are open to foreign nationals, though no encouragement is given for such persons to use the service.

Passing the GED test at a location overseas will not directly enhance anyone's immigration status. It can, however, help a newly arriving immigrant get a job. As this word leaked out, nonmilitary use of the GED exam at overseas testing centers began to increase even without promotion. Demand grew for the opening of additional testing centers to serve these new clients. Concerned about increased hazards to test security and possible misuse of its credential, the testing service decided to take no action until it could more fully consider the implications of an expanded overseas effort.[17]

How Many Immigrants in the United States?

Nearly 10 million legal and illegal immigrants entered what many of them considered to be the "golden doors" of the United States during the 1980s, a period during which 22 million persons were added to the nation's population. With its sizable illegal component (approximately 2 million), this figure exceeds the previous peak high of slightly more than 8 million immigrants for the decade that ended in 1910.[18]

As the 1990 immigration law's provisions take effect, the Immigration and Naturalization Service projects that legal immigration to the United States will climb to more than 700,000 per year.[19] Estimates of future illegal immigration vary. Urban Institute researcher Jeffrey Passel believes that between 150,000 and 250,000 persons are now entering the United States illegally each year. Given troubled conditions in many of the world's countries and the relative ease of crossing U.S. borders, there is reason to believe that illegal immigration will increase in the years ahead. Barry Edmonston and Passel are predicting that by the year 2005, immigration will be at a level of about 1.125 million annually, including 855,000 legal immigrants, 200,000 net illegal immigrants, and a net gain of 70,000 from civilian and Puerto Rican movements.[20]

All of this activity is producing dramatic changes that need to be noticed and taken into account by the nation's educators. The 1990 census shows a significant alteration in the ethnic makeup of the United States, much of which can be attributed to immigration during the prior decade. The percentage of the U.S. population that is white and non-Hispanic continued to decline to 80.3 percent in 1990, down from 83.1 percent in 1980. The percentage of United States residents who are black increased slightly from 11.7 percent in 1980 to 12.1 percent in 1990. The Census Bureau reports that the number of Hispanics in the United States during the same decade grew more rapidly than expected—by more than 50 percent.[21]

If the children of immigrants are included, according to an Urban Institute study, about one-fourth of the Hispanic population in 1990 was the product of immigration in the 1980s. Some 43 percent of Hispanics in the nation are immigrants from the 1970s and 1980s.[22] The number of Asian-Americans, meanwhile, more than doubled in the decade following 1980. Some 43 percent of them as of 1990 came from immigration in the 1980s; 70 percent were from immigration in the 1970s and 1980s.[23] The census figures also show that Asians and Hispanics are beginning to spread themselves more widely throughout the country, quite far in some instances from the places to which they immigrated.[24]

Foreign-born residents, educators should note, have quite a different age distribution than does the total U.S. population. Most are young adults, with the higher concentration being in the 15–29 age range. Some 43.5 percent of immigrants arriving in the 1980–86 period were in this age category, compared to only 25.4 percent of the total population of the country.[25] As young adults, many of these new residents are contributing disproportionately to the nation's rate of population increase. In 1986, according to the Census Bureau, one in every ten babies born in the United States was born to an immigrant mother, up from 7.5 percent in 1983. In the same year, foreign-born

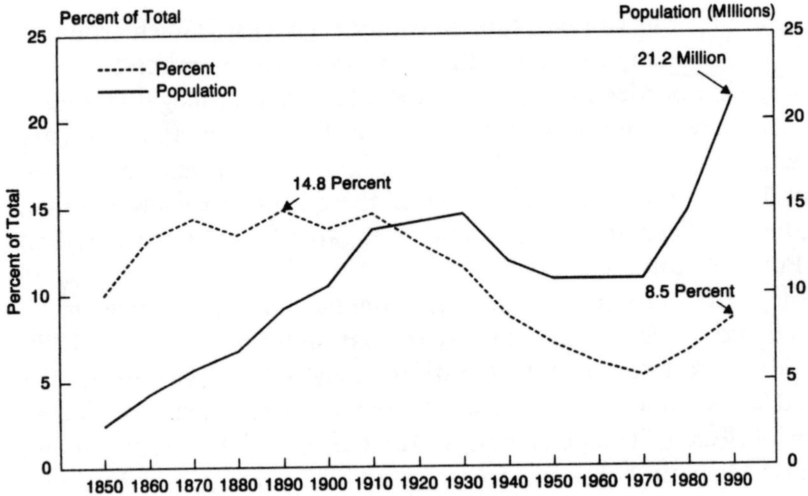

Figure 2–1. Foreign-Born Population of the United States: 1850–1990

Source: The Urban Institute, Washington, D.C.

women averaged 98.9 births per 1,000 women, while U.S.-born women averaged just 67.5 births per 1,000.[26]

At 21.2 million in 1990, the foreign-born population of the United States is more numerous than ever before. This is not, however, the highest percentage of foreign-born residents as a proportion of total population in the nation's history. Some 8.5 percent of U.S. residents were foreign-born in 1990; the comparable figure in 1890 was 14.8 percent.[27] Figure 2–1 shows the patterns over a 140-year period.

Geographic Locations for Immigration

Although immigrants are relatively small as a percentage of the total number of residents in the nation, they are very significant in the geographic areas where they are concentrated. As is shown in figure 2–2, newcomers do not distribute themselves evenly throughout the United States. Just six states—California, New York, Texas, Florida, New Jersey and Illinois—are the home of more than 71 percent of all new immigrants to the United States.[28] Other states that receive large

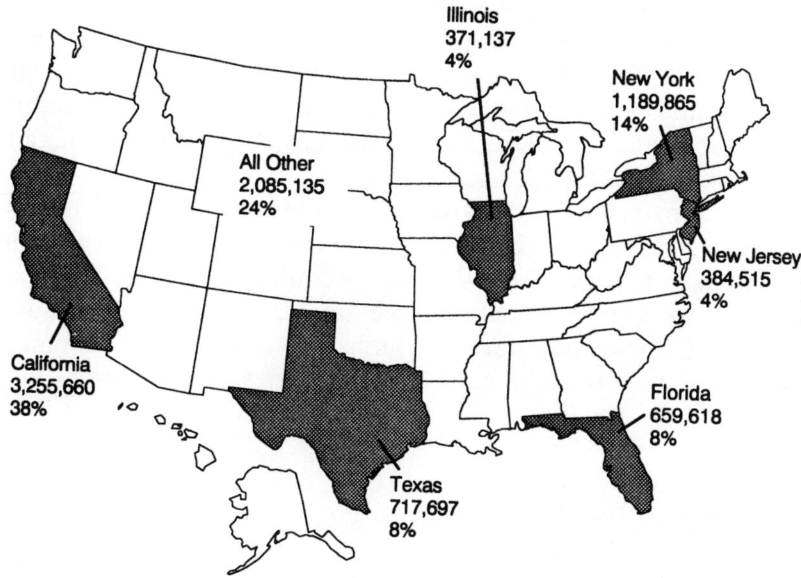

Figure 2–2. Immigration by State, 1980–90

Source: The Urban Institute, Washington, D.C.

numbers of immigrants include, Massachusetts, Pennsylvania, Michigan, Washington, and Virginia.[29]

The Center for the Continuing Study of the California Economy reports that more than 250,000 immigrants arrive each year as newcomers to California, one-fourth of the nation's total of immigration. About half of all new California residents hail from other nations.[30] California is the overwhelming first choice of most immigrants from Asia, a fact that has changed the face of the state as well as the nation. For example, by 1980 there were more Filipinos in California alone than were residing in all of the United States in 1970.[31]

Most of the other newcomers are from Mexico. Today non-Hispanic whites account for only 56 percent of California residents, down from 77 percent in 1970. The balance of the state's population is as follows: 26 percent Hispanic, 10 percent Asians (including Pacific Islanders and Native Americans), and 7 percent blacks.[32] If present trends continue, California will soon be the first state in the continental United States where a majority of the residents can claim a Third World ethnic heritage.

The immigrants are overwhelmingly urban dwellers, with approximately 40 percent of them residing in either greater Los Angeles or New York City (where about one of every five persons is foreign-born). An additional 20 percent of the U.S. foreign-born population resides in greater San Francisco, Chicago, Miami, Houston, and Washington, D.C.[33]

Chinese from countries all over the world are also coming to New York City's Chinatown in record numbers and have swelled its population to at least 100,000 officially counted residents. Some say the actual number is as much as three times that if illegal immigrants are counted. These immigrants are served by eleven Chinese-language newspapers, twenty-eight banks, more than 450 restaurants, and several hundred small garment factories.[34]

Educational Attainment

How much education one tends to have before immigrating to the United States varies widely depending upon the nation of origin. Figure 2–3 shows patterns of educational attainment for foreign-born persons 20 years of age and older as of 1988.[35]

Figure 2–3a shows the distribution of foreign-born U.S. residents who have less than a high school education, along with their nations of origin. The most arresting aspect of this presentation is the disproportionate number of Mexican immigrants—more than 76 percent—who do not have a high school diploma. This reflects the high volume of illegal immigration by persons from the most disadvantaged sectors of Mexican society. Many are farm workers who may never have attended school. Persons born in Vietnam (30.9 percent) and Cuba (35.1 percent) are also less likely than the native-born (21.1 percent) to have a high school education. This can be accounted for by the large numbers of refugees from less advantaged classes who left those nations in the 1970s and 1980s.

Very few persons having less than a high school education have left India, Japan, or Korea for the United States. There are two reasons for this. First, none of these nations in recent years has experienced war or the kind of cataclysmic crisis that generates forced moves for low-income people. Second, they are located at a great distance from the United States, which presents barriers not encountered by immigrants from nearby nations such as Mexico. Figure 2–3b shows the distribution of foreign-born residents who have a high school educa-

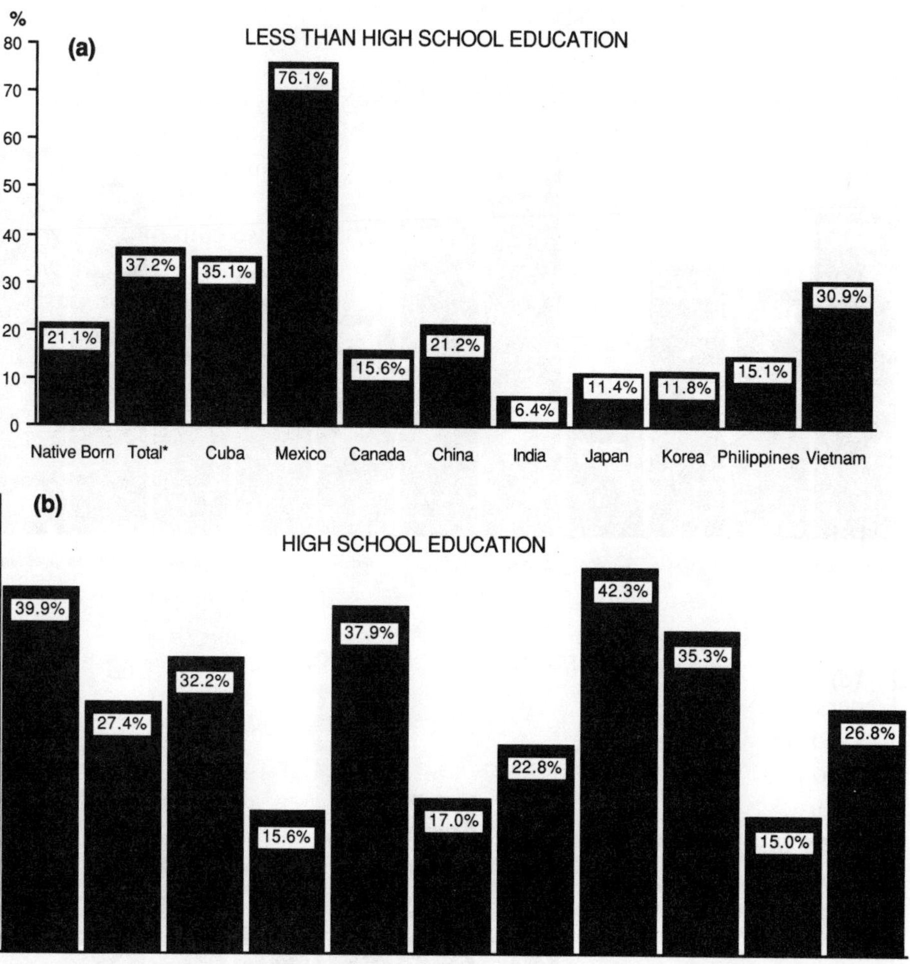

Figure 2–3 (a–d). Distribution of U.S. Foreign-Born Population Twenty Years Old and Over by Place of Birth and Education, 1988 (a–d)

*Total foreign born, including countries not shown separately.

Source: Amara Bachu, "Profile of the Foreign-Born Population in the United States," *Studies in American Fertility*, Series p. 23, No. 176, U.S. Government Printing Office, Washington, D.C., 1991, Table C.

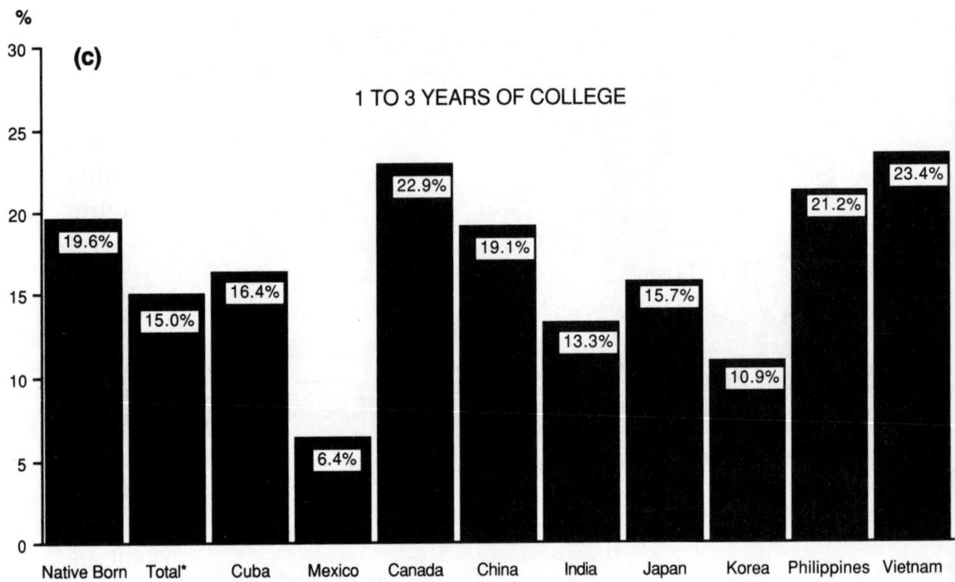

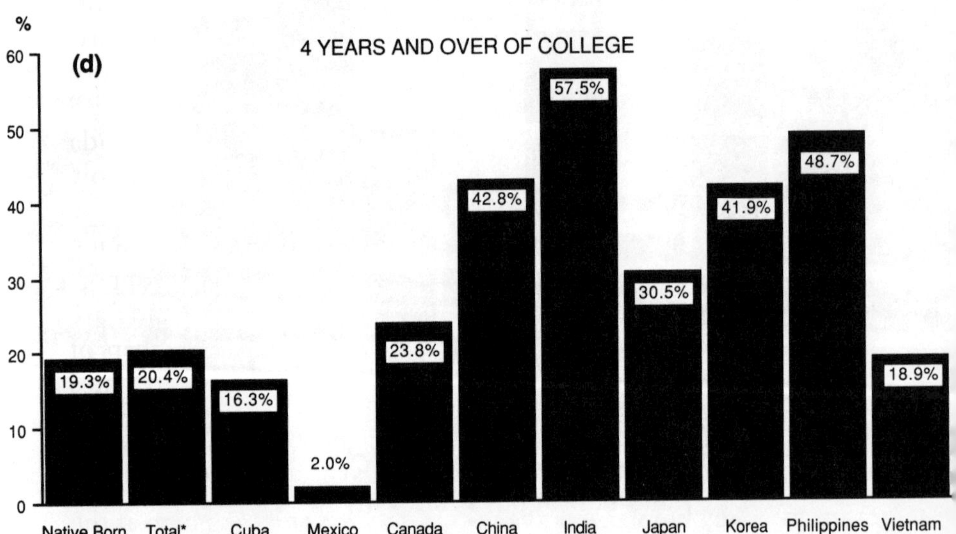

Figure 2–3 (a–d) continued.

tion. In this group, only immigrants from Japan (42.3 percent) are more likely to have a high school diploma than their counterparts in the native-born population (39.9 percent).

Colleges and universities that offer degree completion programs may be especially interested in the nationality patterns for immigrants having one to three years of college education, as shown in figure 2–3c. The individuals most likely to have prior education at this level come from Vietnam; 23.4 percent of these immigrants have at least one year of college work. Other nations where the comparable percentage is relatively high include Canada (22.9 percent), the Philippines (21.2 percent), and China (19.1 percent). All of these approximately equal or exceed the native-born proportion (19.6 percent) who have one to three years of college education.

The "brain drain" in certain sending nations is very evident in figure 2–3d. Professional and business people in India are flocking to the United States, a phenomenon reflected in the 57.5 percent of natives of India now resident in the United States who are college graduates. In contrast, only 19.3 percent of native-born U.S. residents have a college degree. The percentage of college graduates in cohorts of five other sending countries also exceeds that of the U.S.-born cohort. These include the Philippines (48.7 percent), China (42.8 percent), Korea (41.9 percent), Japan (30.5 percent), and Canada (23.8 percent). Only 2 percent of persons born in Mexico and now residing in the United States have a college degree.

Not all of the inflow of business and professional people is coming from poverty-stricken nations such as India and China, where opportunities for advancement are sparse. Korea, Japan, and Canada are prosperous nations; yet they are exporting relatively large numbers of college graduates. The economic and societal lure of the United States remains strong for college-educated people even in some lands of relative affluence.

The patterns of education for all nationalities of incoming immigrants are oddly bipolar relative to the native-born population at the upper and lower educational levels. As show in figure 2–3a, the foreign-born are much more likely than the native-born to have less than a high school education (37.2 percent versus 21.1 percent). The same pattern, though to a lesser degree, is evident at the upper end, where the foreign-born are more likely to have graduated from college (20.4 percent) than native-born residents (19.3 percent).

In evaluating these data, it should be kept in mind that average levels of education possessed by immigrant groups do not remain constant over time. The immigrant groups first arriving from a sending country typically have much higher levels of educational attainment than do their counterparts in succeeding waves of arrivals from the same nation.

Immigration and Illiteracy

There are links between illiteracy and immigration—especially illegal immigration to the United States. The U.S. Department of Education's *Update on Adult Illiteracy* (illiteracy being defined as inability to read at all, or reading below the fourth-grade level) reports that 37 percent of all persons considered to be illiterate in the U.S. speak a language other than English at home. Of these non-English-speaking residents, 82 percent were born outside the United States, with only 14 percent of this group being literate in their home language.[36]

The states ranking first, second, third, fourth, and fifth, respectively, in population of illiterate adults 20 years of age and older are the high-immigration receiving states of California, New York, Texas, Illinois, and Florida. New Jersey, the other major receiver of immigrants, ranks eighth among all states. Texas and New York share the highest levels of illiteracy (16 percent each); Florida is at 15 percent, and California, New Jersey, and Illinois share a 14 percent level.[37]

Hispanic immigrants in particular often arrive without the most basic literacy skills. Of all Hispanics living in the United States, 56 percent are functionally illiterate in English according to a report released in 1990 by the National Council of La Raza.[38] This disadvantage is a source of concern for their advocates in this country. In a statement before a congressional committee reviewing issues bearing on immigration and education, Congressman Edward Roybal (D-California) cited statistics compiled by the National Association of Latino Elected and Appointed Officials (NALEO). These indicated that 20 percent of all illiterate adults are immigrants who had come to the United States within the prior six years. Also, according to NALEO, "only 23 percent of Mexican immigrants have a reading ability in English."[39] Citing a "looming crisis," Congressman Roybal went on to urge action aimed at the educational needs of applicants for amnesty under the legalization program for undocumented immigrants initiated under the Immigration Reform and Control Act of 1986.[40]

Why are so many persons without basic education skills immigrating to the United States? One way of framing the answer: our present economic enterprise wants their lack of skills. The premium in the present era is on washing dishes, making beds, running vacuums, and pumping gas. This practice raises some troubling ethical questions. Educators in the United States would do well to think carefully about their role in facilitating what is in some ways an exploitive national arrangement.

Education as Motivation

The educational opportunities of the United States in no small measure are a drawing card for today's immigrants. Examples are not hard to find in interviews with immigrants. "I didn't see any way to send the kids to school," reported one Haitian father awaiting deportation at the U.S. naval base at Guantanamo Bay, Cuba, in 1992. "I see that when kids go to school, at least you won't be pulling a cart in the road like an animal," he continued.[41] A Korean immigrant put the case a bit differently: "At home, Koreans have to fight for an education. They see America just giving this stuff away."[42]

3
The ABCs of Immigration Law and How It Works

Few, if any, pieces of federal legislation explicity addressing education have had as much effect upon the system of education in the United States as the immigration laws; yet the nation's educators tend to be absent when immigration legislation is discussed. This is a gulf that needs to be bridged.

Three pieces of federal legislation undergird U.S. policies governing the admission of immigrants. All of them are amendments to the most basic legislation, which is the Immigration Act of 1952: (1) the Refugee Act of 1980, (2) the Immigration Reform and Control Act of 1986, and (3) the Immigration Act of 1990. These basic enactments are supplemented by more specialized amendments, such as the Cuban Adjustment Act of 1966, the Amerasian Immigration Act of 1982, and the Immigrant Nurses Relief Act of 1989.

Immigration Act of 1990

It is the Immigration Act of 1990, signed into law on November 29, 1990, by President George Bush, that constitutes the centerpiece of current U.S. law governing the admissions of immigrants. It is a statute that has massive implications for all sectors of the national education enterprise.[1] Not only has it increased the number of persons permitted to enter the United States by almost 40 percent, it also represents an effort to change the ethnic and skills mix of the immigrant pool.

The bill had something for everybody except those urging more stable levels of immigration. The previous annual ceiling of 500,000 visas was increased to 700,000 through 1994; thereafter it is to drop to 675,000.[2] The actual number of immigrants will be higher than this figure, which does not include refugees, asylum seekers, unauthorized entrants, and certain family members to be admitted outside the cap.

Per-country levels under the new law are set at approximately 25,000, with no single country receiving more than 7 percent (or a dependent area more than 2 percent) of all family and employment-based visas combined. Would-be immigrants from Europe and Africa are given incentives designed to facilitate their entry, but Latin American and Asian groups who constitute most of the present inflow gained advantages, too. Raul Yzaguirre, President of the National Council of La Raza, a Hispanic advocacy group, had called the new policies "fair, humane, [and] generous."[3]

The 1990 act removed the former six-category preference system and substituted three immigration tracks, those of (1) family sponsorship, (2) employment skills, and (3) diversity. The new law did not change the definition of "immediate relatives" who are admitted automatically. This definition still includes spouses and minor children of U.S. citizens and parents of U.S. citizens who are over 21 years of age. Also admitted in limited numbers are more remote relatives of U.S. citizens (such as brothers, sisters, married children) and spouses and unmarried children of permanent residents. These individuals are admitted under the "family preference" category.

Some 520,000 visas in fiscal years 1991 through 1994 are reserved for family-sponsored immigrants. This includes 465,000 for immediate relatives of U.S. citizens and family-preference immigrants and 55,000 so-called transition visas for spouses and children of newly legalized aliens. In fiscal year 1995, the ceiling on family-sponsored immigrants is to increase to 480,000 (not including transition visas, which will no longer be available). There is no numerical limit on immediate relatives, but they are included in the family-preference total until only 226,000 visas remain for the standard family categories. When this "floor" level is reached, immediate relatives are no longer counted toward the family cap. They are nonetheless admitted, and it is this provision that results in "piercing the cap" to admit more immigrants than are specified in the law's stated limits. If this provision were not in place, the ever-increasing number of immediate relatives would eventually entirely capture the family-preference category.

The new immigration law increased by nearly three times (to 140,000) the number of immigrants allowed to enter under employment-based categories. It opens up more opportunities for persons who have no relatives or prior employment contacts in the United States. Under the old law, a very few immigrant slots were reserved for immigrants with special skills, and the emphasis here was on *very* special skills. Soviet ballerinas, Romanian Olympic gymnasts, and Japanese scientists tended to have little trouble. On the other hand, it was much more difficult for ordinary workers of whatever variety to enter. An applicant would first have to have an assured job in the United States, and the prospective employer would have to assure the government through an elaborate labor certification process that a U.S. citizen was not qualified and available to fill particular job.

Five employment-based categories give new emphasis to professional and occupational skills in the law. "Priority workers" is the first of these. This term refers to persons with "extraordinary ability" in arts, sciences, education, business, or athletics. Sustained national or international acclaim is required, with achievements recognized through extensive documents. In addition, the person must have the intent to work in that area of ability to make a contribution that would "substantially benefit prospectively" the United States.

Priority workers also include "outstanding professors and researchers." Required of them is international recognition as outstanding in a specific field, at least three years of experience in teaching or research in that field, and entering a tenured or tenure-track teaching position or comparable research position. Also in the priority-worker category are certain multinational executives and managers who required employment with a sponsor for at least one year in the three years preceding application and intent to continue to work for that employer (or a subsidiary or affiliate).

The second employment-based immigrant category is that of "professionals holding advanced degrees (or equivalent) and aliens of 'exceptional ability'." The exceptional-ability proviso requires more than a mere degree or license and requires that the person's presence "substantially benefit" the United States. The third category is "skilled workers, professionals holding basic degrees, and 'other workers'"—basically those unskilled. The fourth category is for "special immigrants," such as ministers and religious workers. The fifth employment-based category is that of "investors," who are defined as those with $1 million in capital and who employ ten or more persons eligible to work in the United States (with variations to encourage investment in targeted areas).

The new goal of "diversity" under immigration cannot be equated with diversity as generally applied in contemporary culture in relation to efforts to increase the proportionate numbers of women and minorities in educational and employment settings. Diversity for immigration purposes must be read to mean increased numbers of visas granted to persons from countries from which immigration has been lower than 50,000 over the preceding five years. In practice, this will mostly benefit prospective immigrants from nations in Europe and Africa who have been less likely than Latin Americans and Asians to gain entry under the preference systems in previous immigration law.

Diversity immigrants under the new law must have a high school education (or its equivalent) at the time of application , or two years of work experience in an occupation that requires at least two years of training or experience. It is likely that most immigrants applying for these visas will be young, either single or young marrieds. Diversity visas, with 55,000 available annually, won't take effect until 1995. In the meantime, some 40,000 "transitional" visas are being created for applicants from a selected number of "traditional source" countries such as Ireland, Poland, and Italy that were "adversely affected" by the 1965 Immigration Law. Of these, 40 percent must go to Irish applicants—a provision that is designed to benefit the fairly large number of Irish citizens already residing illegally in the United States.

Diversification to the extent advertised may not occur under the 1990 law, at least not in the near future. A number of Latin American and Asian countries were given short-term advantages that will assure a continued heavy inflow from those regions. It was made much easier for relatives of permanent residents from "high demand" countries (primarily Mexico, the Philippines, and the Dominican Republic) to enter, reducing waiting periods that had mounted to as much as fifteen years in some instances.[4]

The British crown colony of Hong Kong is to be treated as a separate foreign state for immigration purposes. A significant number of provisions in the 1990 law specifically facilitate immigration to the United States by Hong Kong residents.

Refugees, Asylees, and Humanitarian Admissions

Within the generic category of immigrants are refugees and asylum seekers (or "asylees"), whose admission is primarily governed by provisions of the Refugee Act of 1980. All such individuals are admitted over and above the limits imposed by the laws governing admission of other categories of immigrants. A ceiling on refugee admissions is determined by Congress and the president on a yearly basis; in 1991, the ceiling was 131,000.[5]

The United States in the last twenty years has admitted more refugees than any other receiving nation. But only in relatively recent times has the nation moved to bring a degree of order to its policies and practices with respect to the admission of refugees. The Refugee Act of 1980 was designed to accomplish this objective. The definition for *refugee* in the law is quite specific: to qualify as a refugee, someone seeking to enter the United States must be a victim of persecution in his or her own nation or must have "a well-founded fear of persecution on account of race, religion, nationality, membership in a particular social group, or political opinion." The president of the United States is also given some leeway to designate persons or groups as refugees.[6]

Refugees seeking escape from a country in economic turmoil do not qualify as refugees under the 1980 law. For that reason, legal entry is often denied to persons who seek release from the poverty of their nation (such as Haiti) unless they can prove themselves in danger of persecution upon their return.

Unlike refugees, asylees are persons already in the United States who, if deported, would face persecution in their home countries because of nationality, race, or political or religious beliefs. When granted asylum, a person has the same rights as a refugee. The number of persons admitted as asylees is unlimited; however, the number permitted to adjust their status is limited to 10,000 per year.

Other humanitarian immigrant admissions categories are (1) humanitarian parolees, who are granted entry on a temporary basis pending congressional action on their rights as a group to adjust to permanent status; (2) Cuban/Haitian entrants; (3) extended voluntary departures, which are a suspension of deportation to citizens of particularly troubled countries; and (4) temporary protected status, which provides "safe haven" to citizens from countries affected by natural disasters, armed conflict (for example, El Salvador, Liberia, or Kuwait), or other troubles.

There are fourteen major categories of nonimmigrant visas that nonetheless have the effect of admitting persons who may later become immigrants, either legal or illegal. Tourist or temporary business visas are used to admit the largest such group. Foreign students and their families are issued another major category of such visas; "treaty traders" and investors and temporary workers of various kinds may also qualify. Nonimmigrant visas are temporary, but most of them can be extended. Changes can also be made to shift an individual from nonimmigrant to immigrant status. What generally happens is that a person enters the United States under a nonimmigrant visa, for example, as a student, tourist, or temporary business transferee. He or she then links up with an employer who eventually initiates the change process. Waivers for tourist visas in recent years have been granted to nations having a low record of visa overstays; essentially, this includes the countries of western Europe and Japan.

How Immigration Works

The Immigration and Naturalization Service (INS), an entity within the U.S. Department of Justice, is charged with the responsibility for monitoring the process by which citizens of other countries are admitted to the United states and prepared for naturalization as citizens. The much-prized "green card" (actually, the 1990s version is salmon-colored) issued by the INS is essentially a visa for permanent residence in the United States. Once issued, the green card entitles the holder to work and live in the United States permanently. Permanent residents may not vote and are prohibited from holding certain types of government jobs; however, they have most of the other rights accorded to citizens. A legal immigrant is, by definition, a permanent resident alien and may apply for citizenship after five years of official permanent residency.

If entry to or continuing residency in the United States is illegal, the individuals are subject to deportation. Essentially a forced departure, deportation is a long administrative procedure that must be taken by the U.S. government in getting a court order issued. It is expensive, time-consuming, and does not always result in success, given the safeguards for rights of aliens that are built into U.S. immigration law.

It is generally acknowledged that the INS, especially its enforcement branch, has functioned with severe fiscal restraints. This has made it difficult for the agency to initiate or enforce deportation orders. With the right legal advice, it is not very difficult or expensive to arrange matters so that forced departure is unlikely. For example, the mere act of applying for asylum in effect guarantees a person permission to remain in the United States (with a work permit and six-year suspension of deportation) while the application is pending. With a current backlog of more than 111,000 cases, years of residence in the United States are virtually assured.[7]

Formal deportation, however, is not the usual method for arranging exit of illegal immigrants. Far more common is the action of "voluntary departure." The advantage to this for the illegal entrant is that it carries none of the penalties of deportation, which bars a person from applying for a U.S. visa, usually for about five years. By departing voluntarily, illegals can apply for legal entry at any time. This is the option chosen by almost all of the one million or more persons being apprehended annually for illegal border crossings in the early 1990s. Many such persons try to cross the Mexican border on many occasions and may exercise the voluntary departure option each time.

It is not easy for the government to force illegal immigrants to leave, even when conditions change for the better in their home countries. There should not, for example, be any surprise at the lack of a voluntary mass exodus from the United States of Nicaraguans following the return of democracy in that country. In a walking tour of Sweetwater, the nearly 100 percent Nicaraguan suburb of Miami, journalist Pete Hamill was unable to find anyone who wanted to go home. "Nobody wants to go back," a used-car salesman told Hamill. "And the reason is simple. They didn't come here because of the Sandinistas. That's all politics and bullshit. They came here because of poverty. Here they have jobs, they have places to live, they have cars, they have their kids in good schools, they think it's paradise. Why would they want to go back? And how can the Americans force them to go back?"[8]

Many of the Nicaraguans now living in the Miami area entered the U.S. illegally and applied for political asylum, which they will not likely get under present conditions. Mass deportation might be legal but is undoubtedly infeasible politically. Nicaraguans, along with Cubans, tend to have ties to the Republican party, which controlled the executive branch until January of 1993. (Mexicans, on the other hand, have traditional links with the Democrats.)

The INS is well aware that it has a major problem with fraudulent documentation used by persons desiring to enter and remain in the United States. A major cottage industry is built upon the creation of bogus documentation that can be presented to employers as evidence of legal residence in the United States. False papers (social security cards, birth certificates, alien registration cards, and the like) are not expensive to obtain. In 1991, for example, the U.S. Postal Inspection Service obtained convictions of three men arrested for selling such identity cards for $100 to illegal aliens in the Des Moines area.[9] Prices as low as $3.00 for such cards have also been reported.[10]

Sanctions apply to employers who knowingly hire illegal immigrants, but employers often do not consider it their responsibility (or in their interest) to review documentation in anything other than the most casual manner. Even with the 1986 Immigration Reform and Control Act penalties in effect, many employers are reported to be none too scrupulous about checking the fine points.[11]

Schools or other educational agencies may be unwittingly caught up in the INS's immigration enforcement efforts. The INS has been accused by immigrant advocate groups of harassment, or even abuse and brutality. At a Dallas public hearing held by a Texas gubernatorial task force, it was charged that the INS had conducted a "raid" at a Dallas elementary school . Parents who were taking their children to school were allegedly apprehended by INS officers, and Hispanic teachers in the school were questioned. INS officials told quite a different story, indicating that their officers did not conduct any such raid. In the Dallas incident, the agency said, the INS vehicle happened to be parked near the school only so it would be out of sight of a place of employment then under investigation for hiring undocumented workers.[12]

The Future

Given the new law and present trends in immigration, educators in every sector can expect a substantial share of their clients to come from other countries. Immigration in both its legal and illegal manifestations will rise to the highest levels in the nation's history.

Somewhat greater diversity as to ethnic origin can be expected with larger numbers arriving from the continents of Europe and Africa. The preponderance of immigrants, however, will continue to come from nations in Latin America and Asia. This will significantly alter the racial composition of the nation. In a 1991 study of the immigrant population for the Urban Institute, Barry Edmonston and Jeffrey Passel projected that the white, non-Hispanic population of the United States will continue to decline as a proportion of total population in the years ahead. The Asian and Hispanic populations will grow substantially, both in numbers and proportionately. The number of blacks will increase, but their proportionate share of the population will increase only slightly. Hispanics will increase to a number exceeding blacks by about 2010.[13]

Although a larger number of highly educated immigrants are on their way, an even greater flow of illegal immigrants will enlarge the nation's pool of illiterate or poorly educated residents. The continued emphasis upon family reunification will also bring large numbers of immigrants who will tend to have less education than the original entrants. A recent Census Bureau study indicates that as many as 20 million people worldwide may be eligible to enter the United States because of family relationships.[14] Educators in the United States thus need to be ready to serve an even more diverse clientele in the years ahead.

4

Immigrant Education and the Courts

Immigrant rights are protected by the federal government, which has almost exclusive power over the states in this realm. Generally, states are not permitted to apply policies or practices that discriminate against aliens.

Four federal court decisions have particular relevance for education issues involving immigrants. In other cases, the courts have interpreted laws on civil rights and rights of the handicapped in ways that have importantly affected immigrants.

Meyer v. Nebraska

An early landmark is *Meyer v. Nebraska*, a 1923 U.S. Supreme Court decision that struck down an earlier Nebraska statute barring individuals and schools from providing instruction in a language other than English to any student who had not completed the eighth grade. The defendant in *Meyer* was a teacher in a parochial school in a Lutheran church who taught the German language to a ten-year old boy who had not passed the eighth grade. The text used, a book of biblical stories written in German, was for the purpose of giving religious instruction. Some members of the congregation had difficulty understanding sermons in English and consequently couldn't give their children religious instruction in English. Their desire, according to the pastor, was simply that of having their children learn enough German to worship together as a family.

The *Meyer* decision put a stop to what had become a national trend. Nebraska had passed its English-only statute in 1919, and fourteen other states had followed its lead. Some had gone so far as to declare English (or "American") to be their official language.[1] What was gained in *Meyer* was the right to use a language other than English in the classroom, a right that still stands.

Plyler v. Doe

Texas school districts were among the first to experience strains caused by illegal immigration. In response, the state legislature in 1975 enacted laws under which state funds could not be used for the education of students who were not residing in the United States legally. Under the same law, local school boards could refuse to enroll such children or could charge them tuition. As was inevitable, these strictures resulted in a number of lawsuits, which ultimately reached the United States' high court and were decided in June 1982 in a ruling known as *Plyler v. Doe*. In making its *Plyler v. Doe* decision, the Supreme Court put its emphasis on the rights of children rather than upon the sins of their parents. At issue was the question of whether the children of illegal aliens had a constitutional right to free attendance in the public schools. The state of Texas, in presenting its case, had argued that it was necessary to preserve the state's limited resources for the education of its own citizens. The Constitution's Fourteenth Amendment was cited by the plaintiffs as their ground of support by virtue of the wording, "Nor shall any state deprive any person of life, liberty or property without due process of law, nor deny to any person within its jurisdiction the equal protection of the laws."

The Court's majority determined that "equal protection" under the Fourteenth Amendment "is not confined to the protection of citizens." Both the equal protection and due process clauses of the Constitution, the court declared, "are universal in their application, to all persons within the territorial jurisdiction, without regard to any differences of race, color, or of nationality; and the protection of the laws is a pledge of the protection of equal laws."

The Court's majority opinion in *Plyler v. Doe* contains rather dramatic and elegant language highlighting the public-interest aspects involved. Penalizing children for the illegal entry of their parents would mark them with the "stigma of illiteracy for the rest of their lives." If education in the United States is not a fundamental right, the opinion continued, "neither is it merely some governmental 'benefit' indistinguishable from other forms of social welfare." Was it not instead, as labeled in prior court opinions, "the most vital civic institution for the preservation of a democratic system of government," as well as the chief means of transmitting "the values on which our society rests"? Also underlined by the Court majority was that "we cannot ignore the significant social costs borne by our Nation when select groups are denied the means to absorb the values and skills upon which our social order rests." They added, "It is . . . clear that whatever savings might be achieved by denying these children an education, they are wholly insubstantial in light of the costs involved to these children, the State, and the Nation."

The majority acknowledged that illegal aliens might have a negative net impact upon the economy but did not buy the argument that barring their children from public education would have the effect of discouraging illegal entries, "at least when compared with the alternative of prohibiting employment of illegal aliens." The majority further indicated that they would not be impressed even if the state could have proved that the quality of public education was improved by excluding a certain group of children from educational opportunities. The state, they reasoned, had not justified its selection of this particular group.[2]

As a result of the Supreme Court's *Plyler* decision, no school in the United States may legally deny immigrant students admission on the basis of their undocumented status, nor may they treat undocumented students differently. Even inquiries about a student's immigration status can be touchy if they can be interpreted as having a "chilling" effect on the student's right of access.[3]

The National Council of La Raza, the major Hispanic immigrant advocacy group, instructs its members to insist that school officials stay out of enforcement procedures that are explicitly delegated to the Immigration and Naturalization Service. School boards are further admonished that they should enact and enforce policies clearly forbidding any "vigilante" action on the part of local staff who might decide to require documentation of persons enrolling in school-sponsored activities. La Raza warns school districts that INS agents should be allowed on school property only with a specific warrant authorizing their presence and naming specific individuals. Neither are school records to be made available to INS officials without a similar warrant. Districts are asked to document their interactions with the INS in the event a challenge to actions or policies should be deemed appropriate. La Raza also urges its members to make public protests in the event the INS stages "raids" just outside school property, with the target being mothers or baby sitters bringing children to school.[4]

How then may a school district proceed in obtaining background information that can be helpful in providing appropriate educational experiences for the children of illegal immigrants? The National Coalition of Advocates for Students concedes that under "very carefully restricted and monitored situations," an exception might be made so that schools can document a student's country of origin.[5]

If the *Plyler v. Doe* decision grants rights to the children of undocumented immigrants, it imposes a responsibility as well—namely, the duty to attend school. Like their native-born counterparts, immigrant children must attend school until they reach the age mandated by the state of residence. Schools, too, have a responsibility to encourage attendance. Some fail by their inattention to opportunities for outreach.

Plyler v. Doe does not apply to higher education or to adult education settings. Undocumented immigrants are seldom, if ever, treated differently from citizens or permanent residents when applying to noncredit adult learning programs. Higher education is another matter, and it is nearly certain that the U.S. Supreme Court will hear one day from illegal immigrants asserting that *Plyler v. Doe* should equalize their access to colleges and universities also. In the view of one legal author, such a suit may well be brought by an immigrant who has been served in adult basic education classes offered by a community college that then denies the same individual admission to a degree credit program.[6]

Lau v. Nichols

Language-minority students achieved more protection than was probably anticipated at the time the Civil Rights Act of 1964 was passed. The provision here was Title VI, which prohibited discrimination on the basis of national origin. On May 25, 1970, the director of the

Office on Civil Rights sent a memo to school districts whose national origin minority-group enrollments exceeded 5 percent. To clarify federal policy on issues concerning the responsibility of school districts to provide equal educational opportunity to national origin minority-group children, the memorandum outlined four basic school district responsibilities.

First, each district was to take "affirmative steps to rectify the language deficiency in order to open its instructional program" to students with limited English proficiency. Second, school districts were prohibited from assigning national origin minority-group students to classes for the mentally retarded on the basis of criteria essentially measuring or evaluating English language skills. Third, ability grouping or tracking systems for students with limited English were to be designed to meet language skill needs as soon as possible "and must not operate as an educational dead-end or permanent track." Fourth, school districts were ordered to notify the parents of limited English speakers of school activities, using a language other than English if necessary.[7] This turned out to be a very significant communication from the federal government, but its full import would not be noted until after the Supreme Court's *Lau v. Nichols* decision.

In 1970, a class action suit was entered against the San Francisco school system. The charge was that the district was failing to provide English language instruction to approximately 1,800 students of Chinese extraction who did not speak English and that they were not otherwise provided with adequate instruction that would assure them of "education on equal terms" (the standard used by the high court in *Brown v. Board of Education*).[8] In affirming that this was a violation of Sec. 601 of the Civil Rights Act of 1964, the U.S. Supreme Court in 1974 (*Lau v. Nichols*) declared:

> "There is no equality of treatment merely by providing students with the same facilities, textbooks, teachers, and curriculum; for students who do not understand English are effectively foreclosed from any meaningful education. Basic English skills are at the very core of what these public schools to teach. Imposition of a requirement that, before a child can effectively participate in the educational program, he must already have acquired those basic skills is to make a mockery of public education. We know that those who do not understand English are certain to find their classroom experiences wholly incomprehensible.[9]

The Court added: "Teaching English to the students of Chinese ancestry who do not speak the language is one choice. Giving instructions to this group in Chinese is another. There may be others."[10]

The commissioner of education in August 1975 issued guidelines for assuring compliance with Title VI of the Civil Rights Act under the *Lau* decision. The "Lau guidelines" or "Lau remedies," as they came to be called, were quite comprehensive and very specific. Schools were told how they could identify and evaluate national origin minority-group students' English language skills, determine appropriate instruction treatments, decide when limited-English-proficiency (LEP) children were ready for mainstream classes, and identify professional standards for teachers of language-minority children.

But the Lau guidelines went well beyond the legal bounds of the *Lau* decision to state that schools should provide instruction to elementary students in their strongest language until they could effectively participate in English-only classes. English as a second language (ESL) courses were specified for every student for which English was not the strongest language. Furthermore, any school district that intended to use ESL exclusively was required to demonstrate that their programs were as effective as the types of bilingual programs described in the guidelines.

Although they were never published in the *Federal Register*, the Office for Civil Rights (OCR) staff began using the Lau guidelines as de facto standards to measure compliance with Title VI under *Lau*. The medicine was bitter for some districts, but in the face of losing federal funds, they swallowed hard and signed up as sponsors of bilingual education. During the five-year period between 1975 and 1980, voluntary compliance plans were negotiated with some 359 school districts. It is understandable in such circumstances that many such programs were given stepchild status and that momentum for revenge aimed at the federal government began to build.[11]

The backlash officially came in 1978 when the Northwest Arctic School District in Alaska contested OCR's use of the Lau guidelines, arguing that the guidelines had never been published in the *Federal Register* or promulgated as formal regulations. The suit was successful. It was agreed that new guidelines would be developed, and on August 5, 1980, the newly formed Department of Education published in the *Federal Register* a new set of proposed guidelines that required school districts receiving federal aid to provide special instruction to all students with limited English proficiency.[12]

Comments were invited and were received—some 4,000 of them. Most were critical of some provisions as being too prescriptive. Hearing these unfavorable reactions from many of their constituents, members of Congress were quick to respond. After conferring with congressional leaders, Secretary of Education Shirley Hufstedler suspended work on the guidelines and withdrew them.[13] After the election of Ronald Reagan in 1980, the new education secretary, Terrel Bell, in an unnecessary but symbolic gesture also withdrew the guidelines in order to underline the new administration's opposition to them.[14]

In 1985, OCR issued still another set of procedures for school districts to use in complying with Title VI of the Civil Rights Act. This document reaffirms that school districts must take "affirmative steps" that will facilitate instruction for students with limited English proficiency. Left unstated are any prescriptive measures; the districts "may use any method or program that has proven successful, or may implement any sound educational program that promises to be successful." But they must "evaluate the results to make sure the programs are working as anticipated, and modify programs that do not meet these expectations." The current guidelines have never been published in the *Federal Register*, but they stand as OCR's announced policy.[15]

Teresa P. v. Berkeley Unified School District

It is ironic that one of the first school districts in the country to introduce a program of native-language-based bilingual education should run afoul of contemporary advocates of that system of instruction. Proponents of the system suffered a major setback in February 1989 when a federal district court in California found in *Teresa P. v. Berkeley Unified School District* that the Berkeley schools' English-based bilingual education program did not violate federal law. The laws in question were Title VI of the Civil Rights Act of 1964, which forbids discrimination against students who are limited in their English proficiency, and the Equal Educational Opportunities Act of 1974, which requires school districts to remove barriers to non-English-speaking students' access to equal educational opportunities. A group representing some students with limited English proficiency argued that only native-language instruction by teachers especially trained in this work should be permissible. The district offered both, with native-language instruction favored mostly by Hispanic parents and the English model by Asian parents.[16]

Reflecting the intensity of the debate in this matter, the trial attracted a host of witnesses on both sides, with their five weeks of testimony ultimately filling fourteen volumes. Judge D. Lowell Jenson noted that it was unlikely that Berkeley could find teachers at all of the various levels who spoke and could instruct in all 38 languages represented in the Berkeley schools. The judge found that "the educational theories upon which [the district's] programs are grounded are manifestly as sound as any theory identified by the plaintiffs." The judge also accepted state tests that indicated that LEP students from Berkeley schools did as well or better than students in schools with native-language bilingual models that the plaintiffs held up as models.[17]

Opponents of native-language-based bilingual instruction were elated after the *Teresa P.* decision, claiming that it bolstered their claims that such instruction doesn't work. Bilingual advocates concede that it was a major defeat for their interests; but the debate continues.

Limited English Proficiency as a "Handicap"

Public Law 94-142 mandates that students be evaluated in their native language or mode of communication. But real difficulties present themselves in the way of anyone trying to determine whether students of limited or no English speaking proficiency should be designated as exceptional. There are no normed or validated tests available for many of the languages now represented in the nation's schools.[18]

Nonetheless, failure to comply can be costly, as the Boston public schools now know. The Massachusetts education department began withholding federal special education funds from the Boston public schools in July of 1990 when they judged the schools not to be providing special education services in a timely fashion. The problem, in part, was the district's alleged slowness in translating students' individualized education plans into Spanish. Mary-Beth Fafard, the associate director for special education at the Massachusetts Education Department, said the funds withheld ($863,000) would be given to the district after it submitted a plan and resolved the issues.[19] The money was restored by December when a court-ordered monitor reported that the battered district had made progress, eliminating a backlog by translating individualized education plans.[20]

In January 1991, the Office of Civil Rights in the U.S. Department of Education told the nation's school districts that they could expect closer scrutiny of their bilingual education programs. The OCR said it would be looking at three issues: (1) LEP students who were placed in special education programs merely because of their lack of language skills, (2) disabled LEP students excluded from special education programs because of language problems, and (3) disabled LEP students enrolled in special education programs but excluded from bilingual programs. In support of its agenda, the OCR cite a 1988 survey showing about 20,000 LEP students with disabilities nationwide.[21]

Incipient Issues

Some school districts, particularly in California, have developed "newcomer schools" that typically serve only immigrant students as they enter the system. Such districts may, however, find themselves facing legal challenges—even where such programs are limited to one year, as has been customary in California. Title VI of the Civil Rights Code specifies that programs and activities receiving federal financial assistance may not discriminate on the basis of race, color, or national origin.[22]

Recently the Office of Civil Rights announced the result of its three-year investigation of charges that a newcomer school for recent immigrants in Sacramento was created in violation of federal desegregation laws. It found that the newcomer school did not segregate students solely on the basis of race or ethnic group. In citing its findings, the OCR noted that enrollment in the school is voluntary, that children stay there for less than a year, and that its offerings are comparable to those offered elsewhere in the Sacramento Unified School District. The federal officials stated, however, that they continued "to have some serious reservations" about the existence of such a program at a separate site.[23]

5
Refugees: Special Needs and Issues in Education

The world is brimming with refugees. As of 1992, an estimated 16.6 million persons were living away from their homes as refugees because of war, strife, or political persecution. Who are they? Afghans, Palestinians, Mozambiqueans, Liberians, Somalis, Ethiopians, former Soviets, Sri Lankan Tamils, Cambodians, Vietnamese, and Laotians, among others, according to the U.S. Committee for Refugees.[1] New outbreaks of violence in what was Yugoslavia are adding even more to the roster of the world's displaced.

Which refugees get resettled in the United States? Humanitarian concerns are not the only determinant; politics are in fact a prime consideration. Refugee acceptance is at times an instrument of foreign policy. It is also a way of settling political debts with ethnically rooted home constituencies.

A person seeking admission to the United States, in addition to meeting the definition of *refugee* specified in the Refugee Act of 1980, must be (1) among the types of refugees determined under explicit provisions in the law to be "of special humanitarian concern to the United States," (2) admissible under U.S. law, and (3) not firmly resettled in any foreign country. Even if a person meets all of these criteria, however, he or she has no automatic entitlement to enter the United States.[2]

Refugee Nationalities

Cubans are the largest group of refugees to be admitted to the United States since the end of World War II; more than a million of them now call the United States of America home. About 850,000 persons from Southeast Asian nations have been admitted. Between 1975 and 1986, 109,000 Soviet refugees came, along with 30,000 Poles, 26,000 Romanians, 21,000 Afghans, 18,000 Ethiopians, and 6,000 Iraqis.[3]

In addition, some persons have been granted extended voluntary departure (EVD) status or have applied for asylum after arrival under nonimmigrant visas. Still others reside in the United States illegally but have many of the characteristics typical of refugees; many hundreds of thousands of Central Americans fleeing war or poverty in their nations fall into this category. Beginning in 1992, between 200,000 and 300,000 Salvadorans currently in the United States illegally will be eligible for temporary protected status.

The lines classifying persons residing in the United States officially as refugees, asylees, humanitarian parolees, "Cuban/Haitian entrants," and holders of the temporary protected status of extended voluntary departure status are blurred to say the least.[4] The texture of this flow has in any event changed forever the description of what it means to be "American." A brief description of some key groups of refugee entrants begins to fill in the emerging national portrait.

Three significant waves of Cuban immigration can be identified. The first immediately followed the Castro-led revolution between 1960 and 1963. Another wave broke on American shores between 1966 and 1972. The third wave—mainly the Mariel refugees (a reference to the Cuban port city from which most of them embarked)—came to the United States in 1980.[5] It was the Mariel refugees who presented the stiffest test to the nation's education institutions. On May 6, 1980, then-President Jimmy Carter told the world that the United States would welcome the Mariel refugees "with open arms and open hearts." And so the nation did, but it was a welcome that would wear a bit thin as some 125,000 Cubans took the president up on his offer and entered the United States between April 1980 and the year's end.[6] Fidel Castro with apparent gusto dumped amid the refugee flow some unwanted elements of his society, including hard-core criminals and mental patients. Some 7,200 Haitians also were also admitted in this period as "Cuban/Haitian entrants—status pending," a term unique in immigration law.[7]

Once swamped by the Mariel crisis, Florida moved quickly in an effort to protect itself against future floods of immigrants. Castro was cast as the villain by Florida Senator Lawton Chiles, who said he had watched his state "struggle to bring some kind of makeshift order out of the chaos visited upon us." He pointed to the education and public health services that were strained beyond capacity, and the state, county, and city budgets that were drained. Everyone in Florida began talking about increased levels of crime, business decline, and lost tourism. Senator Chiles sadly noted that the Miami area had become known as a "gun belt" as citizens armed themselves in the face of the crime wave that was stimulated in part by entry of former inmates from Cuban prisons.[8]

Leonard Britton, superintendent of the hard-hit Dade County public schools, told a congressional hearing something about the strains his system was experiencing because of the Mariel boatlift. On April 28, 1980, just a week after the port of Mariel was opened for exits by fleeing Cubans, 27 Cuban refugee students were enrolled in the county's schools. By June 1, the total was 1,000, but by June 11 (the last day of the school year), the numbers had swelled to 6,000.[9] But this was nothing in comparison to what was coming. When the schools again opened on the day after Labor Day, more than 13,000 refugee students were enrolled—none of whom had been in the United States five months before. By the end of the semester, the total had reached 15,000; of this number, 13,500 were Cubans. The others were 800 Haitians, 600 Nicaraguans, 50 Indo-Chinese, 26 Russians, and 25 students from six other nations.[10]

Saigon fell in April 1975, and so began a massive flow of refugees from communist Vietnam, along with Laos and Cambodia, that continues to this day. Of the nearly 300,000 refugees admitted to the United States in the 1976–80 period, 90 percent were from Southeast Asia (with more than 70 percent coming from Vietnam). These immigrants arrived in four recognizable waves. Relatively young, better-educated, and relatively skilled refugees were present in generous numbers in the first wave, which began in 1975 and extended through 1978. Some 125,000 of the total number of 131,000 of this group were Vietnamese.[11]

The "boat people" who began their voyages of escape in September of 1978, and others who arrived with the second wave in the earliest years of the 1980s, tended to be quite different from the prior arrivals. In general, they were from the less economically and socially advantaged classes in their home nations and were less likely to speak English. Again, most were from Vietnam (about 40 percent of them ethnic Chinese), but a large number of Cambodian and Laotian refugees also came with this group.[12] With this second wave, starting in 1980, also came a large number of unaccompanied minors. Many had little schooling because of constant displacement in their home nations. They were agonizingly unprepared for the rigors and culture of schoolrooms in the United States and consequently had more than their share of difficulties with school officials and law enforcement authorities.[13]

The third wave of immigration from Southeast Asia began in 1982 with establishment of the Orderly Departure Program. As relatives of permanent residents they technically hold legal immigrant rather than refugee status.[14] Educators in the United States were ill prepared to receive these early waves of Southeast Asian refugees. For example, the Lowell, Massachusetts schools were nearly overwhelmed when large numbers of Southeast Asian refugees arrived almost overnight in the early 1980s.[15] The nation's schools were particularly lacking in an understanding of the educational background of this group of students. To help them, the Center for Applied linguistics (CAL) even reprinted Vietnamese school textbooks in English so that the teachers would know more of what their new students might previously have learned. But sometimes there was virtually no "educational background" to evaluate.

In the mid-1980s, teacher groups consulted by CAL reported difficulties with an increasing number of refugee children who had virtually no education because they had been in transit as refugees for as long as ten years. Teenage young people from Laos and Cambodia were particularly at risk in the schools on this account. The same condition is currently being reported for many new arrivals from Central America, where youngsters have often bypassed the education system altogether.

A fourth unique wave of refugees, composed of Amerasians (young people with native mothers and U.S. serviceman fathers) and numerous accompanying relatives, entered this country from Vietnam between 1988 and 1990. In order to appease the government of Vietnam, Amerasians are given immigrant (rather than refugee) status. Upon arrival, however, they are given the same benefits accorded officially designated refugees.

Some of these refugees came from cultures with almost no prior ties to the United States. Their presence in this country has transformed entire communities. In early 1981, Fresno, a city of 280,000 inhabitants in the Central Valley of California, had almost no Hmong residents (immigrants from the highland areas of Laos). Two years later, 12,000 had settled there, almost all of them via secondary immigrant routes from other parts of the country. In very short order, the elementary schools were forced into year-round sessions.[16]

Few African refugees—except some who managed to get out of Marxist Ethiopia—have reached the United States, in spite of the approximately 4 million persons who have been displaced from their homes on that troubled continent. Neighboring African countries have, to date, been quite generous in accommodating the castoffs from their neighbors. But another reason for lack of admissions has been the absence of a strong pressure group advocating their cause in the United States.[17]

Until the democratic revolutions at the turn of the 1990s, the Soviet satellite nations of eastern Europe were heavy contributors of refugees to the United States. For example, 33,000 Poles and 29,000 Romanians reached American shores in the period between 1980 and 1988.[18] Troubled Middle East and South Asian nations have also contributed many thousands of their citizens as refugees to this country. Between 1980 and 1988, the United States received 24,000 Afghans, 24,000 Iranians, and 6,000 Iraqis.[19]

At the moment, the most rapidly increasing refugee population in the United States is that coming from what was the Soviet Union.[20] In 1989, several new groups of Soviet refugees began arriving in somewhat larger numbers. These included Armenians, Zoroastrians, and Pentacostals. As the former USSR restructures itself, pressures for admission to the United States of many more displaced groups will build.

English Language Instruction

A study prepared for the Office of Refugee Resettlement in 1985 reaffirmed earlier findings that English language proficiency is of "overriding importance" as a predictor of self-sufficiency for refugees.[21] Proficiency in English has been found to affect labor force participation (those working or seeking work), unemployment rates, and earnings. A 1989 report on refugee resettlement showed that for those refugees who judged themselves to be fluent in English, the labor force participation rate was only 8 percentage points lower than that for the overall United States population. The comparable figure for the entire refugee sample was a gap of 29 percentage points below the overall population. Of the refugees who spoke no English, only 10 percent were employed or seeking work.[22]

The Office of Refugee Resettlement specifies that a competency-based English as a second language (ESL) curriculum based on life-skill performance objectives be followed by all programs for which it provides funding. Recipients of these funds include mutual assistance associations (refugee self-help organizations), church groups, and community agencies.[23]

How do refugees proceed when they want to improve their English language skills? Not always by means of classes, according to a survey of refugees undertaken by the Office of Refugee Assistance. Some 75 percent of refugees said they attended ESL classes, but 66 percent mentioned watching television and listening to radio broadcasts, 40 percent practiced with native-born citizens, 10 percent practiced with members of their own household, 20 percent employed a tutor, and 10 percent chose to live in a predominantly nonimmigrant residential area. Planners of language programs for refugees would be well advised to take into account this rich mix of preferred learning alternatives.[24]

Pre-Entry Education

The typical refugee begins life in the United States with fewer advantages than does the typical legal immigrant. Most of them do not have prior ties to this country and are less likely to have skills that are transferable. Furthermore, refugees are not as apt to have a well-established community of compatriots in the United States, nor are they able to maintain economic or social ties with their home countries.

Refugees almost invariably need to have a variety of education and training experiences before they can be truly successful in entering the national mainstream. Providing an appropriate response on

American shores has been a major challenge. In an effort to gain a head start on this task, the U.S. Department of State decided to install education and training programs in camps located in countries of first asylum. This enabled refugees to use what had previously been wasted time in the months prior to arrival in this country. At present, this program is run at two sites in Southeast Asia. Bataan in the Philippines and Phanat Nikhom in Thailand. Instruction is provided in English, U.S. culture, and work orientation.

Federal Policy on Refugee Education

Current federal policy governing refugee education programs has generated controversy. The arguments often center on the place of vocational education in the curriculum, though as is usual in such debates, the underlying philosophical concerns run much deeper. Jobs and education are linked in the regulations pertaining to targeted assistance funds (TAP) of the Refugee Assistance Extension Act. At least 85 percent of such funds must support projects "which directly enhance refugee employment potential, have specific employment objectives, and are designed to enable refugees to obtain jobs with less than one year's participation."[25]

The range of allowable educational activities is quite closely circumscribed. Included may be job-related and vocational English, short-term job training specifically related to opportunities in the local economy, on-the-job training, on-site employee orientation, and vocational English training.[26] General or remedial educational activities, such as adult basic education or preparation for a GED high school diploma, may be provided though "only within the context of an individual employability plan for a refugee which is intended to result in job placement in less than one year."[27] In such a "front-loading" vocational education program, success is measured "in terms of job placements, job retention, and reductions in cash assistance—the principal objectives of the authorizing legislation," in the words of the administrative regulations.[28]

The federal government's policy of specifying vocational training at the outset for refugees is based on the assumption that more generalized education and training programs tend to delay entry to the labor market and reinforce dependency. Economic adaptation is therefore given preference over cultural adaptation in many of the refugee resettlement programs in the United States; typically, refugees are encouraged to take the first job that comes along. Thereafter, they are encouraged to upgrade their knowledge and skills by taking English language and occupational training. Professional people are encouraged to seek certification to practice in the United States.[29]

At least some studies suggest that this approach, if evaluated only against its stated objectives, is not without merit. The Refugee Policy Group, an independent and nonprofit organization, evaluated the Refugee Early Employment Project (REEP), which has as its aim to promote early employment and economic self-sufficiency among eligible refugees. The results were "impressive" according to the study, with higher levels of employment for refugees and lower costs to the resettlement system.[30] A series of interviews with twenty former staff members of the Overseas Refugee Training Program who are now working with refugees in the United States also offers a positively view of educational programs as accomplished in the overseas holding camps. Several excerpts will provide a flavor of these findings.

Steven Epstein, a coordinator of job training for refugees in San Diego, reports a "phenomenal difference" in refugees who have been through the Overseas Refugee Training Program and those who have not. "Employers really want employees they can talk to," he reports. "Language is a barrier no matter how diligent or conscientious the applicant is. We had one student, a very smart guy, a mechanic, and he never missed class. But we couldn't place him—no English. If he'd had the 20 weeks of language training, we could have gotten him a job."[31]

Much the same report comes from Jenny Jensen, who is a case manager in a Hmong mutual assistance association in Appleton, Wisconsin. She observes a difference not only in language skills but in attitudes toward work among refugee graduates of the overseas program. "Those Hmong who came before the training program started are much more dependent on the government," she says. "They see welfare as an acceptable life-style. The graduates can see beyond that." She further notes that it is the Hmong women who appear to exhibit the most pronounced differences.[32]

Criticisms of Federal Policy

The severest critic of federal policies affecting refugee education is James Tollefson, director of the master's program in teaching English as a Second Language at the University of Washington, who worked for sixteen months in refugee camps in Southeast Asia in the mid-1980s. In a hard-hitting attack, he places the educational programs used for Indochinese refugees in the tradition of the Americanization movement. Such programs, he charges, assume that the refugees must assimilate on the lowest rungs of the social and economic ladder and "change who they are if they are to overcome their difficulties in the United States." The task for the nation's education system becomes that of bringing about change in individual and group identity. If the Americanization movement focused on traditional citizenship as the price of admission to mainstream culture, the refugee education programs are focusing on "*functional citizenship*" [emphasis in original] or "the ability to become a consumer in a consumer economy."[33] Tollefson faults the overseas camps as instruments in a national policy that uses "large scale migration and poorly funded educational programs as mechanisms for achieving labor policy objectives."[34]

There is some truth in these charges, even though they are in some instances grossly overstated by their proponents. Front-loading programs emphasizing high-speed education and training only in the context of acquiring job readiness run the risk of emphasizing the needs of employers rather than the refugees. Job placement, even if it brings self-support and a degree of self-assurance, may not be a satisfactory end in itself. Early employment too often tends to be in marginal jobs where opportunities for advancement are limited; an immigrant may settle into such a job and fail to secure education or training that could lead to something better. More emphasis ought to be placed on identifying existing skills and experience and helping the individual enter the labor market at a higher level where possible.

There are further dimensions to this problem. The welfare dependency rate for refugees in the state of Massachusetts is one of the highest in the nation. One factor contributing to this is that when a refugee goes to work, all welfare benefits, including training, transportation, and child care, are terminated. Many refugees, especially highly motivated arrivals from the former Soviet Union, opt not to take a low-paying, entry-level job when it means giving up their only chance at free training for a more responsible job in the future. The message being given to the refugees is that it is to their advantage to remain on welfare for as long as possible.[35] Educational programs for refugees should also be evaluated to ensure that they contain appropriate components of assertiveness training. Refugees, in common with citizens of the United States, need to learn how to gain more control over the direction of their lives.

Current federal policy affecting refugee education is shortsighted in its preoccupation with early employment goals. Employment, even early employment, may be an appropriate goal of an educational program. But most, if not all, refugees and immigrants unfamiliar with U.S. culture need *both* education leading to employment and education designed to advance them as human beings—just as citizens of the United States do. "Education is not just about making a living; it is also about making a life."[36] In spite of the appearance of this statement in President Bush's *America 2000* education report, the humanistic aspects of this equation are virtually ignored in federal policy pertaining to refugee workers. The implicit assumption seems to be that refugee men and women are not much more than a labor force. Adult and vocational educators should closely examine their role in any process that makes them nothing more than complaisant suppliers of cheap labor.

Aside from philosophical concerns about its goals, federally supported vocational training is not being used by all refugees who might benefit. A study of Southeast Asian refugees for the Office of Refugee Assistance showed that those refugees having the least education and the fewest marketable job skills were also likely to be receiving fewer services than more advantaged refugees. This was especially true of a most important educational service, vocational training. Vocational training was in fact found to be used almost exclusively by males with at least some secondary education and who were professionals, military personnel, or students.[37] This presents a dilemma. The service is being used by those perhaps best prepared to make use of it, but the less advantaged—those most in need of vocational training—remain adrift. More aggressive outreach programs aimed at the most disadvantaged potential clients are an obvious need.

Education as Motivation

If U.S. educators are having difficulty in determining the educational approach that will best meet the needs of refugees, many of the refugees themselves are taking perceived quality of educational opportunities into account in making their own decisions. A study of moves undertaken by refugees resettled in this country shows that educational reasons were a prime motivator in 13 percent of the situations. This was the fourth most important reason for moving, with those listed as more important being a better climate (19 percent) and to join other family members or to get work (17 percent each). In the same study, the need to obtain vocational training was cited as a reason for moving by 2 percent of those surveyed. Among those refugees planning a move, education was cited as a reason by 5 percent.[38]

Cha Yang, for example, did not like heat or gambling—two good reasons for not wanting to live in Las Vegas, where he had initially been settled as a refugee. But the real reason for his move to Long Beach was that he heard it had a better GED high school diploma program than was said then to exist in the Nevada city. Soon after moving, he began studying for the GED examinations for four hours each night after studying English as a second language for eight hours of each day. It took about a year, but he got the GED and eventually started his own business (a mini-mart grocery) in the California community of Fresno.[39]

It took just one look at a classroom in the Philadelphia high school attended by some of his ten children for Kue Chaw, a Hmong leader, to reinforce his feeling that he ought to take his family elsewhere. Might the day come when his children would behave in the manner of the native-born students he observed—with their feet on the desks, chatting with each other during class, and ignoring or even talking back to the teacher?

Kue Chaw didn't like Philadelphia's crowds, noise, pollution, or "fast way of life" either. He gave up a good job as an outreach worker and moved his family to a rural North Carolina community, where he found a house with a combination of omens considered likely to confer good luck on the inhabitants. Some forty Hmong families followed him there. Many of his compatriots still talk about returning to Laos. To them he says, "First we must work hard and give our children a good education. If some day the situation in Laos changes and we can go back, let's go back as teachers, engineers, nurses, doctors, businessmen."[40] In whatever situation they find themselves, refugees determined to succeed in their adopted country cannot ignore education. Most understand that it is their ticket for economic and social advancement.

6

Out of the Shadows and into the Classroom: Educating Illegal and Newly Legal Immigrants

It is relatively easy to enter the United States illegally, and in the last twenty years many millions of people have done so. Most enter by crossing the porous Mexican border, often aided by "coyotes" whose business is that of managing illegal entry to the north. This is the usual mode of entry for illegal entry from Mexico, El Salvador, Guatemala, other South and Central American countries, and even China, where a thriving industry aimed at delivering impoverished immigrants has recently developed.[1] Others, many of them desperate Haitians or Cubans, undertake a sea voyage and arrive surreptitiously on U.S. shores in Florida or elsewhere on the Gulf or Atlantic coasts. "Entry without inspection" is the official INS parlance for this form of access.

Still others enter the United States legally, often on tourist or student visas, and simply overstay the time period of their visa. This is called "visa abuse" by the INS. Document fraud is the another means of illegal entry. An increasing mode of entry in recent years is that used by would-be immigrants who arrive at U.S. airports without valid documents and then claim asylum.

Officials of the U.S. government typically refer to individuals who cross the nation's borders without authorization as "illegal aliens." Some immigrants, Hispanics in particular, object to this term, considering it to have wrongly criminal (as well as "un-American") connotations. Since many clandestine border crossers are otherwise law-abiding and are often would-be citizens, they reason, a more accurate term is *undocumented workers*. This is also the term officially used by the Mexican government. Even so, it can be argued that this term should not be used generically, because it is inaccurate in reference to someone who comes into the country with a legal visa (and then violates its terms and overstays) or who enters with fraudulent documents. Fortunately no longer in official use is the definitely pejorative term *wetback*, which was derived from the condition of persons arriving in the United States after crossing the Rio Grande without the benefit of bridges. In the 1950s, the federal government was even so insensitive as to name one of its mass deportation programs "Operation Wetback."

Once the border is crossed, little risk attends the process of illegal entry. If apprehended, most individuals are simply given an attractive alternative to formal deportation: the option of voluntary departure. If taken, this alternative does not prejudice their chances for legal entry later. The Border Patrol, the semiautonomous arm of the INS charged with border-crossing enforcement, is not equipped to stem the tide completely. Even with a somewhat beefed-up cadre of personnel, it is estimated that for every illegal immigrant apprehended, another one crosses unimpeded.[2]

It is, of course, impossible to obtain precise statistics as to the number of persons living illegally in the United States. Jeffrey Passel, a researcher at the Urban Institute, estimates that the current number is between 3 and 4 million. The Center for Immigration Studies places the numbers a bit higher, between 4.5 and 5 million (excluding the more than 3 million who filed legalization applications in the late 1980s).[3]

A study of apprehensions of those attempting to enter may indicate the approximate composition of those who actually succeed in bypassing entry regulations. Of those apprehended in fiscal year 1991, almost 94 percent were from Mexico. El Salvador, Canada, Guatemala, the Dominican Republic, and China account for the next highest numbers.[4]

The Immigration Reform and Control Act

The nation as a whole has long been concerned about the extent of illegal immigration, but getting appropriate legislation on the books was quite difficult in light of the opposition by employers in search of cheap and reliable labor, as well as ethnic advocacy groups. Ultimately, the forces favoring some semblance of control on illegal immigration prevailed. The 1986 Immigration Reform and Control Act (IRCA) authorized legalization to certain undocumented aliens but at the same time imposed sanctions on employers who thereafter hired persons without appropriate documentation. The idea was to accommodate a widening of the nation's front door (realized through more generous legal immigration limits) by closing the back door being entered by illegal immigrants. This analogy was framed by Theodore Hesburgh, former president of the University of Notre Dame, who chaired a committee that advised the Carter administration on immigration policy.[5]

IRCA subjected employers to civil fines if they knowingly hired undocumented workers or failed to request some evidence of eligibility to work from new hires. Employers found to engage in a "pattern and practice" of hiring undocumented workers were made subject to both fines and imprisonment.[6] Illegal aliens who could prove continuous residence in the United States since January 1, 1982, and who otherwise met criteria for admissibility as immigrants were granted the right to adjust to lawful temporary residence within the year following May 5, 1987.

In addition, the IRCA legislation allowed two groups of farm workers to adjust their status. Individuals who had worked in agriculture for at least ninety days from May 1985 through May 1986 could apply for temporary resident status and be eligible to adjust to permanent status after two years if they met other eligibility criteria. A second group of farm workers who had worked at least ninety days in agriculture in each of the immediately preceding three years could apply for temporary resident status and adjust to permanent status after one year in most instances.[7]

In the months that followed enactment of this law, schools in many areas found themselves inundated with requests for documentation of U.S. residency.[8] School attendance and related records of one or more children were in many instances the tickets that ultimately permitted entire families to achieve legalization.

Title II of the Immigration Reform and Control Act contains important provisions affecting educational opportunities for previously illegal immigrants. It specified that all applicants for permanent residence in the United States (except for agricultural workers, who were exempt) were expected to possess basic English language skills and an understanding of U.S. history and government or be "satisfactorily pursuing" attainment of such knowledge. Moreover, the Congress authorized $4 billion in State Legalization Impact Assistance Grants (SLIAG) for this purpose for a four-year period.

Once available only on an hours-of-instruction-per-student basis, SLIAG funds were eventually opened for use by organizations serving eligible students enrolled in any educational program currently funded under the Adult Education Act—including English as a second language, literacy, GED high school diploma, and other nonvocational courses. Courses on preparing taxes or buying a car could also be covered. Some states authorized SLIAG fund use for activities related to recruitment and retention of students. Coordination of child care and transportation services could also be arranged.[9]

SLIAG provisions were modeled after comparable provisions of the Emergency Immigrant Education Act. The instigator was former House Speaker Jim Wright, whose action in this respect was initially viewed with suspicion by some Hispanic groups. "We initially viewed it as just another hoop to jump through," says La Raza's Cecilia Muñoz, "but when funding was not only authorized but appropriated, the same groups began viewing it as an opportunity."

Implementing Amnesty

How did one meet the IRCA education requirements and become legalized? There were a number of options. The most commonly used one was that of taking forty hours of English language, history, and government courses approved by the state attorney general. No federal regulation specified the ratio of ESL to civics and history in such curricula. In practice, program directors tended to emphasize English instruction and life skills for students at lower levels of educational attainment. Civics was generally emphasized with students with more prior education.[10]

Among the other options deemed acceptable for meeting the education requirement were (1) answering questions from the IRCA Section 312 citizenship test in front of an INS examiner, (2) taking the IRCA Test for Permanent Residency, (3) taking standardized tests developed by the Educational Testing Service or the Comprehensive Adult Student Assessment System in California,[11] (4) presenting a

U.S. high school or English language GED diploma,[12] or (5) taking employer-based courses that met certain criteria.

Passage of IRCA, with its modest education requirements for those seeking legal permanent residency, touched off a rush for immigrant adult education. Long waiting lines for ESL classes built up rapidly in such high-impact areas as New York, San Francisco, and Houston.[13] But it was in Los Angeles, with its huge population of illegal immigrants, that the real crush came. At the zenith of the amnesty education program in April of 1989, the Los Angeles Unified School District had enrolled 121,000 in nearly 5,000 classes. About 3,000 teachers were employed, and twenty-four-hour service was provided at one location, the Evans Community Adult School.

Los Angeles had more than its share of difficulties in meeting the onslaught of demand for classes that would meet the IRCA requirements of forty hours of instruction. Federal funds were not immediately available, necessitating an act of faith in putting up state or local funds to the program started. But very real trauma ensued when a two-week teacher strike hit in May of 1989 at the very height of the amnesty demand. District administrative personnel were forced into marathon performance in classrooms jammed to the rafters with immigrant students anxious to qualify for amnesty. In spite of these problems, the district met the demand. None of its institutions was permitted to place any amnesty student on a waiting list.

ESL classes were another matter. Fueled to a large degree by pent-up demand from previously illegal immigrants, a huge demand arose, resulting in a waiting list of 40,000 persons in 1986.[14] In view of its inability to enroll all applicants in its ESL classrooms, the district turned toward other methods of instruction. It developed an amnesty citizenship preparation video program for use by community agencies.[15]

Throughout California, long waiting lists for English language classes were the rule. At one point, would-be enrollees were in sleeping bags as they waited in line overnight. It was estimated that in 1986, between 80,000 and 116,000 adults were on waiting lists for English language courses that were already filled to capacity. Fully 80 percent of California's adult literacy funding was going for ESL courses during this period.[16]

All of this was enough to trigger a lawsuit filed by some public interest groups to force the Los Angeles Unified School District to provide more classes. It did not succeed. In an ironic commentary on the result, a lawyer for the plaintiffs said she found this to be a "double message" in a state that had just voted to make English its official language.[17]

Finding enough teachers for the new amnesty clients was an obvious priority in every locality where eligible immigrants resided. All too frequently, persons without adequate training in work with adults were pressed into service. To meet the need, the Los Angeles Unified School District took any of its already-employed ESL teachers who applied. Next in line for selection were moonlighting elementary school teachers. Special arrangements were made so that such teachers could work as many as 30 additional hours per week (normally, only 12 hours per week for nontenured teachers, or 20 hours for those with tenure, were allowed). Only credentialed teachers were hired.

Recognizing the need for flexibility, the Texas Education Agency waived its more rigid requirements for persons teaching in the amnesty education program. In McAllen, every teacher in the regular adult education program was required to have the appropriate degree and, preferably, to be certified. In the amnesty program, there were no requirements except that a teacher had to have at least a high school or GED diploma and have experience in teaching adults. Even so, more than 90 percent did have college degrees and were also certified, because most recruiting was done from the ranks of school district personnel. In some instances, degreed professionals from fields other than teaching were employed if they had appropriate experience in work with adults. Many such persons had worked as volunteers in church or community organizations.

Working with amnesty clients was a unique experience even for longtime educators of adults. "I've been in this business for seventeen years, and it was the first time where I've ever gone into a classroom where all of the students stood up," notes Noe Calvillo, administrator at the Hidalgo-Starr Cooperative for Adult Education Programs in McAllen, Texas.

Given the circumstances, it is not surprising that complaints about the quality of teaching in some programs have been heard. A representative of a Texas Hispanic immigrant group reports that he observed a class where the teacher had been asked the meaning of an "s" added to the end of a word. The answer: "Don't worry about it. That's a preposition." Of course, the same types of complaints are being lodged against some teachers in K–12 programs also.

Proponents of community-based education for immigrants say

that too many schoolteachers or others who were not close to the immigrant community tended to be bombarded with questions they could not answer. One such advocate recalls being called for help by an amnesty education teacher who could not answer questions about what her students needed to do to apply for the second stage leading toward permanent residency under immigration law.

If they were sometimes critical of SLIAG-financed programs, immigrant support groups nonetheless wanted to keep the program going and lobbied against a Bush administration move to remove all funding in 1991. There is already talk of an extension that would allow for vocational training (presently prohibited) and training for new family members expected to immigrate under family reunification provisions.

Problems

In view of its scope and complexity, it is not surprising that a number of administrative problems beset the amnesty education program. For example, undocumented immigrants could not be served unless they had been issued the 1680-A temporary residence card (not to be confused with the "green card" that bestows permanent residence). The process for approval was in some instances quite slow, however, with the result that some immigrants found themselves in a kind of educational limbo until one was issued.

Study materials were another difficulty. The INS was also quite late in issuing textbooks specifically designed for amnesty classes; these didn't come out until 1989, about a year after they were needed. Once issued, not everyone found them entirely suitable for this very unique group. In McAllen, Texas, Noe Calvillo at the Hidalgo-Starr Cooperative found the INS materials pitched at a level much too difficult for the clients served in his centers. His organization developed their own materials at three progressive levels with the level of entry determined at the outset. Carol Mares of the amnesty education staff at the Los Angeles Unified School District also found the INS curriculum materials wanting in terms of being too uneven in the levels of difficulty. Accordingly, the district developed its own materials, which were provided free to students.

Some of the federal regulations governing use of SLIAG funds also posed difficulties, in the view of some educators. In testimony before a subcommittee of the House Committee on Education and Labor, then-Superintendent Leonard Britton of the Los Angeles Unified School District cited a number of what he perceived as "constraints" imposed by the new federal immigration law.[18] First was the $500 annual cap per eligible alien on funding for educational services to teach basic English and related knowledge. Equating this with about two-hundred hours of instruction, Superintendent Britton said it would require an average of four-hundred instructional hours to prepare most aliens, and this did not take into account related costs such as curriculum development, teacher training, material development, equipment, housing, clerical and coordination support, and administrative personnel. In Los Angeles alone, he reported, these latter costs during the first year were estimated in excess of $47 million if all who were eligible participated in the program.

Britton also criticized the limit on the use of amnesty grants to those applicants who had attended school in the United States for fewer than three full academic years. This constraint was designed to rule out the provision of services to persons who presumably already possessed sufficient English skills to qualify for amnesty. Still, many lacked history and civics knowledge. "Experience shows that the proficient acquisition of a second language takes longer than three years, especially by an adult," Britton asserted.

The requirement that other available federal funding be exhausted before SLIAG grants could be used also drew Britton's ire. Use of such funds, notably those available under the Jobs Training Partnership Act and the Adult Education Act, would deprive other target populations. Britton asked, why not instead use these funds in addition to the SLIAG funds for the amnesty population?

Another administrative roadblock for some was the IRCA requirement that SLIAG funds could be used only for persons eligible under IRCA legislation. Institutions and agencies attempting to serve the eligible undocumented immigrants, however, often found that this group did not neatly separate from others. Comparable educational needs were being expressed by aliens not eligible for legalization, as well as by permanent U.S. residents and citizens. Some pastors in the Rio Grande Valley, for example, found they could arrange education for only some of the many in their congregations who desired it. Rather than incur the resentment of those who could not be served, some elected to do nothing at all.

If persons did not sort themselves out in neat categories, neither did programs. Amnesty education classes have sometimes exacerbated existing tensions between groups representing immigrants and the establishment's adult education system. Some group representatives in Texas are bitter about what they perceive as the system's rigidness. Community groups might whet their appetites by providing amnesty education and adult basic education classes only to be denied opportunities to obtain public funding for other types of instruction. Commented one such group representative, "The education system says, wait a minute. Now you are trying to get into GED, and you aren't qualified to teach that. We're supposed to turn around and put these motivated adult learners into their system. And it is the same system that never invited them in. And we lose them. Sure, you can refer them to the standard GED program in the community, and they are going to be turned off. They are going to be told, 'Our hours are only from 6 to 7 or 6 to 8, and we don't do Saturdays and, no, we don't do Sundays.'"

In efforts to facilitate and coordinate arrangements for use of SLIAG funds, a number of state governments reached out to local communities. For example, the Texas Education Agency set up a group to advise it on expenditures of SLIAG monies. Half of the 17 persons invited represented advocacy or private groups. The other half represented local education groups. The process was not all smooth, however. Some of the advocacy groups rebelled at having to work through the state-sponsored regional cooperative agencies. They wanted direct funding from the state. At its source, this complaint stemmed from a natural desire on the part of groups representing immigrants to have quick and easy access to federal funds that can be used to serve their constituencies; bureaucracies tend to get in their way and slow them down. As for the advisory group convened by the Texas Education Agency, one immigrant advocate retorted, "They can say they are doing something. It has been good for pacifying the masses."

In some states, community groups with close ties to immigrants perceived themselves as unfairly disadvantaged in competing with publicly supported agencies and institutions for SLIAG funds. In Texas, for example, some such groups believed themselves able to serve clients that the regular adult education system had never been able to reach, yet they were unable to get funds under terms acceptable to them. The "bureaucratic hoops" required by the Texas Education Agency for groups administering SLIAG money were seen as excessive by this group.

It is natural that tensions develop between a bureaucracy charged with disbursing federal funds and representatives of the intended beneficiaries of such funding. Community groups do not always understand or appreciate the need for adequate safeguards against misuse of public funds. State and federal officials do not always appreciate the unique capacities of community groups to serve clients who have stronger ties to them than to public agencies with which these groups may have in the past had uneasy, even hostile, relations. But these two perspectives are not irreconcilable. As some states have demonstrated (New York is one example), it is possible for a state agency to cooperate with community groups and to engage their energies productively in educational programs for once-illegal immigrants. Community groups need to understand that good and accountable management is not too high a price to pay for their use of public monies.

Because of delays and administrative difficulties, many of the SLIAG funds were not spent, in spite of the great need. In the present era, however, money appropriated but not spent does not remain in that category for long. In the summer of 1989, Congress passed an amendment taking $550 million away from SLIAG and shifting it into other areas.

Educational Deception and Fraud

Immigrants, especially those long used to existence in the shadows, are not prone to complain about the services they do receive. Far too many of them, however, were victimized by marginal or exploitive agencies promising "instant English" or other survival educational services. The evidence of such fraud is ample enough to make it clear that the federal government cannot be casual in its development of regulations designed to protect often inexperienced consumers of educational services.

Aggressive advertising campaigns aimed at the amnesty population were launched by many of California's proprietary schools. While the promises and academic offerings of some such institutions were perfectly valid and respectable, many other programs were shameful. According to a *Los Angeles Times* story, many such programs in that area were of very poor quality. One English language class basically just viewed rented videotapes of such movies as *La Bamba*. "We've been literally inundated with complaints," reported

Margaret Reiter, a deputy state attorney general.[19] In the view of La Raza's Cecilia Muñoz, many proprietary schools simply "took the money and ran" after offering amnesty education classes.

In the face of highly public criticism, California's proprietary schools took strong exception to the notion that they might exploit amnesty education students by providing inadequate instruction. One representative of such schools offered to open facilities to inspection and investigation but suggested that public institutions also be subjected to like scrutiny. Admitting that courses made available through proprietary institutions would be more costly than most members of the newly legalizing population could afford, he promised efforts in the direction of limiting costs and providing classes at very low profit margins. In the absence of federal grants based on students per class hour, he added, "we cannot be blamed for providing a needed service to our community at some profit."[20]

Results

Within six months after the new law granting amnesty to certain categories of illegal immigrants passed, the INS opened one hundred new offices, hired and trained two thousand people, printed millions of forms, and put on a massive publicity campaign.[21] How successful was this massive effort? Immigrant advocacy groups are not in the habit of praising the INS, and their evaluations of the agency's outreach efforts to implement the amnesty provisions of the Immigration Reform and Control Act generally do not break this pattern. But by several well-researched accounts, the INS did its work reasonably well.[22] Certainly it gained the confidence of a large share of the immigrant community. Some 86 percent of the more than three million applicants for legalization came directly to the INS for services;[23] the remaining applicants were processed by various church and other groups.

A real flaw in the IRCA legislation, in the eyes of some, is the lack of any incentives for immigrants to continue their education by taking courses in literacy, ESL, high school completion, or vocational education. Dropout rates of students who complete forty hours of instruction have been high even in the best-run programs.[24] Pavlos Roussos, educational program director at the Texas Education Agency, estimates that about 16 percent of their amnesty education clients quit after the required forty hours of instruction. About 54 percent took between forty and one-hundred hours; some 30 percent went beyond one-hundred hours. While disappointing, these are not unusual outcomes in programs serving persons in the lowest economic and social sectors of society. Education is never the first priority for those struggling merely to survive.

The news is not all unsatisfying, however. The mostly young, single men in the seasonal agricultural worker (SAW) population in Texas turned out to be more oriented to education than had been expected. Although they were not required to participate in amnesty education classes, some three-hundred-thousand of them did so in the first two years.

What is success in an amnesty education program? There was some tension between immigrant advocacy groups and the INS over what constituted "achievement" in the 40 hours of required amnesty education. After being threatened with legal action if a test was required, INS finally defined achievement as satisfactory progress "to the best of ability." In practice, this meant that class participation, learning efforts, and even attendance might be taken into account in determining "satisfactory pursuit" as stated in the law. Almost no one was failed. This situation raises several questions. Is it possible for anyone to learn anything worth learning about English, civics, and history by taking just forty hours of instruction? If there is no test, can the educators involved document that any learning has taken place? Is this exercise nothing more than what some have called "green-card English"?

Perhaps these are the wrong questions to ask in classrooms peopled by some of the most disadvantaged groups in society. The important considerations here may not be learning outcomes in the usual sense. Were it not for the amnesty program, illiterate or marginally literate adults who entered the United States illegally might never have seen the inside of a classroom. This class of clients, even those who are native-born, is extremely difficult to attract to adult classes. With the incentives provided by the legalization provisions in IRCA, hundreds of thousands—perhaps millions—of functionally illiterate persons were injected into a formal learning setting, if not into actual learning, for the first time. There is reason to believe that some will continue, and this in itself is an important achievement.

There were other positive outcomes as well. A very large number of persons (about 50 percent) qualifying for amnesty education in

Texas had children in school. Local school officials saw this as an opportunity for them to develop some basic skills so they could help their children with schoolwork. Some suggestion of greater assertiveness on the part of amnesty clients is reported as indicated in increased willingness to use health facilities, to complain about substandard housing conditions, to participate in labor union activities, and leave sweatshop-style jobs.[25] No claim is made that such activities can be directly traced to amnesty education, but some links are not unlikely.

Social, as much as educational, goals were in evidence in many amnesty education classrooms. Long in the shadows, many immigrants welcomed the chance to get out to meet and speak openly. Since most persons in the classes were of a shared Hispanic origin, socializing was natural and easy.

Stimulus (if not yet tangible action) toward further education may be another positive note. A study by the City University of New York of amnesty clients in four literacy provider agencies revealed that 36 percent intended to continue with basic education classes, 35 percent planned on studying citizenship, 39 percent planned to attend high school completion classes, and 37 percent intended to take job training-related classes. Only 7 percent said they intended to take no more classes after acquiring permanent residency.[26]

Amnesty Education Clientele Profile

Whatever the outcomes, the amnesty education effort of the Immigration Reform and Control Act surely qualifies as one of the most massive adult education programs in American history. Just over 3 million persons filed for temporary resident status under the Act. Of these, about 1.8 million asserted their eligibility as residents of the United States prior to 1982. The other 1.3 million were seasonal agricultural workers. Approximately 94 percent of applications by persons residing in the United States prior to 1982 were approved by the INS; SAW applicants had a 93 percent approval rate.[27] The majority of approved applicants (55 percent) resided in California, and another 31 percent were in Texas, Illinois, or New York. More than one-third of all applicants lived in the Los Angeles-Long Beach area. Chicago, Houston, and New York each attracted more than 100,000 applicants.[28]

Applicants for legalization were primarily young (the median age was 30). Some 58 percent were males. About half of the legalized population was married, and Spanish was the native language for 85 percent.[29] Most applications filed under the amnesty program were from citizens of Mexico (70 percent) or Central American countries (13 percent). Another 8 percent came from elsewhere in the Western Hemisphere; 9 percent were from the Eastern Hemisphere.[30]

Generally low levels of education are typical for the newly legalized population. Applicants reported an average of seven years of education, with this figure varying considerably by country of origin. The comparable figure for U.S. residents is thirteen years of education. While only 7 percent of the U.S. population is estimated to have six or fewer years of education, some 48 percent of the legalized population reported leaving school by the end of the sixth grade.[31] Applicants from Mexico tended to have the least education, while those from the Eastern Hemisphere tended to have the most (more, in fact, than the U.S. norm). Visa overstayers and persons who had settled in Miami and New York tended to have relatively high educational levels.[32]

Data collected at the time of enrollment showed that 86 percent of IRCA applicants in California were Mexican; 71 percent were between the ages of twenty-two and thirty-nine; and 64 percent had attended school for six years or less. Of this last group, about 49 percent were illiterate. Most did not speak English, were illiterate in their own language, and did not have basic skills.[33]

In the state of New York, the vast majority of aliens legalized under the IRCA law resided in New York City. More than 130 countries of origin were reported, with the top three being Mexico, El Salvador, and Haiti. New York's newly registered residents spoke 133 languages in addition to English, with Spanish, Haitian Creole, Korean, and Mandarin Chinese being the most commonly spoken.[34]

Illegal Entry: A Continuing Problem

The Immigration Reform and Control Act and its amnesty education provisions will hardly be the last word on the matter of illegal immigration. Illegal entry continues. In many cities, the population buildup of illegal residents is very large. In the Washington, D.C., area, for example, only 55,000 of the estimated 200,000 Salvadorans residing in the area are thought to be in the United States legally, according to testimony presented to the U.S. Commission on Civil Rights in 1992.[35]

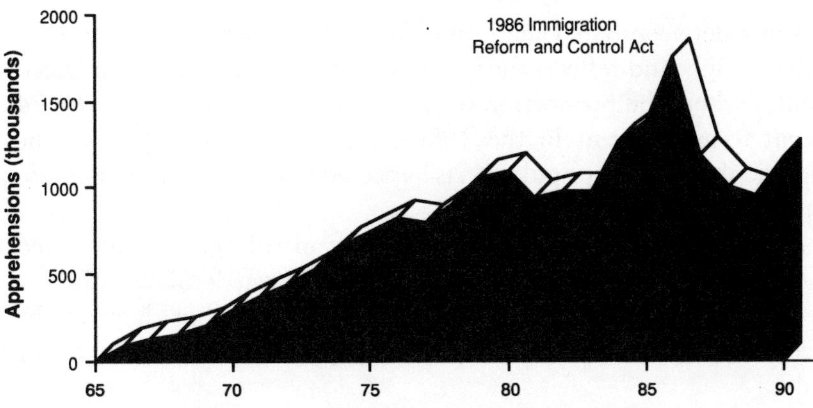

Figure 6–1. Illegal Alien Apprehensions (1965–90)

Sources: *1987 Statistical Yearbook of the Immigration and Naturalization Service* and INS Statistics Office.

As shown in figure 6–1, IRCA was at least marginally successful initially in its goal to reduce illegal immigration, as measured by a drop in the number of illegal border crossings from Mexico. In 1986, a record number of 1,679,000 apprehensions was reported, but in 1987 the number dropped to 1,149,000. The number continued dropping during 1988 and 1989. In 1990, however, the number of apprehensions rose sharply to 1,087,768 million—with a further increase (1,145,691) reported in 1991.[36] Because of variations in the intensity of Border Patrol activities, among other reasons, the number of border apprehensions is not necessarily an accurate indicator of the number of successful entries. It is, though, an indicator of continuing immigration pressures.

The ease of obtaining fraudulent documents is cited as the principal reason for the increase. It is possible, for example, to rent fraudulent documents on the streets of Southern California cities for as little as five dollars an hour.[37] According to one study, 32 percent of immigrant workers admit to having them, though the figure is thought to be even higher because many workers are embarrassed to admit their use. Continuing poor economic conditions in Mexico also account for the renewed inflow.[38]

At times, the border locale between Mexico and the United States resembles a war zone. Hostile and even violent confrontations have been frequent between large groups of illegal immigrants and the Border Patrol or U.S. citizen groups in an area noted for illegal crossings between San Diego and Tijuana, Mexico.[39] The mood is decidedly ugly and reflects the increasing ethnic tensions in San Diego County, where the proportion of whites is expected to drop from 74 percent to 60 percent in the 1990s. During the same period, the Hispanic share of the population is expected to rise from 14 percent to 23 percent.[40]

Clearly the Immigration Reform and Control Act has not solved the problem of illegal border crossings. Some new federal initiatives to stem the tide are inevitable—though it is unlikely that they will be successful, given current conditions and pressures on both sides of the border.

Issues to Be Addressed

Development and enforcement of immigration laws are responsibilities of the federal government. It is obvious that these tasks are being imperfectly performed, but educators must look to the human and civic concerns that attend neglect of the educational needs of anyone who resides within our national borders.

The Immigration Reform and Control Act of 1986 granted amnesty to more than 3 million previously illegal immigrants. But many others never came forward. What is to happen to the estimated 4.5 to 5 million aliens who were not eligible for amnesty under the IRCA or who chose not to apply for it? With employer sanctions now in effect, it was assumed that many such persons would leave the country, but this has not happened. On the contrary, the influx of illegals appears to be continuing at levels equaling or even exceeding those of earlier years. Most have little education, few skills, and do not speak English.[41]

These immigrants have undeniably broken U.S. law in entering the country surreptitiously, and it is obviously not good for the United States to have such massive levels of illegal immigration. But the fact is many millions of such people are here. And it also does not bode well for the nation to have in its midst a large and educationally deprived underclass who inhabit a netherworld where they cannot fully engage themselves in programs of the nation's educational system.

What responsibilities does the nation have to educate the continuing flow of illegal immigrants? A democracy such as the United States cannot be indifferent to the educational needs of any of its residents, regardless of the legality of their status. The governing principle must be that anyone residing on the soil of this country should have access to appropriate learning opportunities.

Thanks to the *Plyler v. Doe* Supreme Court decision, the schools cannot deny an education to the children of illegal immigrants at the K–12 levels. This is admittedly an expensive effort if done properly, but funds must be found and applied to the task. Adults require comparable attention. The lessons learned with amnesty education should not be forgotten. Already, pressures are building for a new amnesty, with proposals being advanced by National Council of La Raza, among other groups.[42] It is likely that these efforts ultimately will succeed.

The U.S. Congress need not grant permanent residence status to an illegal immigrant, but in the absence of a deportation order it should not deny him or her the chance to learn. Illegal immigrants should, to the extent possible, be encouraged and accommodated when they seek educational opportunities.

It is crucial in any event that the matter of education for illegal immigrants be placed on the national agenda as it now is not—perhaps in the vain hope that problems will not surface. And the nation's educators must insist that they be part of whatever new approach is devised.

7

Schools: Pressures on a Weak Institution

Two reports issued in Texas in the late 1970s were among the first to document the effects of the influx of immigrant students on U.S. schools ill prepared to receive them. One study by the Texas Education Agency showed that approximately forty-five thousand such students were enrolled in the Texas schools during the 1975–76 school year, with about 26 percent of these having been enrolled for less than one year. A second study showed that about 60 percent of Texas immigrant students were enrolled in the sixty-one school districts immediately adjacent to the Mexican border. This study reported that high percentage enrollments of immigrant students had a negative impact on the receiving district in the areas of funding, personnel, space utilization, and educational programming.[1]

Neither of these studies, however, was designed to determine the specific impact of immigration in each area. Accordingly, in 1977 the Texas Education Agency published a follow-up case study of the impact of students from Mexico upon a typical Texas border school district—that of Rio Grande City, where a relatively stable school enrollment had been established prior to the 1975–76 school year.[2] Virtually all of the immigrant parents in the Rio Grande City area were found to be very poor; almost all were looking for employment as agricultural laborers. Most resided with friends or relatives or in substandard housing and so did not affect the tax base of the district. All spoke Spanish as their first language; it was estimated that about

85 percent did not speak English.[3] Interestingly, most of the new immigrants stated that one of their primary reasons for coming to the United States was to assure their children of a better education than would be possible in Mexico. Consequently, it was typical that one of their first acts upon entering this country was to enroll their children in school.[4]

Only about 10 percent of the immigrant students had English skills that were sufficient for them to function in the regular school programs. Most were assigned to special state or federally funded academic programs designed to facilitate their entry to this country's education.[5] Nearly all (97 percent) immigrant children were found to be on the free-lunch program and were provided breakfast through a federally funded program.[6] The younger students were fed and clothed with federal funds originally designated for other purposes.[7] As a result of the immigrant inflow, five of the six elementary schools experienced total enrollments that exceeded both their program and their building capacities. One junior high school had a total enrollment that exceeded its program capacities.[8] While the new immigrants were generally well accepted (Rio Grande City was 99 percent Mexican-American, and Spanish was the predominant language), the arrival of so many new residents imposed added fiscal demands upon an already very poor district.[9] The report noted that the Rio Grande City School District was "faced with problems unknown to most school districts in Texas" and that financial assistance was needed to alleviate their impact.[10]

Other districts in Texas and elsewhere in the United States would soon enough find that they, too, faced a challenge and would need help—often even more help, because the new immigrants would be entering communities less culturally attuned to their needs than in Rio Grande City. A review of school enrollment patterns in some of the big immigrant-receiving states fills out this picture.

California

By the turn of the 1990s decade, California was receiving more than one-third of all immigrants (legal and illegal) coming to the United States. Immigrant children were enrolling in the state's schools at an incredible rate. More than 16 percent of school children in the state were foreign-born (in contrast to 4 percent in 1973). In all, more than

25 percent of all recently arrived legal immigrants and more than 50 percent of all illegal immigrants resided in California. California accepts a disproportionate number of immigrants, and these new residents have disproportionate numbers of school-age children.[11]

California's secondary schools now enroll nearly one-quarter of a million students with limited English proficiency. Twenty-one of twenty-seven schools reported unanticipated and dramatic growth in their secondary-level LEP enrollments, and an increase of 42 percent in such enrollments has occurred in the past three years. One LEP program director commented, "It's like being in the middle of a tornado; you don't know where or when you'll touch down."[12]

In 1986, California Tomorrow, an advocacy group for immigrant needs in that state, launched a massive and well-designed study of the social and educational experiences of immigrant children and of the schools' response to the task of serving them. Completed in 1988, the results of this effort (which was directed by Laurie Olsen) were startling. The number of immigrant children in California schools had increased two and one-half times in the previous decade. It is expected to continue to grow at a rate of 5 to 7 percent annually over the coming decade. The majority of immigrant students, the report stated, did not receive English language instruction that was sufficient to enable them to engage productively in an English-taught curriculum. Little or no instruction or academic support services were provided in native languages. The result was a "huge academic gap" between students who were immigrants and their U.S. native counterparts.[13]

In 1989, California State Superintendent of Education, Bill Honig acknowledged that his schools were facing "the biggest population explosion since the post–World War II baby boom," a growth that exceeded all expectations. "California already has the nation's most crowded classrooms, averaging more than twenty-seven students in each," Mr. Honig went on to say. "If we started today, we would have to build almost thirteen classrooms every day through 1996 just to stay even."[14]

California Tomorrow, in one of its research reports, estimated that one in six children in the state's public schools was an immigrant. A foreign language is spoken in the home of 29 percent of California's school children. In some school districts, as many as 80 percent have few or no English language skills. At least one in ten students in about one-third of California school districts has only limited English proficiency.[15] In the 1988–89 school year, the number of white children in California school fell below 50 percent; given immigration patterns in which Hispanics and Asians predominate, this trend will continue.[16]

Spanish, the language spoken by 73 percent of the LEP population, is by far the most significant language group represented in the California schools. Vietnamese is spoken by 5.4 percent, Cantonese by 3.5 percent, Cambodian by 2.5 percent, and Filipino/Tagalog by 2.4 percent. Many other languages are also spoken by California school students."[17]

A 1989 survey by the Los Angeles Unified School District showed a population of approximately 61,000 students classified as "immigrant," meaning that they had been born in other countries and had been in a U.S. school for less than three years.[18] More than half of the elementary students are identified as speaking no or limited English.[19] In 1992, about two of every three students in Los Angeles come from families where a language other than English is spoken. Some 81 different languages are represented in the Los Angeles school population.[20]

By far the largest component of increased enrollment in the Los Angeles schools comes from the children of recent arrivals from Mexico. According to one study, no other school system in the United States has ever experienced such a concentrated influx of students from just one nation.[21] It is not surprising that callers to the information line of the Los Angeles Unified School District hear a bilingual Spanish-language recording if the operators are too busy to receive the call—a service much appreciated by Hispanic parents.

The Garvey Unified School District in Los Angeles is growing at almost a classroom a month.[22] In nearby Long Beach, the school district has a population that is 71 percent minority, including the largest population of Cambodians outside that country's capital city of Phnom Penh. "The challenges are greater than at any time in my twenty-four years as a school superintendent," says the school district's head, Tom Guigni. Many of his challenges stem from accommodating a fast-rising tide of immigrants with very little education.[23]

Large cities such as Los Angeles and San Francisco are relatively experienced at accommodating immigrants within their school systems, but for many school districts in California the experience is a very new and unsettling one. In the Stockton Unified School District, for example, the LEP student population is four times what it was five years ago, and it includes a very large Southeast Asian population that did not even exist in the area ten years ago.[24]

New York

In the 1990–91 school year, the New York City public schools experienced a sudden and quite unexpected spurt of growth—almost all of it attributable to the beginning of a new wave of immigrants. In the spring of 1992, it was announced that 120,000 immigrant students from 167 nations had enrolled in the prior three-year period. It is expected that the inflow will continue, with the city's public school enrollment possibly hitting more than a million students by the year 2000.[25]

Crowding in the New York City public schools has been endemic in the immigration era. Robert F. Wagner, Jr., president of the school board, remarked in 1989, "Until you see it, it's hard to appreciate how awful it is for the kids." At one school visited by Wagner, five newly arrived Haitian youngsters were actually being taught amidst the stench of a urinal because of lack of any other space. "It's not just the crummy facilities but the message it sends: the society, the schools, don't care," Wagner said.[26] At Public School 102 in Queens, for example, 900 students were using space that served only 650 four years previously. ESL classes were being held in vestibules.[27]

School officials are worried that class sizes may burst the mandated 25-pupil maximum. The newcomers could not be arriving at a more inopportune time. The new wave of immigrants hit a school system in a state of fiscal crisis and in the process of cutting back on the number of regular teachers, yet the inflow of LEP students has required the concurrent recruitment of bilingual teachers.[28] Moreover, the district's capital expenditures budget of $4.3 million through 1993–94 is based on projections accomplished before the surprise surge in immigrant enrollments.[29]

Students with limited English proficiency in New York state schools come from 130 nations and speak a variety of 160 different languages, including Azerbaijani (Iran, Some republics of the former USSR), Bhili (India), Jonkhan (Bhutan), Malinke (Guinea, Guinea-Bissau, Senegal, Gambia), Quechua (Peru, Bolivia, Ecuador), Urdu (Pakistan, India), Tamazight (Morocco), and Yoruba (Nigeria, Dahomey). This exotic array brings new dimensions to any concept of bilingual education.[30]

Texas

The state of Texas continues as one of the magnets among states in attracting immigrants. By far the largest numbers are coming from Latin America, primarily Mexico. Between 1976 and 1986 alone, 6 percent of the state's public school membership shifted from white (or "Anglo," as all non-Hispanic whites are generally called locally) to Hispanic.[31] In the fall of 1990, the continuing inflow of Hispanic immigrants created a "minority majority" in the state's public schools for the first time. Although the percentage of black students declined, a 4 percent increase in Hispanic students inched total minority enrollments to just over 50 percent.[32]

Border crossing is routine all along the Rio Grande. Children gain immediate U.S. citizenship if born on U.S. soil, so maternity wards in hospitals in El Paso, for example, always have women from nearby Ciudad Juarez.[33] Children born on the north side of the river are eligible to attend schools in the United States; so are the children of anyone who can prove residency on the U.S. side of the border, regardless of the legality of such residency.

Many of these newcomers are showing up at U.S. schools that are already grossly overcrowded and taxed by the continuing inflow. The public school system in the Texas border town of Brownsville, for example, admits more than two thousand immigrant children (mostly from Mexico) every year. "It's almost a new school coming in per year. We're building all the time," reports Alejandro Perez, supervisor for admissions. It has been an expensive proposition for the city to build and support facilities to accommodate all of its children. Brownsville's population has increased by 13 percent during the decade, according to the Census Bureau, but some local officials believe the true figure is closer to 18 percent.[34]

In Hidalgo, a town about seventy miles upstream from the mouth of the Rio Grande, school officials concerned about unauthorized enrollments of Mexican residents went so far in 1985 as to conduct "bridge raids." According to Superintendent Alejo Salinas, he would post teachers on the bridge leading from Mexico at seven o'clock in the morning. They would try to spot their pupils from among the carloads who came across to go to school. The students would be dismissed from school if their parents could not be located as living on the U.S. side of the border. "It sounds cruel," Salinas told a local newspaper, "and it is sad. But it's necessary. I have no choice. There are a half million kids across that bridge who want to come here to school. I don't have enough room for the two thousand students who are legal, much less the ones who aren't."[35]

Florida

Florida schools have at times been overwhelmed by the rush of immigrants from Central America and the Caribbean. Senator Connie Mack (R-Florida) reported that the Dade County, Florida, public schools during the 1988–89 school year registered new immigrant children (many of them illegal) at a rate of 755 per month, requiring the system to add "virtually two new teachers per day and one new school per month." The cost, said Senator Mack, "exceeds $27.5 million, or $3,900 per student."[36] By 1990, the schools of Dade County were absorbing more than 200 additional schoolchildren a month at an average annual cost of $4,000 per child or $33 million per year.[37]

Massachusetts

By the middle of the 1980s, Massachusetts had 65,000 students (nearly 8 percent of the enrollment in its public schools) whose first language was not English. In many instances, enrollment growth of immigrant students was meteoric. In the Lowell public schools, for example, there were 2,000 students from Southeast Asian countries, up from just 98 in 1980.[38] As former Massachusetts Commissioner of Education Harold Raynolds described the staffing difficulties experienced at one school district in his state, "There were 100 students registered that were unexpected each day of the first five days, and then the next week, a couple of hundred more. Where do you find teachers to teach 700 additional people? Twenty-eight to thirty teachers who can deal with children who speak predominantly a southeast Asian language?"[39]

Nowhere was the influx more dramatic than in Lowell, a town that received many thousands of Hispanic and Southeast Asian immigrants in the last decade and a half. In 1975, Lowell's school population of minorities was only 4 percent. By 1987, minorities, half of whom were LEP students, constituted 40 percent of enrollments. In 1987, a big immigration year, as many as 35 to 50 southeast Asian students were arriving in the city's hard-pressed schools each week.[40]

In 1989, the teachers' union filed a grievance against the Boston public schools, charging that some bilingual education classes had more than twice the number of students allowed under state law. Overcrowding was allegedly centered on South Boston High School, where about 230 of the city's Cape Verdean students had been assigned to a bilingual education program after another comprehensive high school had closed. Ethnic gang fights were also said to be a major difficulty for teachers at South Boston High. Earlier in the year, 130 students had walked out of the troubled school to underline their concerns about safety, overcrowding, and sanitation.[41]

Illinois

Illinois has more than twenty one thousand LEP students in districts outside Chicago and another twenty nine thousand in Chicago. Some eighteen language groups are represented in the Chicago schools, including Arabic, Assyrian, Cambodian Khmer, Chinese, Greek, Gujarati, Haitian Creole, Hindi, Italian, Korean, Laotian, Polish, Romanian, Russian, Spanish, Serbo-Croatian, Urdu, and Vietnamese.[42]

Washington, D.C.

Washington, D.C., is doing a poor job in serving the needs of the immigrant children who compromise about 10 percent of the local school district's enrollment. A consultant's study in 1989 noted that the ratio of immigrant students to bilingual teachers was about seventy-five to one and that immigrant students often lacked access to early childhood, special education, and honors or remedial programs. Furthermore, the district did not do much to assess the progress of immigrant students after they were placed in the classroom. The report recommended that the system's bilingual education division be reorganized and better staffed to serve more effectively a group of students that is rapidly growing in number. The study was triggered by the district's disputes with immigrant groups about its performance in teaching LEP students.[43]

The Washington, D.C., suburban area of northern Virginia acquired more new people in the 1980s than at any time in its history. This explosive growth was to a large degree fueled by an inflow of immigrants. School officials there report growing pressures not only for additions to existing schools buildings but also for English as a second language, multicultural curricula, and programs designed for minority students.[44]

A National Challenge

No official tally of the number of immigrant students in U.S. schools exists, though counts of *school-age* foreign-born students from the 1990 census will be available in 1993. Walter Haney of Boston College in 1987 offered the first estimate of the total number of school-aged immigrants (five to eighteen years old) in the United States. By his calculations, the total at that time was between 2.1 and 2.7 million. This figure was, however, based upon a conservative estimate of the number of undocumented immigrants having children in the schools. Given the uncertainties of counting this population, it is likely that the actual total of school enrollments was and is higher.[45]

The National Coalition of Advocates for Students in 1988 issued a comprehensive study of immigrant students in the nation's public schools based on two years of research, including public hearings held in five gateway cities. They concluded that the U.S. school system was "unprepared and overwhelmed" by the new challenge of educating immigrant children.[46] School officials attending a 1990 national forum on personnel needs described themselves as overwhelmed by demands posted by rapidly increasing numbers of LEP students. Severe teacher shortages were reported, along with difficulties in recruiting bilingual psychologists, physical therapists, vocational education and special education instructors, and speech pathologists.[47]

These conditions are exacting a toll on the morale of teachers and staff in too many schools. One California school administrator acknowledged to me that many teachers in her system have negative attitudes toward immigrant students, "not because they are bad people but because they have problems [with immigrant students]." What forms do such problems take?

No sooner is the classroom organized than three more students come in from, say, Nicaragua. The teacher already has an ESL cluster going, but these new kids have never been to school. They don't know how to hold a pencil, and one of them is very dirty. They don't speak English. A Spanish-speaking teacher's aide has to be brought in and oriented to her job.

In the meantime, parents of the other students hear complaints from their children because the class has to be reorganized. Some children even have to be transferred to another classroom in midsemester, which brings more protest from parents. At this point (the semester is still not over), four more students enter the class, though none of them on the same day—two of them Soviet Jews, one from Bangladesh, and another from the Philippines. None of the immigrant children presents any behavior problems, but all require extra time and special attention that the teacher feels ill prepared to give. Parents also complain to the teacher about dangers to their children from ethnic gangs in and around the school. It is not surprising that teachers in these circumstances become tired and discouraged.

These reports are not encouraging, but the picture is not entirely bleak. Assertive and often innovative actions are being taken by administrators and teachers in some school districts in their work with immigrant students. Some of these activities are described in the chapter that follows.

8

Schools and Immigrant Children: Creative Responses

In their efforts to better serve immigrant students, some schools have come up with well-conceived, even innovative programs and institutional arrangements. These include specialized assessment and placement centers, language proficiency assessment systems, newcomer schools, year-round school calendars, parental outreach programs, and partnerships with community agencies and organizations.

Specialized Assessment and Placement Centers

The first day at a new school is inevitably a traumatic experience even for native-born children, but consider the additional strains on the immigrant child. A Vietnamese girl doesn't eat lunch; no one told her that's what is done at noontime. Once steered to the lunchroom, she doesn't know what food to eat or how to eat it. A boy from El Salvador uses the shrubbery outside the school as a bathroom because that's what was done at home. A Mexican girl is mystified when fellow students leave to go to other classrooms. What is that bell, and why is everyone leaving? She is used to sitting in one classroom all day.

Chinese parents may have a good idea when they put good-luck talismans into the pockets of their youngsters as they go off for that crucial first day. Fresh green onions, which symbolize intellectual potential, are a favored item; they may be tied with a red string for an extra measure of good luck.[1]

How can a school adequately serve an immigrant child beginning on the first day? In best practice, the process leading to this decision substantively involves the parents. In the Los Angeles Unified School District's student guidance, assessment, and placement center, families may spend two or three days as they progress through four stations. These include intake, academic and language assessment, the health center, and the counseling and guidance center, where the families are seen by staff including a social worker and academic counselor. Bilingual aides provide essential support services throughout this journey.[2]

If California's findings are an indication, the nation's schools have much to learn about identification, assessment, and placement of incoming immigrant students. Forty percent of immigrant students interviewed believed they had not been placed at the appropriate grade level; age or English language proficiency often appeared to be the only factors considered in placing a child. For example, a ten-year-old Laotian youth, though ignorant of the ABCs, was enrolled in the fifth grade. A seventeen-year-old Filipino student was bored by tenth-grade work that essentially was a repeat of what he already had learned in the Philippines.[3]

Too often the identification process, with its subtleties, is delegated to school secretaries or office personnel. In filling out the home language survey, these frequently untrained persons either complete the questions using guesses as to a child's English fluency or simply leave the forms blank. Sometimes, if the child can recite the ABCs or answer several questions in English, he or she is assumed to be sufficiently proficient in the language.[4]

Equally sloppy procedures were found in the area of assessment, the process of determining where in the academic program a child should be placed. Too frequently, assessment is accomplished by an untrained staff person who makes decisions based on a brief conversation that centers on impressions of the student's ability to speak English. Little or no use may be made of standardized tests of language skills, evaluation of literacy and academic background in the native language and English, or physical and mental health screening.[5]

California's experience suggests that placement of immigrant students is severely hampered by the unfortunate fact that programs appropriate for meeting the needs of such students simply do not exist. As a consequence, many students find themselves oddly mismatched in academic terms. Sophisticated and flexible approaches to English language development are an obvious need. Also needed are support services that take into account the social and affective adjustments required for entry to a new learning environment. Standardized tests are not the only instruments for assessing the learning of immigrant students in the best-run assessment and placement centers; alternative forms of assessment—portfolios put together by the students, for example—are also used.

It is not only academic placement that must be accommodated by schools serving large numbers of immigrant students. Immigrant students from poor countries frequently appear at the doors of U.S. schools with severe health problems. One California teacher who encountered such students found it necessary to call 911 five times during a ten-day period. Malnutrition, anemia, dental cavities, communicable diseases, parasitic diseases, tuberculosis, and untreated ear infections are not uncommon. Teen pregnancies are also common among many groups of immigrants.[6] The need for appropriate referrals to a variety of social agencies is often pressing. Home-school liaison personnel with appropriate language skills and cultural sensitivities are needed to assist homeroom as well as classroom teachers.[7]

One of the great problem areas in the realm of placement for immigrant students is what to do with teenage children who have had little or no schooling in their home countries. They can hardly be enrolled in the first grade; yet they are clearly unprepared to study with their own age counterparts. In the worst-case examples, such students may simply be placed in classrooms with their age peers, even though such action is clearly damaging not only to the immigrant newcomers but to the classroom environment into which they are so thoughtlessly injected. Another inappropriate "solution" is that of funneling them mindlessly into vocational education programs that also may not meet their needs.

One need that many such students have at the time of entry is mere survival education. The term *survival*, incidentally, is being interpreted by at least some high schools to mean survival to the end of the day. The immigrant who has little or no prior schooling but is nonetheless enrolled in a U.S. high school is not going to graduate with a high school diploma. He or she may, however, learn enough

English to serve on the job that night, to get the car fixed, to help a younger sibling enroll in school, or take someone to a hospital.

Emergency measures aside, it is clear that innovative thinking is needed to manage this now-common situation in many of the nation's schools. The development of new programs especially designed for older students is an obvious necessity. Specially designed curricular materials are urgently needed, as is training for teachers to work with this population. Successful implementation of such programs requires a careful integration with the adult high school completion programs that must be employed if the students eventually are to earn their high school diplomas.

Language Proficiency Assessment Systems

Many schools are not receiving passing marks for their performance in meeting the needs of limited English proficiency (LEP) students. In 1982, Secretary of Education Terrel Bell noted that "although local school districts and states are making an effort, schools in general are not meeting the needs of LEP students." Bell also asserted that "many schools are not assessing the special needs of language-minority children. They are not assessing the English language proficiency of these children, much less the home language proficiency, as a basis for planning programs and providing services." Only one-third of those students identified as LEP were receiving either bilingual instruction or instruction in English as a second language without the use of their home languages.[8] A subsequent study published in 1985 by the Educational Testing Service affirmed as well that "unique needs of pupils whose home language is not English are currently not being served sufficiently by the nation's educational system."[9] This finding is echoed in a 1990 report issued by the Council of Chief State School Officers.[10]

The state of Texas has addressed this issue by requiring that each local school district establish a language proficiency assessment committee to review the language proficiency and achievement-level data for each student in the district whose primary language is not English. Such committees may be established on either a district-level or school-level basis. The law specifies that the members of the committee must be broadly representative of persons having a direct interest in the successful academic performance of the affected children.

In Edinburg, Texas, such committees at each of the schools include the principal, a bilingual teacher, a regular classroom teacher, an instructional specialist, and the parent of an LEP student. The committee has responsibility not only for classifying students and recommending appropriate placement, but for notifying parents of action taken. The committee is also charged with periodic review of each student's progress for purposes of reclassifying or arranging exits from bilingual instruction. Follow-up instructional activities are designed to reinforce the chances for student success.

Newcomer Schools

The concept of newcomer schools that serve only newly arriving immigrant students is a pioneering idea. Of the schools of this kind I have seen, Newcomer School in Los Angeles stands out. Newcomer is one of two schools intended only for immigrants in the Los Angeles Unified School District (LAUSD). The program extends for not more than one year so as to avoid charges of segregation. Assignments come from an assessment center especially tailored to meet the needs of immigrant students located in the heart of the city, where most immigrants live. At the center, newcomers receive physical examinations, are interviewed to detect psychological or other problems, and are given a test in their primary language where possible. A review is done of how much education, if any, young people of high school age have acquired. Referral to Newcomer School is presented as an option to the parents.

A narrative account of my visit at Newcomer may be the most effective means of communicating the mission and operation of an institution of this type. Driving out from Los Angeles's central city along Sunset Boulevard en route to Newcomer School, one savors the flavor of what is to come. Armenian, Cambodian, Vietnamese, Nicaraguan, Honduran, and Chinese neighborhoods succeed each other along the route, which extends into funky West Hollywood and ultimately wealthy Beverly Hills. It is a short drive off Sunset into the canyons of Bel Air to reach the steep hill on which Newcomer School is located. The array of buses parked outside have just discharged their young cargo, some of whom have ridden for several hours.

The posh Los Angeles suburb of Bel Air is an odd location for the Newcomer School, as virtually none of the immigrant children whom it serves live nearby. But it is in affluent neighborhoods such as this where vacant or low-enrollment school buildings are located; this one once rang with the shouts of upper-middle-class white children. These days, the building bustles again but with a very different kind of inhabitants: a polyglot group of children from the dozens of nationality groups now pouring into Los Angeles.

The neighborhood in which Newcomer School is located was not enthusiastic, to put it mildly, when they were told how the then-vacant building would be used. At a neighborhood meeting, they voiced fears that students would return at night with spray cans and knives to damage or steal local property. This has not happened. Newcomer students are new to the United States, generally well motivated to learn, and young enough to be not yet caught up in the notorious Los Angeles gang culture.

The principal objective at Newcomer School, which incorporates grades four through eight only, is English language training plus counseling designed to ease their eventual enrollment in a regular classroom. Nurses come in to give often much-needed health care education. Learning how to take a sponge bath is one early lesson; many of the youngsters go home to a garage, where bath or shower facilities don't exist. A number of children have been found to have tuberculosis. Many know nothing about disease control. Others, Cambodians especially, arrive without ever having seen a flush toilet.

Hispanic children are clustered in classes where they receive all academic instruction in Spanish. All of the others receive instruction in English; teachers are helped by aides who speak the appropriate native language. Lila Silvern, who directs the Emergency Immigrant Education Assistance Program for the LAUSD at Newcomer, notes that "of course, we know that the children in the mixed class are going to learn English a lot faster." Still, she endorses the bilingual program for Hispanic students and tends to agree with her colleagues in the office of bilingual/ESL instruction who believe that "a little delay" in learning English is compensated for by benefits related to learning in subject-matter areas. She also notices that "the kids feel good about themselves, and they have a good attendance record. . . . We are learning that a sense of pride in culture is important to share."

In their first days at Newcomer School, immigrant children often reveal homesickness. In one class, children were asked to come to the front of the room and pick out the flag of their home nation on a large poster. A Chilean girl found her flag, kissed it, and began to cry.

Counseling of children may take place in "magic circles" where the youngsters are encouraged to share their feelings, usually around a theme. They may be asked, for example, "Who are the people you miss in your homeland?" or "What was your first impression of the United States?" This is done with students all the way from the first to the twelfth grades. When they sense the presence of traumatic feelings in students, counselors will follow up with teachers or make appropriate referrals.

Usually, children are pleased to be asked to describe something good about their home country. But not always, as with one girl recently arrived from the wreckage of Nicolae Ceausescu's Romania. "In my country," she said, "we have *nothing*. I never want to go back."

The United States is not necessarily a haven for students from war-torn countries, for they may enter a new war zone—the inner city. "Los Angeles, with its gangs, is even worse in some ways," believes Lila Silvern. An important part of the orientation process for these students is instruction in survival techniques. To be effective, this also requires participation by their parents. A number of fairly successful parent meetings have been held at the Newcomer School in spite of the necessity for most of them to travel long distances to reach the school. Sessions for them are arranged with teachers, counselors, and nurses. One such session was on gang warfare and was conducted with the assistance of Korean, Armenian, Russian, and Spanish translators.

The concept of immigrants-only newcomer schools is well established in California. At least twenty school districts in the state have them.[11] No evaluative study of these unique institutions, however, has yet been accomplished, according to a spokesman for the California State Department of Education. The time is ripe for such an endeavor.

In McAllen,Texas, I visited another newcomer school that serves a somewhat older student body and has a more limited mission—that of serving incoming students whose command of English has been identified by the McAllen Independent School District main office as insufficient to enable them to attend regular classes. Here, this translates into a student body that is mostly young people from Mexico. The appearance of what McAllen calls Magnet School is not prepossessing. Located in a rundown neighborhood, the 1930s-era building has seen better days. Inside, though, the atmosphere is more heartening. Principal Wilbur Harper is enthusiastic in describing the basic mission of his school as that of teaching the English language.

The ages of the student body range for thirteen to twenty-one. Thirteen-year-olds are generally grouped together for instruction, as are fourteen-year-olds and those fifteen or older. The program ordinarily lasts for one year before students leave Magnet School to attend regular school classes. In some instances, two years are allowed, but Harper does not recommend this, having observed that students work harder and achieve more if they know the program is to last just one year. Although the focus of instruction is always on English, the curriculum is currently being stretched a bit to include other content in the sciences and mathematics. Harper observes that many of his students have had fairly good preparation in mathematics in the schools of Mexico.

Enrollment growth at the Magnet School has been explosive, fueled not only by illegal immigration but by an influx of workers to McAllen's growing twin-plant Mexican border industries. In the spring of 1990, 18 teachers were providing instruction to an enrollment of 327 students. Dr. Eva Hughes, director of language response programs for the McAllen School District, developed this specialized institution when she found that many children arriving in McAllen did not really fit into either bilingual programs (as then structured) or ESL classes. What should be tried, she believed, was the magnet school concept, where such students could spend a full year there before being shifted to the regular high school program.

The subsequent course of events was not entirely smooth. Dr. Hughes had to put a stop to the practice of automatically assigning older newly arriving immigrant children to Magnet School on the assumption that they knew no English. This was not necessarily so, she had discovered. Therefore, the registrations of all newly arriving immigrant children are channeled through Dr. Hughes's office. Efforts are made to secure transcripts from Mexican schools where this is possible, and credit is given for Mexican courses. Equivalency examinations are also given. The students may be assigned to a neighborhood school, depending upon their English proficiency and prior educational attainment.

As an additional mission, Magnet School is providing an option for many of the older young people arriving in McAllen who do not have sufficient educational background to enter a high school in this country. Such young people (aged 15 and over) are counseled that because of their age at entry and lack of basic skills, they probably won't be able to finish high school under the usual arrangements. In many cases, they still wish to proceed and learn as much as they can in the time available. They are able to do so at Magnet.

Year-Round School

School overcrowding is a common denominator in many cities faced with a rapid influx of immigrant students. One solution to this problem is that of extending school sessions for all students over the entire calendar year. Summer vacation for most students goes by the board; instead, different groups of students will be granted vacation time during each session of the school year. More efficient use of facilities and resources can be effected under these arrangements.

The Los Angeles Unified School District implemented a year-round school calendar beginning in the summer of 1991. The measure was necessary to accommodate accelerating enrollment growth, much of it the result of immigration.[12] Many students, teachers, administrators, and parents alike were dismayed at the decision to begin year-round classes. Yet, year-round schooling seems to have taken hold without too much trauma in Los Angeles. Students, as well as parents, got used to it in the areas where it was initially tried. Most Los Angeles teachers appear to love it. According to teacher union official John Perez, only about 5 percent of teachers initially employed on a year-round basis wanted out. The evened-out pay schedule is the prime reason; teachers like receiving thirteen yearly paychecks (one each four weeks) and do not miss the long summer and early fall paycheck hiatus of a traditional teaching schedule. The only significant complaint thus far has been about summertime work in schools without air conditioning—something that likely will not be acquired soon, in view of the estimated $300 million cost of installation.[13]

There is no great outcry among teachers or administrators, or even the city's citizenry, for a return to a traditional schedule. Former Superintendent Leonard Britton is one of many who believes year-round scheduling is the wave of the future. This opinion is echoed by Dr. Jeremiah Floyd, associate director of the National School Boards Association, who predicts that by the year 2001, nearly all schools in the United States will be on such a calendar.[14]

Parents

Immigrant parents and schools alike report problems in their interactions (or lack of interactions) with each other. Many of the difficulties involving immigrant schooling relate to the parents, who are often baffled by the new environment into which their children have been injected. What their children learn at school sometimes turns out to be a mixed blessing when applied at home. There is plenty of evidence that some immigrant parents are unhappy with the way in which some school districts are meeting the needs of their children.

In 1989, officials of the Florida Department of Education began a thorough study of its bilingual education policies in the face of lawsuit threats by Hispanic and Haitian advocacy groups who charged that local districts were slow to identify language-minority children. The groups were also unhappy with the quality of instruction and lack of access to special education and dropout prevention programs. In Dallas, Hispanic parents charged that school employees would either hang up or place a call on hold for an extended period of time if a person called and asked in Spanish to speak to the principal.[15]

Reaching deep into the individual psyches of parents is the awkwardness, and often the humiliation, experienced when they find that their children have learned "too much" in terms of the mother culture. "This country can easily alter a young mind," is how a youngster (newly arrived from India) in a New Jersey school put it.[16] It might be added that immigrant parents do not always like what they see in those altered young minds. They are often resentful—even intimidated—as they watch their youngsters become more like their native-born counterparts.

Role reversals are typical of immigrant students and their parents. It is not unusual for a teacher to have an absence explained as resulting from having to take a parent to see the doctor; with U.S. students, the responsibility for this chore would be the other way around. The concept of the child as interpreter is one that is forces itself on many immigrant families. A study of immigrant households showed that 49 percent of immigrant schoolchildren performed this function; the figure was 69 percent in Hispanic families.[17] If this causes disturbance for parents unused to looking up to a child for important functions, it places unnatural pressure and responsibility on often very young children as well.

Most alert teachers and school administrators are well aware of the rift within immigrant families that can happen when the children acquire skills not possessed by their parents. A number of programs designed to prevent or heal such wounds are funded by the U.S. Department of Education's Family English Literacy Programs. Though anecdotal accounts tend to be encouraging, little is known about the real efficacy of these programs. A study to learn more is under way.[18]

Researchers in a California survey found what they called "a wide gap" between the parents of immigrant children and the schools. School personnel are frequently critical of what they perceive as parental inattention to the educational needs of their children. Conference or parental go-to-school nights tend to be ignored. Hispanic parents in particular are perceived as lacking an appreciation for education.[19]

One reason for the difficulties experienced by schools in involving Hispanic parents is that many of them come from cultures that tend to hold teachers (along with priests, doctors, lawyers, and other professional people) somewhat in awe as people to be respected, not questioned. The parents are not accustomed to being asked for their opinions or certainly not for any involvement in policy-making.[20] The same is true with many parents from lands in Southeast Asia where passivity toward all policy-making is the norm.

In many instances, however, parents are obviously anxious that their children do well in school but do not know how to help. The connection is not necessarily made between success in school and appropriate support at home. Parents interviewed in a survey conducted by the organization California Tomorrow indicated a definite interest but also much confusion about the system that is intended to serve the educational needs of their children.[21]

Parents in this country are expected not only to encourage students to do their homework but to help them with it at times. But this value is meaningless with parents who cannot read English and may even be illiterate in their native language. English language notes or newsletters sent from the school to such parents are quite obviously unhelpful. So are invitations to parent-teacher events if parents are afraid that they will be embarrassed because of language or cultural differences. Responding to the needs of parents who do read but not in English, the California State Department of Education published handbooks describing the structure of the United States school system. These are printed in Spanish, Korean, Vietnamese, Chinese, Hmong, and Laotian, as well as in English.[22]

Schools attempting to arrange meetings with immigrant parents often find major hurdles in the way. Transportation is often a problem. The parents may not own cars; schools are often located at some distance from their homes. There are a number of possible solutions to these difficulties. School personnel, often bilingual aides, may phone the parents. Or, since many low-income immigrants don't have phones, aides or even teachers may be employed to call on families at home during evening hours. Free transport is arranged by some schools. Sometimes parent meetings are held at locations in the neighborhoods where immigrants live.

One approach for encouraging parent involvement is to give them nonthreatening options for participation. Parents may become paid or volunteer teacher aides, for example, or be asked to serve on an advisory committee. Their help may be sought in organizing multicultural events. Of course, they may be enabled to visit classes, to attend discussion sessions, or to be involved in school governance of decision making. Although immigrant parents of students at South Junior High School in Edinburg, Texas, seldom attend PTA meetings (which are conducted in English), with assertive outreach endeavors they can sometimes be attracted to open houses. On these occasions, they are addressed in their Spanish language and outreach opportunities are provided through home-school parenting efforts.

Asian parents may be very quiet, even submissive, in their demeanor. Yet this exterior may mask a passionate interest in the educational welfare of their children. Teachers and counselors need to be very prudent in choosing the words that will be used to describe the problems of Asian students in conversations with their parents. Even the most casual word may be taken with undue seriousness. Esther Yao, a researcher in this realm, suggests that a child's strengths be the first topic of conversation. Then problems may be outlined, along with a proposed plan for remediation that will involve support from the parents. Yao also suggests such substitutions as "unfamiliar with American culture" for "rude," "reserved" for "passive," and "disinterested" for "lazy" in these conversations.[23]

It should not be assumed, incidentally, that all Asian parents are "passive." Le Van Tien, a Vietnamese immigrant, arrived jobless in Washington, D.C., in July 1991. But within three months, he had been elected president of the PTA at Bancroft Elementary School, where his son was a third grader. The school has about six hundred students, including children from twenty-eight countries. Tien cites his major task as that of getting parents, including new Vietnamese immigrant parents, involved in the mission of the school.[24]

Passive also would not be the first word applied to the coalition of Southeast Asian and Latino parents in Lowell, Massachusetts, who organized a grass-roots campaign to demand equal access and equity for their children in the schools. The campaign was successful, garnering a thirty-three-point program of educational reform aimed at achieving desegregation and facilities improvement but also addressing issues of personnel hiring and training, curriculum, drop out prevention, special education program development, and parent involvement.[25]

In Alexandria, Virginia, where fifty nations and thirty languages or dialects are represented in one high school, strenuous efforts have been made to involve immigrant parents in the education of their children. An imaginative and successful program at one school was that of sponsoring an international cross-cultural day where parents brought native foods, crafts, and related items.[26]

Direct educational services for the parents may also be offered. Citizenship preparation courses, community service orientation, and adult ESL programs may be offered through parent outreach endeavors.

Community Agencies

Partnerships with community agencies can be a valuable asset for a school enrolling immigrant students. Often their resources may be tapped in support of instruction provided in school. In Los Angeles, I visited a number of organizations in this category. For example, PUENTE, a community organization that largely serves the Hispanic immigrant community, is more than classes. It is very much a social center, with learning and recreation closely related. Fast response to expressed community needs is an objective.

A program of informal instruction in computers began when one parent asked PUENTE to come up with an after-school learning project for her elementary school child. PUENTE promised that if the girl would come the next afternoon, she could learn how to use a computer. The girl showed up—with fifteen friends. The program grew faster than the number of available computers. At the time of my visit, forty-six youngsters were showing up and dutifully taking numbers to await their turn at the computers. A similar program provides a room where high school students may receive tutoring as they do their homework (they tend to come from crowded, noisy homes).

El Centro de Acción Social, originally a settlement house serving Mexican immigrants in Pasadena, was revived in 1967 as a summer academic program for the children of new immigrants. Spurred by the new immigration from Latin America, it now conducts a variety of classes in English and Spanish literacy, ESL, and consumer education.

Parent education designed to address child abuse is a major concern at El Centro. The instruction may also help parents work on problems involving school. Often barriers in communication beset parents, schoolteachers, and officials. At times, a school secretary may serve as translator. Not trained in counseling, she may tend to preach at parents, who then feel stigmatized. El Centro Executive Director Lydia Fernandez-Palmer also helps both parents and school officials to improve communication. At times, this can be a trying task. One parent reported that she had laboriously taken the time to write a note to her child's teacher. The teacher's response was to return the note, with its mistakes corrected in red ink.

In Richmond, Virginia, a comprehensive bilingual vocational education program for refugee youths is operated by Catholic Charities of Richmond. The two-year program of instruction includes one-half day of intensive English as a second language instruction, one-half day of vocational training with bilingual assistance, and three hours per week of training in job readiness and independent living skills. In its first year of operation, this program significantly reduced the dropout rate in the two county school systems it served: 35 percent to 0 percent in Chesterfield County, and 20 percent to 4 percent in Henrico County. Preliminary results of an independent evaluation of the program by Virginia Commonwealth University indicate that 96 percent of the students contacted who have completed the program are either employed or continuing their education.[27]

9
Teaching and Accommodating Diverse Cultures

In the new era of mass immigration, schools in the United States are making changes in their approaches to both curriculum and instruction. These changes in many instances must be much more than cosmetic. Accommodating diversity—and doing so in a manner that can benefit all students, not just those who are immigrants—is a challenge.

It is teachers and instructional support staff who are on the front lines of this great effort. Old methods are being reexamined, and new ones developed and tried. There are plenty of surprises along the way. If this condition is threatening to some teachers and supporting staff, it invigorates others. Work with immigrants can be, and often is, exciting and rewarding.

Teachers and Immigrant Student Cultures

One of the most basic tasks facing teachers in classes that include immigrant students is that of bridging the cultural gulf that separates them from their students. One of the greatest shocks for most immigrant students comes when they observe the relationships between native-born students and teachers. It is all right, even expected, that students disagree with teachers. Class discussion is freewheeling, and it is the student, not the teacher, who is expected to say the most.

There is less emphasis upon memorization without instruction designed to evoke understanding and thought. And, of course, teachers don't receive the respect that is common in most other countries; their instructions are not always obeyed.

This experience can be severely disorienting to students accustomed to a more restrained atmosphere. In one-room West Indian schools, for example, the authoritarian role of the teacher is virtually unquestioned. Children are punished for disobeying rules, including the norm of absolute quiet. West Indian immigrant children who become boisterous, even undisciplined, in the freer classroom atmosphere in this country are reacting to a freedom that they do not understand.[1]

Children raised in a society where frank and open contact between males and females in public is virtually unthinkable will be shocked at the behavior of their native-born schoolmates. They, in turn, may incur ridicule if they hold hands with friends of the same sex, behavior that is perfectly acceptable in most societies in southeast Asian cultures. Boys from Afghanistan, a male-dominated culture, may find it difficult to receive instructions from female teachers or administrators. Girls from strict Moslem cultures may find it agonizing to change clothes or to put on shorts for physical education classes.

The ignorance of natives of the United States as to the history and culture of Southeast Asian peoples is too often reflected in the interactions of teachers with newly arrived students from that region. One of the most common mistakes is that of referring to anyone from the Indochinese peninsula as Vietnamese. Children from Indochina speak different languages and may be of different religions. Their families may have been on different sides of the chronic wars that have long beset the region.[2]

A teacher who affectionately pats a Vietnamese child on the head may unintentionally violate a cultural taboo and get an unexpected negative reaction. It is not customary in Vietnam for any individual to touch the head of another.[3] Pointing one's feet at someone is a grave insult in some Buddhist-influenced Southeast Asian cultures.[4]

Cultural differences can skew instructional outcomes in every sector of the curriculum, even mathematics. Consider, for example, the math teacher who poses this problem to her students: "Suppose there are four blackbirds sitting in a tree. You take a slingshot and shoot one of them. How many are left?" A native-born student is quick to give the "correct" answer, which is three. But an immigrant student from Africa is equally confident in giving the answer zero. The teacher tells him this answer is wrong and that he needs to study mathematics a bit more. The student thereafter ceases participating in class activities. Had the teacher pursued the matter further, she might have gotten this explanation from the student for his answer: "If you shoot one bird, the others will fly away." Nigerian educators frequently use this story to portray the differing cultural perspectives of Africa and the United States.[5]

No teacher can possibly be expected to understand fully all of the differing cultures that will be encountered in today's class rooms. He or she must, however, acquire appropriate awareness and sensitivity. With the assistance of the school administration, parents, and community organizations, teachers and staff can be helped toward better understanding of the perspectives of immigrant students.

Creative Teaching

Though the presence of large numbers of immigrant students in classroom presents difficulties, it also offers imaginative U.S. teachers some unique opportunities. The key is to view these young people (and their parents) as resources, not as problems. Tapping the students' home culture is one sound and basic instructional strategy. Teachers may ask immigrant students to write or speak about their personal histories and their native countries. Native-language newspapers may be brought into class, examined, and discussed. In English class, children may be told to ask their parents to tell them a folktale or story from their own childhood. This accomplished, the children repeat the stories in class and write them up for placement in notebooks. In Appleton, Wisconsin, the school district joined with the League of Women Voters to identify songs, games, artwork, and related activities within the large local Hmong immigrant community. Imaginative projects for all schoolchildren were derived from this endeavor.[6]

Older students often respond well in discussions launched by immigrant student accounts of world events that they have witnessed firsthand. Who better than a recently arrived Soviet Jew, for example, can give an account of daily life in the former USSR? The Persian Gulf War may be seen through quite different lenses by a Palestinian student than by, say, one who is Iranian. Such dialogues cannot help but expand the worldviews of all students in such classes.

Native-born students, too, need to be enlisted as part of the solution. Immigrant and native-born students alike seem to benefit when the sole initiative for interaction is not left to them. Good results are reported when teachers intervene to initiate positive interaction between the two groups. For example, groups may be organized in which young children read to each other. At first, it may be only the native-born youngsters who do the reading; but as time goes on, the immigrant children typically begin using pictures in the books to relate stories and eventually begin reading themselves.[7]

Schoolteachers often find that the "buddy system" is useful as a way of assuring that the immigrant student's basic needs are taken care of. Someone who speaks the student's native language generally works best for learning activities; an English-speaking student can also run interference for more social interactions. Being appointed as someone's "buddy" should be seen by class members as a privilege, not a chore.

JoAnn Crandall of the Center for Applied Linguistics expresses impatience with the notion that native-born school students are harmed by the extra attention that their teachers must give to immigrant students. On the contrary, it is possible to tap into the diversity when those students are put into the business of tutoring their immigrant companions. There is a lot to be said for the idea that you do not really learn anything until you teach it, she asserts.

Teaching English as a Second Language

As they began noticing increasing enrollments of immigrant students in the early 1970s, schools tended to mainstream these students. They were typically looked upon as in need of "remediation" and were assigned to the teacher who did not happen to have a full load just then. This changed when states began requiring specialized ESL certification, a requirement that did not exist anywhere until the mid-1970s. By 1983, about half of all public school teachers in the United States had in their classes students with limited English proficiency. Still, only one teacher in seventeen had taken any course in ESL techniques. Of those actually teaching ESL classes, more than half had no preparation for the task.[8] As of 1992, thirty-seven states require such certification for teachers of limited English proficiency (LEP) students.

In states without a specialized ESL licensure (sometimes called "certification"), trained ESL teachers have sometimes been denied jobs because they lack licensure in a subject recognized by their state as "certifiable." The result in the classroom is too often that instruction for LEP students is provided by teachers who do not have the training to do it.[9] Tensions between content-area teachers and ESL teachers are not uncommon. ESL faculty sometimes report that content-area teachers are not meeting the unique academic needs of the students. Content-area teachers sometimes say that ESL teachers "coddle" LEP students and inhibit them from moving out on their own.[10]

With or without specialized licensure, the professional status of the typical ESL teacher in a U.S. school system tends to be tenuous. Most are part-time, working an average of two times a week for a total of only about three hours per week. Anyone expecting to make a living doing this kind of work must somehow aggregate a number of part-time jobs. Most have no regular classroom space or place to store their supplies. They are, as one knowledgeable observer puts it, "modern-day wandering minstrels." Burn out is a word that is all too apt in describing the reactions of ESL teachers who work in such environments, and it is small wonder that turnover is high.[11] Richard Orem, former acting executive director of Teachers of English to Speakers of Other Languages (TESOL), notes that most people leave the profession unless they can find full-time work within about five years.

An even more marginal status is typically accorded to ESL teachers of adults. According to the U.S. Department of Education, most are women working part-time with low pay, no benefits, little or no support staff, and few instructional materials. Some have no training in either teaching adults or in teaching a second language.[12] Although it is to be hoped that professional upgrading will become more common, adult ESL teaching probably will forever be the realm of the part-time instructor. Typically, adults aren't available for instruction during the day, and even at night demand for classes tends to be uneven. Part-time teachers, often persons who teach in the K–12 program during the day and who see adult work as peripheral, thus will staff immigrant adult ESL programs.

Some ESL teachers work with both adults and children, though the skills and tasks involved are by no means interchangeable. William B. Bliss, an ESL consultant with extensive experience in work with schools, believes it is often easier to train a nonteacher to work with adult ESL students than it is to "deprogram" an experienced K–12 teacher who has built-in convictions derived from experience at teaching at the elementary or secondary levels.

What are the ingredients that make a good ESL teacher? An appropriate academic background in ESL theory and methodology is an obvious asset—and ought to be the norm. So is firsthand experience at learning another language invaluable, especially if this is accomplished while living in another country. A working knowledge of the characteristics and learning styles of adult learners is vital for those working in adult education settings. The teacher also needs to understand that being a student will not be the client's first priority; employment or parenthood concerns will be primary. Attendance will be spotty, with plenty of drop-ins and dropouts.

But in many instances academic background and even experience is of secondary importance, according to experienced educational administrators. It is personal qualities that are of central importance, especially in work with adults. The teacher needs empathy and compassion. A sense of missionary zeal is characteristic of the more successful ESL teachers.

With its vast numbers of new immigrant clients, the ESL profession, though still weak, is gaining strength and moving out of its traditionally marginal status within U.S. schools. It is the ESL teacher who often takes the lead in training other teachers (some of whom are not anxious to be trained) about the special needs of language-minority students. There is still some "dumping" of unwanted teachers into the ESL slot, but not as much.

Specialized state licensure for ESL teachers is desirable as a means of assuring that ESL teachers have at least minimal qualifications. But additional encouragement in the direction of higher-quality performance is needed. A step in this direction is being taken by TESOL, the organization of ESL teachers. They are progressing in a project to develop a professional certification option for ESL teachers. The certificate so issued will not be a substitute for master's degree programs, nor will it replace the certificates for specialized licensure offered by some of the states. It will, however, represent an effort by TESOL to set national standards for quality (not just minimal) performance by members in the profession and to measure attainment of specified skills and knowledge.[13]

In-Service Training

Some school districts have come up with innovative plans for helping teachers learn how to work with their immigrant students. In New York City's Theodore Roosevelt High School, students selected on the basis of their academic performance and language proficiency are helping in the instruction of teachers and other staff members in both the Spanish and Vietnamese languages. The program is conducted after school by an assistant principal; each teacher or staff member enrolled in the class works with an immigrant student partner. There is, of course, no expectation that the program will produce language fluency. Cross-cultural understanding, including an improved ability to communicate with parents, is the basic objective.[14]

In an effort to help its teachers cross cultural boundaries, the Lennox, California, school district has gone so far as to bring in teachers and administrators from the rural area of Mexico that is the source of most immigration to the Lennox area. The two groups have compared notes with the objective of helping the Lennox teachers be more effective in their work with the Mexican immigrant children.[15]

Teacher Aides/Tutors

Teachers, even bilingual teachers, cannot perform all of the tasks required for quality instruction of immigrant students. Bilingual teacher aides can provide valuable support services. According to a report recently issued by the United States Commission on Civil Rights, however, some such aides are not receiving appropriate training. In one school system, teachers gave them routine tasks such as grading homework rather than employing them in direct interactions with the immigrant children.[16] Such pitfalls should be avoided. Teachers, as well as the aides, need training in how to make their partnership work most effectively.

Tutors need not be peers or paid aides. An organization called San Francisco School Volunteers (SFSV) now has more than 2,000 adults working with 33,000 students and 2,100 teachers in the schools of that city. A private nonprofit organization with solid ties to the school district, SFSV matches volunteer tutors (many of whom are senior citizens) with individual children and places them in classrooms as teacher assistants. Many of the students so served are recent immigrants.[17]

Counselors

It is the school's counselor who is most often called upon to assist immigrant students in getting over the rough spots. Frequently, these counselors are as unprepared as their young charges for the encounters that follow; sometimes the initial session is the last one.

Problems of adjustment for immigrant children sometimes play themselves out in unexpected ways. While visiting a school in Los Angeles I was told of an instance where teachers became mildly concerned about a young Chinese immigrant who was having a bit of difficulty in adapting to the norms of a U.S. classroom. He was well behaved but was obviously struggling with the new modes of behavior that he was encountering in a new culture. The teacher discussed the matter with a counselor, who asked the boy's mother to come in for a conference. The counselor, herself an immigrant Chinese, conducted the conversation with the mother in Chinese with appropriate sensitivity, she believed, to the feelings involved. All appeared to have gone well enough, but the boy never returned to school. A phone call to his home revealed the reason: he had been shipped back to China in disgrace "because he caused trouble in school."

Counselors cope with these difficulties in a variety of ways. Some remain inflexible and may attempt to enforce a kind of mainstream counseling designed to "Americanize" an immigrant student as rapidly as possible. Others may bend too far, making what ends up as a pathetic effort to enter the immigrant culture.[18] Derald Wing Sue, a professor of counseling psychology at California State University at Hayward, believes that clients from many minority cultures approach a counselor with serious doubts. Can this person, this process, and even the sponsoring institution be trusted? The experience of many in these immigrant communities suggests to them that the answer may be no.[19]

Counselors in schools with large immigrant student enrollments need a good understanding of the various constituent cultures. A number of training models are available to help them develop cross-cultural competencies.[20] Enlightened by training as to the immigrant culture, the counselor identifies strengths and attitudes that can be applied with success to the new environment. The home culture is seen as a bridge to the new one, not as a barrier to be removed. But mere cognitive understanding is not enough. Counselors further need thoughtful analysis of their own attitudes toward ethnic groups other than their own. Biases, where they exist, must be confronted honestly. Any program of cross-cultural training ought to assist counselors in undertaking this difficult, often agonizing task.[21]

A background in group dynamics is helpful for counselors working with immigrant students. Counselors also should have appropriate links with local immigrant organizations or assistance groups. Developing a mechanism for tying counseling to the ESL program is a strategy that is employed by success by some.[22]

A budding specialty in school counseling is that of work with immigrant students. The T. C. Williams High School in Alexandria, Virginia, for example, employs one counselor to work only with immigrant students who are enrolled in substantial numbers at the institution.[23] Most urban school systems, however, are desperately short of counselors who can meet the needs posed by immigrant students. This absence of attention now will surely exacerbate emotional and physical problems and assure the eruption of trouble for society, as well as individuals, in the future.

Multicultural Curricula

Accommodating diversity in a sound and creative way requires more than enhanced cross-cultural understanding and enhanced techniques of instruction. The curriculum, too, needs enlightened attention, and throughout the United States, schools are wrestling with issues that attend consideration and development of multicultural curricula.

The case for a multicultural curriculum adaptation essentially stems from a belief that children from non-Western cultures asked to study only European values and history may perceive that their own cultural past is deemed unimportant. Most educators agree that curriculum change of some type is warranted, but the great debate begins about how this is to be accomplished.

Like so many words associated with immigrant education, the

term *multicultural curriculum* is much abused and is often equated with unduly particularist approaches that ignore or demean the common strands that define the United States of America. In one justly criticized report released by the New York state commissioner of education in the fall of 1989, residents of the United States were divided into five groups: African-Americans, Asian-Americans, Native Americans, Latinos/Puerto Ricans, and European-Americans. Each of these nonhomogeneous groups was said to have its own particular culture and history. The narrative emphasized differences, historic oppression, and enmities.[24]

At times in discussions of multiculturalism, educators in the United States have permitted the extremes to frame the debate. A false dichotomy is presented in a choice that includes only a narrowly separatist, ethnocentric curriculum proposal and one that rejects multiculturalism altogether. A multicultural curriculum is not by definition narrowly ethnic, for example, or denigrative of western European culture.

Impressive support for a multicultural curriculum in the nation's schools has recently come from no less a source than the executive board of the Organization of American Historians, which issued a statement supporting the importance of studying not only ethnicity but also race, class, and sex in secondary-level history curricula. The statement emphasizes that history courses should "be based upon sound historical scholarship" and rejects any curriculum that "asserts or implies any superiority of one race, gender, class, or region of the world over another."[25] A multicultural curriculum must, in short, contain the unvarnished truth—all of it. The good and bad that is embedded in all cultures will be presented in all of its complexity and richness.

At its best, a multicultural curriculum will reinforce attitudes of mutual respect, progressive social change, and equal opportunity for all who live in the United States. It acts to combat attitudes promoting cultural dominance or ethnic nationalism. It is the implacable enemy of xenophobia and intolerance. It encourages informed thought about differences, as well as about communalities. It helps build bridges, not walls, among young learners. With his usual insight and wisdom, John Dewey put it this way in a 1916 speech in which he discussed "hyphenated Americans" (e.g., Polish-Americans, German-Americans): "The point is to see to it that the hyphen connects instead of separates."[26]

Immigrants, and indeed *all* students in today's schools, need a curriculum that is multicultural in nature. At issue is not whether there should be multiculturalism, but what kind of multiculturalism should it be. At a minimum, the concept mandates a curriculum that takes into account in a real way the minority cultures that help define the society at large. Appreciation for, and at times tolerance of, all such cultures must be taught. It must be supposed as well that any of the disparate societal cultures can be enriched by infusions from the others. Intercultural learning should be an expectation.

At the same time, the shared values of the national culture and the importance of maintaining and enhancing these values need concentrated and informed attention. The United States cannot survive as an enlightened democracy if its history and underlying civic culture is not understood and appreciated within a pluralistic setting. Children must learn at school what it means to be a citizen of the United States. It is the considerable task of today's teachers to see that *all* of these things happen.

10

Troubles and Some Ways Out of Them

Tension and even conflict between immigrant children and others is all too common.[1] Schools do not often report severe problems of socialization between immigrant and native-born students in the lower grades. Segregation and sometimes hostilities begin in the upper grades and high school.

Immigrants and the Native-Born

A report issued by the California attorney general in 1990 records an upswing in hostility toward immigrants and racially motivated hate crimes in schools.[2] Of 651 hate crimes against Latino students in Los Angeles County public schools during the 1988, one-third were anti-immigrant in nature. Half of 308 reported incidents against Asians or Pacific Islanders during the same period were also anti-immigrant.[3] A study by the organization California Tomorrow found that immigrant children in the state almost universally report experiences of violence, intimidation, or harassment. Frequently voiced also were criticisms of student disrespect for teachers, vulgar or abusive language, and absence of appreciation for education and freedom.[4]

The majority of those immigrants interviewed by the California Tomorrow project felt that their native-born counterparts had negative feelings about them. Incidents in the first year of arrival were most common, with almost every immigrant student reporting that he or she had been called names, pushed, spat upon, cruelly tricked, or teased in that unnerving period. "They are afraid we are going to take over" and "They wish we'd go back where we came from" were some frequent remarks.[5] Some 50 percent of immigrant middle school students and almost 70 percent of high school students in the California Tomorrow sample said that severe tensions or problems existed in relationships between themselves and native-born students in their schools. Immigrant students entering elementary schools perceived less hostility but reported feelings of isolation similar to those of the older students.[6]

In a U.S. Department of Health and Social Services survey in San Diego schools, students were asked to comment on the good and bad points of efforts to integrate Southeast Asian refugee students at their schools. Their remarks showed an alarming degree of prejudice toward these newcomers, with about 30 percent of the nonrefugee respondents expressing pointedly racist points of view. Such negative comments came as much from black and Hispanic students as from whites. One in four students stated that refugees were either hated or were receiving bad treatment.[7]

Also in San Diego, a Vietnamese social worker at a junior high school asked a group of refugee students about their experiences of racism. Seventeen of the twenty-four students reported being called names such as Yang, Nip, Chink, and Jap. When called names, nine "swore back," and six fought back. Five other students had observed fights between Vietnamese and nonrefugee students. In all, 46 percent of the group had directly or indirectly experienced physical confrontations as a result of racial baiting.[8] Hispanic immigrant children may get a similar message, as did this Mexican girl who entered a California school in the tenth grade and dropped out at age sixteen:

> 'I dropped out of school because the other students were so rude and mean. The work was hard, too. Nothing was right. I was scared of the girls who act so tough, and embarrassed because everyone knew more than me. When I used to try to speak everyone made fun of me, so I never wanted to try to speak again. I couldn't understand what the teacher was saying. On one test at school I didn't write a single word because I didn't understand. That was the last day I went to school. I felt happier at home with my sister.'[9]

A report of the immigrant experience in New Jersey schools states that the somewhat shy and retiring stance of many Asian students is not always appreciated or respected by the often more assertive native-born, who view the Asians as prim and proper. Asians are aware of these attitudes and feel isolated. A student from India in a New Jersey school describes the experience as feeling "like a chocolate chip in the middle of vanilla ice cream in class."[10]

Native-born students may also feel uncomfortable with, or even threatened by, immigrant students. Unfamiliar languages, foods, manner of dress, smells, personal demeanor, and social expectations can be intimidating on both sides. Children who have difficulty in school, as many immigrants do, sometimes express their frustrations in socially unacceptable ways. Gang formation and behavior is one of these. A first generation U.S. citizen of Hispanic ancestry at a Fairfax, Virginia, high school told a newspaper reporter that she often felt uncomfortable with the "huge number of immigrants from Nicaragua and El Salvador. They dress differently and don't do well in school. It seemed like the Central Americans would come to school to start trouble; they are so insecure that they have to put up a front."[11] It is understandable that native-born children, as well as immigrants, have difficulty in accommodating differences that may in some instances be quite wide.

Immigrants and Other Immigrants

In their nationwide interviews, researchers for the National Coalition of Advocates for Students encountered a troubling pattern of tension between groups of immigrants as well as between immigrants and the native-born. It was Cambodians versus Puerto Ricans in Lowell, Massachusetts; Providence, Rhode Island, schools experienced conflict between Southeast Asians and Hispanics; black, white, Hispanic, and Asian students sometimes resorted to violence in school gymnasiums in Philadelphia, Boston, and California; and native-born and Haitian blacks argued and fought in Florida.[12]

Immigrants and School Personnel

Negative attitudes toward immigrant students are not necessarily limited to other students. The principal of one school in a large metropolitan area was heard to make this remark by one of his teachers: "These Armenians. They're just a bunch of Mexicans." Teachers, too, can be prejudiced or at least resistant to the notion of doing anything special for an immigrant child. Too often there is a tendency to consider immigrants as the responsibility of the bilingual education or ESL teacher.

Immigrant students are sometimes made aware of the difficulties they present for teachers. A Central American newcomer to a Los Angeles classroom was greeted by the teacher with, "Oh no, not *another* one!" Reporting on the incident to a counselor later, this student (who, though wounded, retained a sense of humor) said, "At least she said it in Spanish." Among the unpleasant results of these tensions are hostility and even open conflict, ethnic separatism, and a newly developing phenomenon called "tipping," as English-speaking residents withdraw their children from schools enrolling large numbers of limited English proficiency students.

Hostility and Conflict

War in their native countries has exacted a deplorable toll from the lives of too many immigrant children, especially those from Southeast Asia and Central America. Consider, for example, the troubled and combative eight-year-old from El Salvador who told her Queens, New York, elementary school guidance counselor about the day she saw her father put up against a wall and shot. In Providence, Rhode Island, a Cambodian boy asked what he had been taught in his native land. His bitter response was, "You don't want to know."[13]

Fighting, stealing, withholding of information, and general mistrust of authority figures are behaviors that can be useful in war but extremely damaging in the newly adopted nation. Crime, gang activity, drug use, and family deterioration are all reported in communities where large numbers of immigrants from war-torn nations are struggling to build new lives. And if schools are a problem for some of these young people, so is the city itself. Many have lived only in rural areas at home; they do not know how to read the urban landscape. Often, they have no other family members in this country except perhaps an older brother.

Many immigrant young people from Mexico, having been taught to respect authority, are better behaved than their native-born counterparts. Still, there are those who exhibit "very hostile" attitudes toward the United States, according to one Texas junior high school teacher with whom I spoke. "It breaks my heart," she reported. "I, too, am an immigrant, and I am so grateful to this country. I tell them, 'Look at these books, these supplies, this classroom. The rest rooms are clean. There is everything here for you to succeed.' But to some of them—no, a lot—it makes no difference. They come to this country just for what they can get."

Especially volatile tensions can be triggered by a heavy influx of immigrant students to a school that already has a large enrollment of low-income African-American students. Some such incidents in 1990, the most recent of a dozen or more over a two-year period according to school officials, rocked the Oxon Hill High School in Prince George's County, Maryland, which had in recent years acquired a large number of new residents who are immigrants from the Philippines. Filipinos had come to represent a sizable minority (about 11 percent) at Oxon Hill, where 72 percent of the students were black and 16 percent were white.

Filipino students reported a number of incidents of attack on the school premises, as well as outside. According to one Filipino youth, his attackers were black students who objected to the use of Tagalog, a Philippine native language, in the hallways and lunchroom. He said the blacks accused him and his friends of talking about them. When interviewed by a local newspaper, other Filipino students asserted that some blacks called them "FOBs" (fresh off the boat). Black students charged that some Filipinos called them "peas," a reference intended as an insult to the size of their brains. One black student said that "the black students may have been provoked because the Asian students don't always treat us with a lot of respect. It's like they come here thinking we are all a bunch of dummies who don't do nothing but rap and kill each other."

Whatever the cause, school officials found it hard to finger those responsible for any attacks, because some Filipino students were reluctant to identify their attackers. Some had not reported attacks allegedly occurring over a two-year period for fear of retaliation.[14]

Racial hatred took a horrifying turn for children and their teachers at Cleveland Elementary School in Stockton, California, on January 17, 1989. On that day a deranged gunman, using an AK-47 assault rifle, entered the schoolyard and began firing. The toll was five Indochinese children dead and another thirty wounded. The motive, according to the California attorney general was the man's "particular animosity" toward Southeast Asians.[15]

The reverse side of the equation of violence was illustrated a year later when two Cambodian youths fired on a group of white students outside Central High School in Providence, Rhode Island, missing their targets but killing two bystanders. The Cambodians cited their earlier harrassment by white students at the school as the motive for their response.[16]

Segregation

In addition to violence, subtle segregation is another undesirable outcome of tensions involving immigrant children in U.S. schools; at times, this escalates to become assertive ethnic separatism. True cultural integration often does not exist, even in schools without violence or overt tension. Nowhere is this more evident than at lunchtime, where ethnic groups tend to stick together. There may no overt hostility, but neither is there communication across the invisible lines.

Sometimes immigrant children receive a not-so-subtle message from home that too much communication with the majority culture will not be tolerated. Sikh children (immigrants from the Punjab in India) in a small California farming community were advised by their parents not to mix with white children outside school hours. The penalty for too much fraternization: forced early marriage or withdrawal from school for work in the fruit orchards. "The fields are waiting" was the parental warning.[17]

No organized neo-Nazi or white supremacist activity is yet reported in U.S. schools, but perhaps the final step in the trend toward separateness is represented by the formation in 1991 of a European Americans Club at Anaheim High School in California. The predominantly Hispanic school already had the Asian Club, the Black Student Union, and MECHA (a Spanish acronym for the Southwest American Chicano Education Movement). The organizers of the new club do not have a racist agenda; half of the people who joined the club are not of European descent. One motive for the club's founders was seeking help in preparing for college and obtaining scholarships.[18]

Even noble experiments, such as the newcomer schools designed to meet the needs of incoming immigrants, can carry troubling segregationist baggage. Such institutions can reinforce feelings of separateness in the minds of immigrants and the native-born alike. Pressures may build to extend the period of enrollment in such schools beyond the short term.

The "Tipping" Chain Reaction

With the heavy influx of immigrants to the nation's cities, some urban school systems have experienced a "tipping" phenomenon that is reminiscent of the civil rights era. Today, it is not whites fleeing from blacks, but English-speaking parents who move out of the neighborhood or withdraw their children from schools where larger and larger numbers of students have limited English skills. The problem that these parents perceive is that teachers have less time to spend with native children in the face of heavier demands from the LEP students; they are also uncomfortable with rising levels of tension and violence.

Because of the nature of immigration patterns, immigrant children are never scattered proportionately throughout a school district. Instead, they emanate from clustered groups of immigrant communities that are apt to be in the poorer and more crowded areas. The result is that immigrant children tend to enroll in schools that are already overcrowded, understaffed, and plagued with problems. Where this occurs, the all-too-frequent result is a diminishment of services for all students in the school. In San Francisco, for example, the largest school district on a state list of thirty-two in danger of default, elementary school music programs and all middle school electives have been eliminated, high school sports have been dropped, and some 574 employees have been laid off.[19]

"If you are a parent from the original baby boom who hasn't been in a school since you graduated, you are in for a rude shock," Ed Foglia, president of the California Teachers Association, told a newspaper reporter. "A lot of things that you had just aren't there anymore."[20] Suburban schools, too, are feeling the crunch. In Castro Valley, for example, a school building that was closed for nine years and reopened for 254 students in 1988 was expecting an enrollment of 415 students in September of 1991.[21]

One answer to problems resulting from a rapid increase in LEP students at a particular school is to create at that location a magnet school that will tend to draw compensatory numbers of English-speaking students. But this solution also has its drawbacks. In Fairfax

County, Virginia, a science magnet program was recently installed at Bailey's Elementary School, where English was the first language for only 19 percent of the students (and where twenty-eight other languages are spoken). This may correct an imbalance at Bailey's, which has high enrollment of Hispanic and Asian immigrants, but what of the other eight schools in the county where English is already the second language for 40 percent or more of the students? The magnet school concept cannot be employed at all of them. Language balance thus will have to be achieved in other ways.[22]

Another solution, believed to be the first student-assignment plan of its kind, was announced in January 1992 in LaCrosse, Wisconsin, where a very large inflow of Hmong students to a once overwhelmingly white community has created severe strains on the school system. More than one-fifth of the district's 3,500 elementary school children are being moved to new schools to even out socioeconomic differences in schools throughout the city. This is being arranged by shortening the range of students at each school who qualify for federal lunch subsidies, from 4 to 68 percent to 15 to 50 percent. The plan was described as "crazy" by an opposing citizens group, which accused the school board of being out of touch with public opinion.[23] A voter revolt in July 1992 resulted in recall of 4 of the 9 school board members who had supported the plan. Two more were forced into a run off election.[24]

Solutions

Difficulties stemming from ethnic tensions do not, of course, lend themselves to easy solutions. But they are pregnant with menace to democracy in this country, and there must be solutions if immigrant students and their native-born counterparts are to live in peace and equality.

Four ingredients are typical in situations where such difficulties have been brought under control: (1) problem recognition, (2) an educational agenda designed to effect attitudinal and behavioral change, (3) a continuing mechanism for continuing education and problem resolution, and (4) a resource base that allows special services for immigrant students without diminishment of resources that would otherwise be applied to programs for native-born students.

The first step in solving a problem is to accept that it exists. In too many school districts, denial of problems between immigrant students and others is typical. Native-born students may feel uneasy or hostile in the presence of immigrant students whose culture they do not understand or appreciate. Immigrant students may bring their own set of prejudices and hostilities toward people who are different, including the native-born and other groups of immigrants. The best-intentioned teachers and administrators will admit in private moments their own negative feelings toward some groups of immigrant students.

All of this is not praiseworthy, but it is natural. Cultures differ and will sometimes clash on a number of levels. But negative feelings and impressions are not necessarily mindless, malicious, or permanent. Under skilled and sensitive leadership, these feelings and attitudes need to be brought into the open. The various groups need to have an understanding about why others feel as they do.

It is not enough to understand. The second ingredient of success is that of developing an educational agenda that will effect needed attitudinal and behavioral change. Instruction about culture—immigrant cultures *and* the civic culture of the United States—must obviously be a part of this common curriculum. Achievement of consensus about productive action that will resolve differences in acceptable and, where possible, productive ways is essential. Acceptance and appreciation (or at least respectful tolerance) of cultural differences must be the final outcome.

The third element in successful resolution of group conflict is that of creating a permanent mechanism for problem resolution. One-time or short-term programs—a film, human relations seminar, or school assembly, for example—are insufficient. Diversity is a feature of today's school landscape in the United States, and one of the arts of school administration must be the successful management of this diversity.

Finally, school districts must be able to accommodate immigrant students without impairing opportunities for native-born students. Unless this is done, feelings of resentment on all sides are inevitable. Unfortunately, the means to finance this option have been politically blocked in many school districts, and the unhealthy phenomenon of tipping continues.

11

Adult Education for Immigrants: Curriculum, Sponsorship, Instruction

What subject matters do adult immigrants study as they enter life in the United States? The basic answer is that they learn everything that citizens of the United States learn. But they must also learn more, and often their needs are quite distinct from U.S. citizens in comparable educational settings. A common denominator in many immigrant-oriented curricula is English as a second language (ESL) instruction. Generally, this is integrated with, or closely parallel to, other subject matter offerings. (ESL instruction for immigrants is more fully described in chapter 12.)

Citizenship Education

Some programs are aimed at immigrant clients exclusively; citizenship or naturalization education is the most obvious of these. Persons granted permanent residence in the United States are eligible to apply for naturalization after five years (three years if married to a U.S. citizen). Such applicants must also be at least eighteen years old, of good moral character and loyal to the United States, and willing to take an oath of allegiance to the United States.

Beyond this, certain minimal educational requirements are specified. In general, applicants are required to show some knowledge and understanding of the English language and of the history and form of government of the United States. Although there are some exemptions, the usual requirements are that the applicant has to be able to (1) speak, read, and write simple words in everyday use in the English language; (2) sign his or her name in English; and (3) demonstrate familiarity with the Constitution and the more important historical facts in the development of the United States and with the form and principles of its government.[1] What country did we fight during the Revolutionary War? Who is the Vice-President of the United States? Who selects the Supreme Court justices? Who was Martin Luther King., Jr.? These are typical of the questions reviewed by immigrants studying for U.S. citizenship examinations. It's a rote-memory exercise for anyone new to the study of United States history and government.

At the Alpine Center in Los Angeles's Chinatown, I observed as a group of mostly middle-aged or elderly immigrants prepared for INS citizenship examinations. Most of the group, who obviously enjoyed a warm relationship with their instructor, were from mainland China, the world's most populous nation and increasingly a supplier of immigrants to the United States. They were taught in English, occasionally supplemented by Mandarin Chinese. The instruction on the day of this visit was about how to converse about the weather—and not just that in Los Angeles. "How is the weather in Warsaw?" the instruction asked. Referring to an illustrated paper showing worldwide weather reports, the class responded in unison, "The weather in Warsaw is cloudy." The name "Warsaw" was carefully pronounced, and the class repeated it a number of times. The lesson built on an earlier session covering geography.

How relevant was this to a citizenship examination? Very much so, as it turned out. Instructor Evelyn Dai, herself an immigrant from Shanghai, explained that INS officials may reject applicants informally if they cannot answer in advance of taking the exam a question as simple as "How is the weather today?" The citizenship applicant will be expected to give an accurate description of the current Los Angeles weather.

The purpose of such inquiries is to sort out people who have memorized expected exam questions by rote and have no real working knowledge of English. INS officials may also ask questions designed to document the identity of the person who is applying to take the exam. Attempts to substitute an exam-taker for the actual citizenship applicant are not uncommon.

From a professional adult education perspective, the continuous question-and-unison-response approach carried more than a tinge of nineteenth-century pedagogy. Questioned about this, Ms. Dai explained that Chinese people are accustomed, and expect, to memorize and recite in this manner. She added that they do not like to write.

The prime motivation for the older persons in this class to obtain citizenship, according to Ms. Dai, was the greater ease with which citizens can bring relatives as immigrants to the United States. Many in this class had children and grandchildren in China who eagerly await an opportunity to achieve the American dream. As I left, the class moved to a study of United States history. "What were the original thirteen states?" they were asked. The responses were very good, up to a point: "Virginia, Rhode Island, North Carolina, South Carolina, Tokyo . . ."

Test results announced in April of 1990 suggest that immigrants such as these don't have far to travel in order to match the knowledge of U.S. history and civics possessed by native-born students. Two-thirds of the eighth graders and 62 percent of seniors in U.S. schools were not able to identify the opening passage of the Declaration of Independence. Although 56 percent of fourth graders knew the names of Columbus's three ships, only 36 percent of them understood why he sailed from Spain to the American continent.[2]

Applicants needing instruction in order to prepare themselves for the citizenship examination may receive such help in classes conducted by public schools in most communities. Usually, there is no charge. The federal government also publishes textbooks to assist applicants as they study for naturalization; questions on the examination about the history and government of the United States are taken from information in these books.

The test to determine whether an applicant possesses the required knowledge is given orally by a naturalization examiner. The INS promises that the questions will be asked in simple English and will cover "only subjects with which anyone who has made a reasonable effort to learn should be familiar."[3] Questions designed to uncover "good moral character" are also asked at this time, and the applicant will be asked if he or she believed in the principles of the U.S. Constitution.

The INS has not been rigorous in its administration of its responsibilities with respect to naturalization education. There is no consistent standard to which all applicants for citizenship must adhere.

Most examiners take an evenhanded approach in their assessment of the civic knowledge demonstrated by would-be citizens, looking for evidence of a good-faith effort to learn about the history and structures of the nation. Still, there is the occasional tough, even unreasonable INS examiner. Fearing the challenge, too many immigrants try only once or not at all to demonstrate the required levels of knowledge specified for citizenship.

The INS has absorbed its share of criticism for its citizenship education materials. A few revisionist historians in the 1960s attacked the notion that citizenship education in this country had as its objective the opening of doors to opportunity and success in the adopted country. Instead, these critics contended, such education was a sort of capitalist plot aimed at manipulation and even oppression of the masses.[4]

But there was some criticism in mainstream circles as well. A 1984 survey of eight then-current government publications of citizenship education for immigrants sponsored by the National Council for the Social Studies suggested that there was room for improvement. The author concluded that although all of the texts carried recent copyrights, the general content was from twenty to forty years old. Readability scores indicated that most materials required reading skills of at least junior high school level. The text themes were "patronizing" and stereotypic. The subject matter throughout was laced with "implicit racism and overt sexism." There were no colored illustrations and few maps; drawings generally portrayed only the most conventional image of the United States. Needless duplication was also found to exist.[5] The survey author concluded that a new series of materials should be written "which would assist immigrants to understand not only the pluralistic nature of U.S. society but how these cultural differences have been traditionally imbedded in the documents which shape the values of our society."[6]

The INS responded by developing vastly improved materials for citizenship education, which were released in the late 1980s. The next texts took into account the variety of cultural, ethnic, and language groups represented by today's immigrants. A variety of educational backgrounds and learning styles are also accommodated. Three basic topics are covered in the texts: United States history from 1600 to 1987, U.S. government structure, and citizenship education and naturalization information. Three different versions of these texts are available: (1) English as a second language, (2) reading grade levels one through three, and (3) reading grade levels four through seven. Unfortunately, a number of factual errors cropped up in some of these books, and the INS is currently having them revised.

If the study materials are available, however, they are not used to the fullest extent. In recent decades, the government has done very little to encourage naturalization. The 1990 Immigration Act authorizes funds to the INS to encourage naturalization, but no appropriations have been made for this purpose. Understandably, other concerns within the INS have been seen as higher priority, given limited resources. The INS has also backed off when its efforts to encourage naturalization have been incorrectly interpreted by immigrants as coercive. The absence of speedy naturalization, however, tends to encourage illegal immigration, because it results in long delays before legal residents become citizens who can then bring in relatives through legal means.

The casual INS approach to encouraging naturalization has been noticed by some immigrant advocacy group. In testimony before Congress, the National Association of Latino Elected and Appointed Officials (NALEO) supported a provision in a Senate bill that would have authorized $1 million a year for community-based and other organizations to conduct outreach programs aimed at encouraging naturalization. NALEO has some experience in this realm; it logged more than one-hundred fifty thousand calls on its toll-free U.S. citizenship hotlines between 1986 and 1989, during the period when many persons who had immigrated illegally were applying for amnesty and permanent residence under the Immigration Reform and Control Act of 1986.[7]

Life Skills Education

Instruction in the basic techniques of survival in a society that is often quite alien to a newcomer must be the first order of educational business for many immigrants. Given the hand-to-mouth existence of some groups of immigrants, hard-pressed instructors sometimes find themselves inventing a curriculum of the "putting out fires" variety. The Office of Refugee Resettlement specifies that a competency-based ESL curriculum based on life-skill performance objectives be followed by all programs for which it provides funding. Recipients of these funds include mutual assistance associations (refugee self-help organizations), church groups, and community agencies.[8]

St. Paul, Minnesota, has learned that on-site delivery of educational services is essential for reaching the often-timid Hmong refugees. Classes held in public housing projects provide instruction for the refugees on such basic skills as brushing teeth, shopping, and how to turn on an oven and use a refrigerator. Appropriate attire for Minnesota winters is also given attention.[9]

Such courses as life management, marriage and family living, and life skills are typical these days in secondary and postsecondary education programs in the United States. In many cultures, however, such subject matter is considered to be exclusively within the purview of the family; the school is expected to concern itself entirely with academic matters. The mere existence of a "life skills" program is a radical idea to many groups of immigrants.[10]

Literacy Education

The high rates of illiteracy that now beset many areas of the nation are correlated to a large degree with comparably high rates of immigration.[11] Relatively low levels of educational attainment are especially typical of illegal immigrants and family members enabled by immigration law to join immigrants who have achieved permanent residence in the United States. According to a U.S. Census Bureau study in 1982, about 37 percent of adults with low literacy skills spoke a language other than English at home. Of these, 82 percent were born outside the United States, 42 percent lived in neighborhoods where their home language prevailed, and 14 percent were literate in their own language.[12]

The illiteracy rate among Hispanic adults may be as high as 56 percent.[13] SER, a Hispanic employment group, estimates that about two-hundred thousand Hispanics are added each year to the nation's pool of functionally illiterate persons. Of Hispanic adults 25 years and older, 49 percent have not completed high school, as compared to just under 24 percent for non-Hispanics. The Hispanic school dropout rate is currently about 40 percent, as compared with 17 percent for blacks and 14 percent for whites.[14] Only 39 percent of Hmong adults in a survey of four U.S. cities in 1982 were literate in any language. More than 70 percent of the adults in a West Coast Hmong community had experienced no schooling in Laos.[15]

In 1985–86, according to the U.S. Department of Education, adult literacy/ESL programs were extended to about 1.3 million students. This represented more than 41 percent of the total adult literacy education enrollment. Curricula in these courses usually focus on the most basic English grammar and vocabulary, plus "survival English" built around such topics as health care, money management, and shopping.[16]

The basic assumption of family literacy programs is that parents can contribute to the language development of their children. Many educators have become convinced that an approach that conceives of parents and children as a combined resource for learning is especially suited to work with refugees from Vietnam, Laos, and Cambodia. In these countries, the family, not the individual, is the basic unit of society. Research findings support the idea that the strength of the family bonds can either smooth or obstruct the process of adjustment to the new culture.[17] Family literacy programs facilitate the process for learning by building on structures of interaction and support already existing in many refugee homes. Parents (it is usually the mother) typically receive between five and ten hours of instruction per week in literacy and ESL. The adults are given the opportunity to interact with their children as both work on language development. In a family literacy program in the state of Washington, Hmong mothers and daughters learn to read by following a recipe as they cook or by using a pattern to sew.[18]

A similar approach to literacy education for Hispanic immigrants is exemplified by the Family Initiative for English Literacy sponsored by the El Paso Community College Literacy Center in four local school districts. Typically, five to seven families (including even grandparents as well as children and parents) work together in activities designed to sharpen their oral language skills. The curriculum centers on real-life interests. Instruction includes story telling by family members to give individuals an opportunity to bring their own knowledge and culture into the learning situation. If children get homework, so do their parents, who may be asked to read a recipe to prepare a meal for the family.[19]

A study of the Department of Education's Family English Literacy Program suggests that the projects that seem most effective are strongly tied to the school activities of participants' children. Further, they are linked to community agencies that assist parents in adapting to the school and the community and in providing support for their children.[20]

A number of difficulties beset immigrants seeking literacy or adult basic education. Hispanic immigrants report that they often find themselves barred from literacy programs that require participants to be orally proficient in English before they can be tutored. Private literacy organizations depending upon volunteers often serve a relatively small number of people in Hispanic and other low-income communities because of a lack of volunteers in the areas in greatest need, according to a study by the National Council of La Raza.[21]

Immigrants and the native-born will generally find themselves to be uneasy seat partners in the same literacy education class. Many of the immigrants in literacy programs are not learning the most basic reading and writing skills; they are instead transferring skills already learned in another language. They may consequently outperform their native-born counterparts who are struggling to read and write for the first time in their lives. The U.S. native may view the immigrant with more advanced reading and writing skills as arrogant, and negative stereotyping can develop in the absence of a teacher's constructive intervention.

The same tension may occur as immigrants move from ESL and into mainstream literacy programs and begin to outperform the native-born. Teachers at both levels need to prepare the way; however, the task is not impossible. In the hands of a skilled teacher, true collegiality and sharing may result, with attendant benefits to all of the literacy students in a group.

To date, no national literacy survey has actually determined the rate of literacy in languages other than English. Neither does any popular definition of literacy include a definition of literacy except in the English language. The Hispanic immigrant community in particular is rightly critical of projects in their midst that do not take care to distinguish literacy from English proficiency. Many Hispanics read, write, and speak Spanish but have limited or no proficiency in English. Other Hispanics speak only Spanish but do not read or write either Spanish or English. Still others may not be literate in English but may speak the language perfectly well. All of these differences need to be sorted out in any true analysis of literacy among Hispanic (or other ethnic) Americans.

Adult-oriented Spanish literacy materials suitable for a U.S. setting are few in number. In Los Angeles, I visited a class where immigrant adults used Mexican government curriculum materials designed for children; one lesson focused on the story of three little pigs. Significant challenges face both instructors and students who must use inappropriate materials.

The governments of the United States and Mexico are concerned about the related literacy problems of Spanish-speaking adults in the two nations. An unprecedented two-day conference involving educators and education officials in both countries was held in El Paso and in neighboring Ciudad Juarez across the Rio Grande in October 1991. One outcome of the meeting, which was attended by U.S. Secretary of Education Lamar Alexander and his Mexican counterpart, Manuel Bartlett Diaz, was that the United States would supply money to enhance adult literacy programs in Mexico. Some U.S. educators were not entirely pleased; "I wish they would be as generous with us," was the comment of Superintendent Robert Zamora of the La Joya (Texas) Independent School District.[22]

GED and Secondary Programs

The language learning barrier doesn't just surface in classrooms; it is equally at issue in testing centers where secondary-level achievement is measured. Suzanne Griffin, director of adult education for the state of Washington, in August 1990 presented the problem to a group of advisors to the American Council on Education's GED Testing Service. Her concern was that while many adults with limited English proficiency master the language well enough to perform on the job and even in advanced studies, many of them will never be able to read in English with enough speed to pass the GED test for a high school diploma.

Ms. Griffin believed that LEP adults should automatically be granted extra time on the GED tests to allow them to translate in their heads from English to their native languages. It is, she said, an equity issue for those adults whose native language is neither English nor Spanish. (Spanish language GED tests normed on graduating high school seniors in Puerto Rico have long been available, as have French versions for use primarily in Canada.) "Why," she asked, "should a native Spanish speaker be given an opportunity that a native speaker of Korean is denied?"[23]

The issues surrounding test-taking time allotments are, however, complex. A number of other categories of test-takers might also make comparable demands that could create an administrative nightmare for test administration. Reading speed, for example, is another equity issue. If the language barrier were breached, could not a case be made for the slow reader also? Though sympathetic to the concern, the GED Testing Service denied the Washington request. In the absence of what she considers equal opportunities for all immigrant groups, Ms. Griffin responded by withdrawing authority for use of either the Spanish or French versions of the GED in the state of Washington.

Vocational Education

Immigrants in job training programs may be either mainstreamed or placed in special-track classes. Mainstreaming costs less and offers students a wider choice of subject matter. Special-track-classes, however, are frequently the best means of meeting the specific needs of immigrants who speak very little or no English.

Certainly vocational training for immigrants can seldom, if ever, be successful in the absence of an integrated approach to instruction. In 1976, the Arlington, Virginia, school system got its first assigned task as part of the refugee program—that of training seventy-five boat people for jobs within ninety days. "We demonstrated that it couldn't be done," reports program director Inaam Mansoor with a smile. Doing it right was a longer and carefully crafted process that included teaching English, offering cultural experiences, and providing transportation to the workplace. William B. Bliss, who authored a study of LEP programs for the Southport Institute for Policy Analysis, estimates that it takes about six hundred hours and $1,500 per person to provide basic survival English and workplace-oriented language instruction for each LEP adult.[24]

In bilingual vocational training (BVT), instruction is undertaken in the student's native language as job-related English language skills are also developed. In well-designed programs, use of the native language gradually decreases while use of English increases. The typical BVT learning group speaks the same first language and has a low level of skills in English. Nonetheless, class morale can be good when content can be learned from the very first day.[25] A positive note is also injected if both instructor and students learn to view the native language as an asset, not as an obstacle.

Vocational education programs, although generally delivered by the same school systems and community colleges that deliver other literacy programs tend to be less used by LEP clients. But projects are few in number and do not have the assertive constituency that is typical of such programs at the elementary and secondary levels.[26] Still, there is at least some evidence that bilingual vocational training has helped reduce unemployment and increase earnings of many immigrant groups in the United States. One study of such programs indicated that one year after leaving the program, the rate of unemployment for participants was 40 percent less than what it had been before their participation. Furthermore, the average weekly salary was 16 percent higher. Most individuals were not, however, employed in the jobs for which they were trained—a finding consistent with that for many other employment training programs.[27]

A massive program of short-term vocational training is conducted by the Abram Friedman Occupational Center in Los Angeles. This institution is a favored destination for refugees, many of them Asian, who qualify for tuition-free instruction leading to rapid job placement. Courses offerings include auto body repair, building maintenance, electromechanical drafting, and locksmithing. In a vocational ESL (VESL) at Friedman, I watched as an Iranian woman learned the vocabulary of job application forms. Another student, a young Vietnamese refugee, used a card reader to learn the vocabulary of automobile mechanics. Using cards, each with the picture of an automobile part or tool for repair, he inserted them into the reader, which then "voiced" back the appropriate word (spark plug, wrench, etc.). The student then repeated the word; the machine recorded his response, which was then played back for comparison with the earlier correct pronunciation. No frequent instructor intervention was required. Other Friedman students use audiovisual tapes for learning mechanical nomenclature.

Teaching vocational education to immigrant students presents some different dimensions than are typical in programs for the native-born. Ron Cabrera, an instructor in an apartment-house repair course at Friedman, remarked that some of his Hispanic young men students were reluctant to learn more than their fathers know about the building trades. His imaginative solution: more programs especially designed for the fathers.

Community colleges in Los Angeles are also heavily involved in immigrant education. Nick Kremer, faculty coordinator at the El Camino Community College District, administers a federal grant designed to facilitate the entry of LEP students to vocational education programs at his campus. The objective is to help them improve their English skills as the latter relate to specific classes.

The audience for vocational ESL programs at El Camino is not exceptionally large, at just over three hundred. It is very diverse, however, with a block of Spanish speakers (30 percent) and significant groups of Japanese, Vietnamese, Korean, Chinese, and Arabic students. Thirty other languages are also represented, including Tagalog, Indonesian, Malay, Thai, Tongan, Ibo, French, Hungarian, Haitian Creole, and Farsi.

If the El Camino ESL students are ethnically exotic, they are relatively well educated. A recent survey showed that 95 percent had graduated from high school in either the United States or another country. Another 23 percent had already graduated from college, almost always in another nation. Although these students often possess many transferrable academic skills, however, they have significant language barriers to overcome and face cross-cultural issues brought about by differing educational systems and educational styles. Kremer says his experience with immigrants suggests that the focus in such entry-level courses ought to be that of learning how to use information, not on how to memorize information. Faculty, too, need training in work with students coming from other cultures. They are not necessarily resistant, but are often simply not aware of what approaches may be most appropriate.

If progress is being made, there are still difficulties. Kremer admits to some degree of bafflement as to the intricacies of helping immigrant students make a transition from sheltered ESL entry classrooms to the educational mainstream within his institution: "Whether it's vocational education, literature, or history, we don't really know what it is they run up against that causes problems." Too often, he notes, an institution's open door becomes a revolving door where immigrants are concerned.

Direct translations into some languages are difficult, if not impossible—a fact that presents difficulties in some vocational education settings. In Haitian-Creole, for example, no vocabulary exists that names the parts of a vacuum cleaner, a device that rarely exists in ordinary homes in Haiti. This fact must be understood by those preparing vocational education programs aimed at Haitian maids in hotels and motels.[28]

Newly arrived immigrants from very poor countries often seek work as domestics. Many such applicants come from rural areas where most homes lack even electricity, much less the kinds of furnishings and appliances that are the norm in the United States. Videotapes are available to meet the need for employment training in these situations. One such presentation features demonstrations of how to clean a North American home using various appliances. The video is narrated in Spanish with English subtitles, so that employee and householder can watch together.[29]

Sponsors

Education and training programs for adult immigrants are typically sponsored not only by public schools and community colleges, but by employers and community agencies and organizations. Curriculum and instruction are not the only concerns of the institution or agency working with immigrant students; any organization aiming at success in providing training for immigrants will need to consider appropriate support services. These include outreach, assessment, counseling, child care, cultural orientation, and job placement.

Public Schools and Community Colleges

Public institutions in areas heavily affected by immigration must develop programs tailored to meet the needs of these new residents if they are to serve the community well. The Los Angeles School District operates twenty-seven community adult schools, including six skill centers and six occupational centers. Nearly all of them are heavily used by the immigrant and refugee communities. Substantial pressures on these institutions resulted after 1986 when more than eight-hundred fifty thousand aliens applied for legalization—some 10 percent of the population of the entire county. The county also has the nation's largest legal immigrant population and the largest population of refugees.[30]

El Paso, with its large community of Mexican immigrants, has a formidable problem with illiteracy. Approximately one-fifth of its population is considered functionally illiterate in English because their dominant language is Spanish. The Literacy Center at the El Paso Community College is attacking this problem with a variety of methods, including volunteer tutor training at twenty-four sites, small group instruction at three of its campuses, live interactive televised literacy instruction at eight sites, prevocational classes directed at single parents and homemakers, instruction for parents of preschool and primary school children, and job training and workplace literacy programs in partnership with other agencies and businesses.[31]

Employers

Immigrants often receive occupational training in a work setting, usually without pay. These trainees can see for themselves what a work situation is like and then return to their classroom for discussion of what they have experienced and seen. In classes, the curriculum emphasis will typically be on vocational English as a second language (VESL), and intercultural communication though some skills training may also be provided. It is customary for trainees to spend about four hours in the workplace and four hours in the classroom for each day in such programs.[32]

Ties with private industry can be helpful for literacy educators. The sprawling complex of hotels and motels in Arlington, Virginia (across the Potomac from Washington, D.C.), is largely staffed by immigrant labor. The Arlington Chamber of Commerce is a partner with the Arlington public schools in a workplace literacy program grant with the Arlington schools for immigrant literacy training. All instruction takes place during work hours; more than four hundred students are currently enrolled.

It is not only literacy or basic skill acquisition that is the goal of workplace literacy programs aimed at immigrants. The development of management skills of the sort required in a McDonald's franchise outlet was part of an experimental training program begun in 1989. Van Management, Inc., which operates six McDonald's restaurants in suburban Fairfax County, Virginia, arranged the training sessions through the Fairfax County public schools' adult education program. The classes were taught in the restaurants during business hours as customers munched hamburgers and fries at nearby tables. English comprehension was emphasized in the sixty-course series and included an unusual component, small talk. Sharon Atherton, teacher in the first class, said this skill is something that is important to many U.S. citizens but is not understood by many who did not grow up in this country.[33]

A review of proposals that received funding under the Job Training Partnership Act as "immigrant demonstration projects" reveals close ties with immigrant advocacy groups as a common ingredient. An employer-related agency in Dearborn, Michigan, effected links with the Arab-American and Chaldean Council and the Arab Community Center for Economic and Social Services—groups with strong ties to an immigrant group that is unskilled or semiskilled, according to one study. In Norwood, Massachusetts, where the bulk of immigrants are refugees from the former Soviet Union, the Jewish Vocational Service is the partner. Ties with community-based organizations serving Hispanic and Asian–Pacific Islander immigrant and refugee communities are featured in a project for employment and training of those communities in Seattle. Links of a different kind are used by a grantee in San Diego; a corporate advisory council, the Amigos de SER, is a group of twenty employers who provide expertise ranging from workshops on job search skills to the conduct of mock job interviews with immigrant clients.[34]

Several employers in El Paso, Texas, were among the first to cooperate with the INS in bringing citizenship education classes to the workplace. Mark Ross, director of human resources at the giant Farah USA plant, reports that employees were at first skeptical of any program linked to the INS. Response was sparse at the first meetings, but as trust was established attendance increased at the lunchtime and after-work sessions. Eligible to attend are persons who have been resident aliens for at least five years and who are Farah employees or members of their families. No enrollment fees are charged for the program. Curriculum materials are supplied by the INS; instructors, who must have at least a high school diploma, are from Farah's personnel department. One reason for the program's popularity, according to Ross, is that family members are included.

A similar program of naturalization education classes in 1987, also in El Paso, was offered after work and on Saturdays at seven Levi Strauss and Company facilities to help immigrant employees prepare for the INS examinations. September 1, 1989, was a big day for six-hundred-fifty Levi Strauss employees and family members from twelve countries who became U.S. citizens in a mass ceremony at the El Paso Theater for the Performing Arts.[35]

Educational outreach to immigrants by employers will have to become the norm, rather than the exception, in the near future. By the year 2000, the U.S. Department of Labor expects that one in five prospective entrants into the labor force will be foreign-born.[36]

Community Organizations and Agencies

In many states, adult basic education funding may not be given to community-based organizations. (The state of New York is one notable exception.) Nonetheless, many of these groups are active in literacy and ESL education and often enroll otherwise hard-to-reach persons within particular ethnic communities. Family and job counseling, substance abuse treatment, health screening, and other social services may also be part of the package offered by such organizations.[37]

One highly respected community organization in the Hispanic immigrant community of Los Angeles is PUENTE. The name, which means "bridge" in Spanish, is also an acronym for People United to Enrich the Neighborhood through Education. The driving force behind this thriving institution, which is open from eight in the morning until eight at night, is Sister Jennie M. Lechtenberg, a Catholic nun.

PUENTE began in 1983 as a tutorial program for Spanish-speaking elementary school children. When the parents saw that the program, then staffed largely by volunteers, was helping their children to catch up with or even surpass other children, they became willing recruits for adult classes. Originally the sessions were conducted by PUENTE in public schools—often in closets. Sister Jennie eventually arranged for conversation to classroom space of a former barbershop in the present building, a former Masonic Hall that is now almost entirely occupied by PUENTE programs.

PUENTE justly prides itself on a very low dropout rate from its ESL classes and cites close ties with its constituent community as the principal reason for this. Many of its clients are illegal immigrants who equate public school with the government. They know they can come to PUENTE without fear of the "green and white [Border Patrol] bus that will take them to Tijuana," a staff member told me.

Community-based agencies serving Hispanic clients sometimes find they must tread lightly in work with women. "The women are just like little sponges," one program director reported in describing their approach to learning. "But we can only take them so far because the men don't like it." Some of the women students "sneak into school" during the day when their husbands are at work. At home, their books are hidden away. These women do not give out their phone numbers to teachers or school officials; they do not want calls coming to the home.

This is not a new problem. The history of immigration to the United States is replete with accounts of what were generally called "Old World races" that disapproved of women leaving the home to appear in public. In the early twentieth-century settlement houses, YMCAs and women's clubs reached out—not always with great success—to meet the educational needs of these women.[38]

Teachers for Adult Immigrants

What makes a good teacher of adult immigrants? Cultural understanding, or at least sensitivity, is almost invariably the first trait mentioned by immigrant education representatives to whom this question was posed. Skills and knowledge in effective techniques of instruction for adults is another element. All too many adult immigrants have been bruised in encounters with teachers who treated them as if they were children (not an uncommon experience for native-born adults, either).

If teachers must make some adjustments in work with the immigrants, so too must some immigrants make comparable adjustments. Teachers in most foreign countries are expected to dress formally and to maintain a certain distance from their students. It is a shock, to say the least, when immigrants from these nations see their teachers dressed in jeans and even sitting atop their desks as they instruct their classes.

Most teachers in adult programs for immigrants are employed part-time and do not qualify for the fringe benefit packages available to full-time teachers. This makes it difficult to attract and retain good teachers, especially when they are asked to teach for as many as four nights a week. About six months of this is about as much as most people can tolerate, according to one experienced adult program administrator.

Nonetheless, assertive efforts by dedicated teachers to prepare themselves for work with immigrant adults are not uncommon. Former Los Angeles Superintendent Leonard Britton was surprised one Saturday, upon visiting a school for another purpose, to find between three hundred and four hundred teachers and administrators engaged in learning about presenting ESL for adults. All were there voluntarily. None was being paid; neither were they getting extra credit points on their staff development records.[39]

Adult Education for Immigrants: An Uncertain World

The stepchild status of adult education generally is doubled in spades in too many immigrant education programs. In a letter to the *Washington Post*, Tom Bello, an adult ESL teacher, probably spoke for many in expressing frustration with the situation.

Bello teaches at a school with the largest enrollment of ESL students in suburban Fairfax County, Virginia, representing approximately 30 classes. With an enrollment of six hundred students (and two hundred on a waiting list in September 1989), no more classroom space was available. Efforts to get parking lot lights had been unsuccessful, Bello asserted, and the school had "more roaches than students because the extermination bill had not been paid." He went on to note that almost all ESL teachers worked part-time with scant benefits. Pay, which was by the hour, did not include time for preparation, planning, student-teacher meetings, or paperwork.

Like many of his colleagues across the nation, Bello liked his work in spite of the problems. His plea was for help to institutions and teachers who are struggling to bring immigrant and refugees into the mainstream of life in the nation.[40]

12
Learning English

In the late twentieth century, English is the acknowledged king of languages. English is the first language of more than 300 million people; an equal number use it daily as a second language. Never before in the history of the globe has one language been so pervasive.[1] Also, never before have so many non-English speakers been engaged in efforts to learn English. Many of these are immigrants to the United States.

There are significant differences between teaching English to non-English speakers and teaching it to those who already have it as their native tongue. The emphasis in ESL instruction is on the acquisition of basic English skills, not on refinement of existing knowledge and skills.

Some 31.8 million residents of the United States speak a language other than English at home according to Census Bureau estimates. Of these approximately 6.6 million residents of the United States either do not speak English well or do not speak it at all. Another 7.3 million speak English "well" with the remaining 17.8 million speaking English "very well."[2] Some persons who speak English with difficulty or not at all are native-born, but the majority are immigrants.

By the year 2000, an estimated 17.4 million adults with limited English proficiency will be living in the United States.[3] In the same year, it is expected that fifty-three of the largest metropolitan areas of the nation will have majority populations whose native language is not English.[4] By the same time, LEP workers will constitute more than 10 percent of the national work force.[5]

ESL in the Schools

The number of LEP children is not the same as the number of immigrants in schools. Children born in the United States who speak a language other than English (usually Spanish) are included; not included are immigrant children who do have sufficient fluency in English.[6] The great majority of LEP students, however, are immigrants. On this account, LEP student concerns are essentially immigrant student concerns as well.

How many LEP students are in the U.S. schools? It depends upon what definition is applied; estimates range from 1.2 million to 5.3 million.[7] In 1986, then-Secretary of Education William Bennett said there were between 1.2 and 1.7 million of them aged five to seventeen. This was a considerable step down from the 3.6 million LEP students that the Education Department had estimated in its 1984 report issued by Secretary Terrel Bell, who had also predicted that the number would increase by 40 percent during the next twenty years.[8]

Why the big difference? It stemmed from a narrower definition of limited English proficiency being applied by Bennett in an effort to head off requests for an increased budget for bilingual education. The earlier figure had included children eligible for assistance in school projects funded under the Bilingual Education Act. The new definition included only those "most likely to benefit," with the cutoff point being set at the twentieth percentile rather than the forty-third percentile.[9] The most recent Department of Education estimate is that there are about 2.2 million LEP students in U.S. schools. This is an increase of several hundred thousand over the level reported five years earlier.[10]

The number of LEP children in the United States is expected to increase by about 35 percent by the year 2000; of this increase, about 92 percent will have Spanish language backgrounds. In contrast, the number of school-age children in the general population is projected to increase by only 16 percent during the same period.[11] The need for classes in English as a second language thus will continue to grow. By the year 2000, according to one estimate, the number of

LEP students aged five to fourteen in the nation's schools will approach 3.4 million.[12]

How is it determined that a child has "limited English proficiency?" In California, a standardized test is used for this purpose with students from homes where a language other than English is customarily spoken. Those scoring below a specified percentile are determined to be LEP; as of the spring of 1987, California had so designated some 613,222 of its schoolchildren. Another 568,928 were designated as having "fluent English proficiency" (FEP), meaning that they scored above a certain percentile or received language training and thereafter were determined to be fluent in English.[13]

In 1989, in a move responding to pressures to enlarge the state's bilingual education programs, the New York State Board of Regents approved rules that expanded the definition of an LEP student. The new rules, which became effective for the 1990–91 school year, permit students who score up to the fortieth percentile on English tests to remain in bilingual or ESL classes. Under the previous standard, students whose scores were above the twenty-third percentile were moved to regular English language classes.[14]

In a report issued in 1992, the Council of Chief State School officers calls for a uniform national definition of limited English proficiency. The same report calls for development of a comprehensive model for identifying and assessing LEP students needing different levels of program services.[15]

ESL for Adults

ESL instruction is the fastest-growing sector of the adult education program in the United States. At the national level, a report on adult education programs funded under the federal Adult Education Act indicates that between 1985 and 1989, enrollments of persons with limited English proficiency rose from 29 percent to 42 percent of total enrollments. In 1990, almost 1.2 million were enrolled in federally-funded programs of ESL instruction in adult basic education and adult secondary education (leading to a diploma)[16] (see figure 12–1).

Fiscal year	*Federal expenditures for ESL programs**	*Estimated percentage of total federal literacy/secondary expenditures*
1989	$113,766,714	41.8%
1988	104,090,532	40.2%
1987	87,014,821	31.1%
1986	89,342,045	28.8%
1985	99,052,466	29.4%

Figure 12–1. English as a Second Language (ESL) as a Proportion of Total Federal Adult Literacy and Secondary Education Expenditures, 1985–89

*May be less than dollars appropriated.
Source: U.S. Department of Education.

Persons having limited proficiency in English generally do not engage in other types of learning in this country until they have participated in ESL classes. Of the three million adults served in the state-administered adult education programs in 1988, more than nine hundred thousand were enrolled in such classes.[17] In general ESL classes, instruction is linguistically based; students learn speaking, reading, and writing skills. Some specialized curricula have also been developed for teaching ESL to adults. These include survival ESL, vocational ESL (VESL), and English for special purposes (ESP).

Immigrants enrolled in survival ESL (or competency-based ESL) encounter a program designed to help them learn enough English to survive in the United States. How to use public transit, find a place to live, read an employment ad, or write a check are the typical curricular situations. The emphasis is on situations and not grammar. Although survival ESL is essential for most immigrants starting out in the United States, by itself it is not sufficient for assuring an individual of success on the job.

Vocational ESL (VESL) curricula are also situational, grounded in such specific jobs as nursing assistant, cosmetologist, or automobile mechanic. Instructional materials are most often adaptations of vocational materials used in classes for native English speakers. The intent is that of teaching English related to the jobs at hand—not the job's technical skills, which are taught in a coordinated manner by other instructors.

English for special purposes (ESP) classes are designed for foreign students and are intended to help them acquire English skills needed to function in specified situations. An underlying assumption is that the students have a sturdy academic background and are preparing for careers in the professions. Curricula are situational, unlike general ESL, and are drawn from the worlds of such professions as law, medicine, engineering, and business. An ESP text used by a would-be civil engineer, for example, would teach the language of building tunnels and bridges, of surveying, or of environmental engineering. The grammar is presented in the sequential order needed to pursue objectives of the content area, not from what is easiest to what is hardest in terms of linguistics.

In schools, ESL programs generally are organized as either stand-alone ESL or ESL-plus. In stand-alone programs, LEP students are grouped together and taught in a manner similar to that used in any foreign language class. In ESL-plus, students receive a component of instruction in and about English, but the curriculum also includes a focus on content instruction. Geography, mathematics, and social studies, for example, may be taught in the ESL-plus format.[18]

Adult Program Sponsors

Most ESL instruction for adults in the United States is offered by local school systems and community colleges. Curricula in these courses usually focus on the most basic English grammar and vocabulary of "survival English," built around such topics as health care, money management, and shopping.[19]

Community-based organizations are also active in literacy and ESL education and often enroll otherwise hard-to-reach persons within particular ethnic communities. Family and job counseling, substance abuse treatment, health screening, and other social service may also be part of the package offered by such organizations;[20] such courses typically are offered free or at minimal cost. Colleges and universities are increasingly turning to ESL instruction in their efforts to improve access for immigrant students.

Methods

Several methods have been used to teach English as a second language to immigrants. Heavy emphasis upon English grammar was characteristic of English language programs for immigrants before about the mid-1960s. At that time, the audio-lingual method (ALM) was most commonly used. The objective of this approach was that of teaching English grammar, vocabulary, and punctuation within a context of use in structured activities. These included repetition of words or phrases, memorization of dialogues, and substitution drills. This method, as was all too evident to even the most casual observers in such classes, simply did not work with most immigrant students.

One major flaw was that the situations described by the words being learned did not relate to the real lives of the students—and were in fact often absurd from the perspective of mature adults. Using the early ESL texts, for example, instructors might find themselves drilling a class composed of Iranians and Jordanians to repeat words such as these: "My name is Juan Perez. I come from Venezuela. I live at 2243 Main Street."[21] It is hardly surprising that the completion rates of adult immigrants in these programs tended to be very low.

The more sophisticated ESL programs of instruction that have emerged in the past several decades have been far more effective in work with immigrants. Instruction in the present era is based on satisfying the students' immediate needs. Adults focus on vital vocabulary and learn grammar concurrently; content follows situation, not the other way around.

Successful ESL and bilingual teachers of immigrant students quickly learn to inject the student's first culture into learning activities of whatever kind. Comparisons of several cultures can productively be discussed from the student's perspective.[22] This process requires a teacher flexible enough to allow conversation to diverge at times from the basic textural material presented for discussion.

At Fiorello LaGuardia Community College in New York, the administration has found it better to mix, rather than segregate, ethnic groups in ESL classes. Combining relatively quiet and passive Asian learners with more vocal and assertive Hispanics, for example, tends to create a superior classroom dynamic.[23]

Chris Larsen, instructional developer for the City Colleges of Chicago, has developed what he calls "realia" to help ESL students work on oral skills, as well as real-life reading skills needed for shopping trips. He suggests using food ads to teach the concept of comparison shopping. Milk cartons are rinsed out and brought in to teach the measurements of pint, quart, and gallon, along with such milk terms as whole, skim, 2 percent, and low fat. Cereal boxes, cans, and frozen food packages are used in much the same manner. In class, role playing is encouraged; one student plays the customer, another the cashier. Field trips are made to grocery and drugstores where students look for unit pricing signs and learn to read labels. Costs per pound are discussed, and so are "use by" dates. All of this makes for much faster learning than is possible through exclusive use of grammar-based texts.[24]

It is not at all uncommon for an ESL teacher who speaks only English to have a group of fifteen students who speak ten languages. Sometimes teacher and students have scarcely one word of a common language. Such groups may include persons who are illiterate, as well as those with postsecondary-level training. How does one manage a situation that appears on its surface to be instructionally unmanageable? Even ESL teachers may wonder about the answer to this question. Frequently their teacher training sessions did not prepare them for such extreme situations.

One ESL methodology in these instances employs what is called a "total physical response." Students are involved in body movement to demonstrate comprehension. The teacher acts out a particular concept; students follow. For example, a teacher says to students, "Stand up," and stands up herself. Students respond by standing also.[25] Eventually, and sometimes quite rapidly, comprehension follows. With larger groups, it is possible to separate a class into various levels for specialized attention. Peer teaching, often by volunteers, is a great help. Teacher aides may also be used. Such volunteers and aides need appropriate training for this task, a necessity that is too often overlooked.

Schools and adult education agencies, hard-pressed for assistance in accommodating the huge new demand for ESL, have had to develop a wide array of support. Tests to facilitate placement or measure progress are an obvious first priority need. The Basic English Skills Test (BEST) developed by The Center for Applied Linguistics tests elementary listening comprehension, speaking, reading, and writing. This instrument provides an evaluation of the extent and nature of an adult immigrant's English language proficiency so that he or she can be appropriately placed in a class or in individualized learning activities. It is also used for determining the progress of immigrants as they learn English with respect to survival or prevocational situations.

In addition to BEST, a number of other tests are available to determine language proficiency level. Among these are the Comprehensive Adult Student Assessment System (CASAS) developed by the California Department of Education, the English Language Skills Assessment (ELSA), English as a Second Language Oral Assessment (ESLOA), HELP Test, Ilyin Oral Interview, John/Fred Test, Secondary Level English Proficiency Tests (SLEP), and Structure Tests—English Language (STEL).[26] Instruction by interactive videodisc is an obvious need. No well-designed program of this type, however, exists at the present time.

Demand to Continue

ESL is sure to continue as a growth area within all sectors of the educational system in the United States. Such instruction is required in the most basic literacy classes and even in colleges and universities as immigrants seek access to higher education. Given the surge of immigration by persons whose first language is not English, it is understandable that the demand for teachers of English as a second language is skyrocketing. Teachers of English to Speakers of Other Languages (TESOL), the professional organization serving such teachers, has the largest membership in its history and reported a membership growth of 25 percent between 1990 and 1991.[27]

13
Bilingual Education as an Educational Option

Great confusion clouds too many discussions of bilingual education, much of it caused by imprecise definitions employed by the various adversaries; also, the constructions of philosophy and method are inappropriately mixed. The term *bilingual education* is used to describe a number of educational approaches using another language and English in instruction. True bilingual education programs are those that include (1) use of the students' dominant language, (2) teaching of content subjects through the dominant language, (3) teaching of cultural heritage and history of both linguistic groups, and (4) teaching of English as a second language.

From this definition, it can be seen that it is incorrect to characterize English as a second language (ESL) and bilingual education as competing approaches. The word *bilingual* means two languages; it isn't bilingual education if it doesn't have an ESL component. Teachers of English to Speakers of Other Languages (TESOL), the organization representing ESL teachers, formally endorsed the concept of bilingual education as a method of acquiring a second language in 1976.

The Politics of Language about Language

Extreme caution is advised for anyone walking in the mine field of terms said to define language instruction for immigrant children. The language of bilingual education is politically charged to the point that groups opposing each other's point of view will sometimes not use the same words to describe the topic of their discussion. Many terms have inventors with political, as well as educational, agendas. Few have completely generic connotations. Accordingly, some initial definitions of these and related terms often used in discussions about bilingual education are in order.

The word *immersion* is correctly and nonpejoratively used in reference to English as a second language (ESL) instruction. It is sometimes used in a demeaning sense, however, to imply old-fashioned submersion techniques with no particular accommodations for limited English speakers. In the now-discredited submersion programs, students whose proficiency in English was limited were placed in ordinary classrooms in which English was the language of instruction. They were given no special program to help them overcome their language problems, and their native language was not used in the classroom. Also called (with some justice) "sink or swim," submersion was found unconstitutional in the Supreme Court's 1974 decision in *Lau v. Nichols.*[1]

Proponents of bilingual education sometimes refer to their opposition as the "English-only" movement. This is an unjust label if applied to advocates of well-designed ESL programs. And almost all of the adjective modifiers of the term *bilingual education* (*transitional, maintenance, developmental, bicultural*) have manipulative meanings, depending upon who is using them. For example, opponents of bilingual instruction saw their challenge pick up supporters to the degree they could use the adjective *maintenance* in a derogatory fashion. After watching it function as a red flag, bilingual advocates of the present era have generally stopped using *maintenance* as the label for programs designed to help young people retain and improve their native language. "Developmental bilingual education" is the goal of these programs, according to James Lyons of the National Association for Bilingual Education (NABE). "Either you develop a language or it atrophies. . . . You don't want to maintain, you want to develop."

On the other hand, some advocates of bilingual education assertively proclaim their goals of ethnic consciousness. It is no accident that the titles of some programs now read "bilingual/bicultural education."

Not even the term *transitional* in reference to bilingual education is free of political associations. In the view of some opponents, it was invented in the late 1960s as a way of making bilingual education more palatable to a public that was beginning to perceive it as primarily an instrument for cultural maintenance.[2]

English Immersion Programs

Immersion is the general term used for teaching approaches for language minorities that do not involve using the children's native language.[3] The language is the medium of instruction, not it's object. A proper immersion program requires appropriate materials and methodology; it may also require bilingual teachers. Two forms of immersion language education frequently used in U.S. schools are sheltered English and structured immersion.

Sheltered English

Sheltered English programs, primarily employed at the secondary level, are essentially "alternative content" classes designed for students who lack sufficient English language skills to understand the regular curriculum. The teacher is careful to use only the vocabulary and structures they understand. Content-based courses may parallel nearly all regular academic curricular offerings or may involve only one or two subjects. Teachers must have ESL training but are not necessarily bilingual. There is no arbitrary time limit for such programs; students exit when they achieve a level of proficiency that will enable them to function in the mainstream program.

Structured Immersion

In structured immersion programs, used in both elementary and secondary schools, language-minority students receive all subject-matter instruction in English. Communication is, however, at a level the students can understand. Students may use their native language in class, but the teacher (who is typically bilingual) uses only English in response. Some structured immersion programs include some language-arts teaching in the native language.

Pull-Out Immersion

So-called pull-out immersion programs are typically used in schools that have relatively low enrollments of immigrant students. LEP students are "pulled out" of regular classes for special instruction in English. Such instruction is usually, though not always, provided by a teacher trained in ESL methodology who uses materials specially designed for ESL students. Technically, pull-out programs are not truly bilingual, because only English is used for instruction. This approach, however, is typically included among approaches to bilingual education.[4] In schools with larger enrollments of non-English-speaking immigrant students, English language instruction is more often used in classrooms where mainstream students are also enrolled.

Types of Bilingual Instruction

The labels given the most basic types of bilingual education programs vary, which is one cause of confusion. The following terms probably are those most widely accepted by those engaged in research on the subject. These are (1) transitional bilingual, (2) maintenance bilingual, and (3) two-way enrichment bilingual education. Each of these approaches has different instructional objectives.[5]

Transitional bilingual programs emphasize development of English language skills in order to enable students whose proficiency in English is limited to shift to an all-English program of instruction. Initially, subject matter is taught in the native language until English skills are sufficiently developed for the student to engage in regular classroom instruction. Some programs include English as a second language.

Bilingual education programs at either the elementary or secondary level are classed as "early transition" or "late transition" programs, depending upon the criteria used to determine the potential for success in an all-English program. In early transition programs, students remain until they can demonstrate oral English proficiency. In late transition programs, students are not released to the mainstream until their English proficiency (including reading and writing) is sufficient for them to survive in regular English language classes. In both types of programs, students also receive instruction designed to develop their native language skills, as well as ESL and content-area instruction in either English or the first language. Grouping is according to first language; teachers are, of course, bilingual.

A maintenance (or developmental) bilingual program has as its primary objective the preservation and development of literacy skills in the home language in addition to the acquisition of English. Instruction in such classes is provided in both the native language and English in equal measures for as many grades as the school elects to provide the program. There is no emphasis on leaving the program for English-only instruction, as is the case with transitional bilingual education. An important concern is that of learning English while honoring and using the home language as well.

In a two-way enrichment bilingual immersion program, both language-majority and language-minority students are served concurrently in the same classroom. In the lower elementary grades, all content instruction takes place in the native language of the minority students (generally Spanish), with a short period devoted to oral English. In the upper elementary grades, approximately half the curriculum is taught in the native language and half in English.

In such a program, English-speaking students learn Spanish, for example, while continuing to develop their native English language skills. The immigrant or LEP students learn English while becoming literate in their native Spanish. The objectives of two-way bilingual immersion programs are for both groups to become bilingual while succeeding academically and developing positive intergroup relations.[6]

The Case for Bilingual Education

The case for bilingual education rests heavily on the idea that the ability to use English develops in two stages. Basic interpersonal communications skills (BICS) come first, but although these enable the child to play and interact with other children, they do not translate into success in the classroom. It is cognitive-academic language proficiency (CALP) that must be achieved if the child is to master academic subjects. Developing skills at the CALP level is believed to take between five and seven years and to be most effectively built upon a foundation of the native language, rather than English.[7]

Moreover, advocates of bilingual instruction believe, native language instruction has significant affective educational benefits. In their view, something more than mere language acquisition is at stake. A curriculum with bicultural as well as bilingual content provides an affirmation of the LEP student's personal being and culture. Self-esteem can more easily be enhanced, and the stage is set for a more effective engagement in the process of learning English.[8]

Aside from narrowly educational considerations, bilingual education proponents cite research showing that "substantial and alarming evidence" that English-immersion preschool programs frequently lead to children losing their primary language, and with that the ability to communicate with their parents. In the view of Lily Wong Fillmore, a professor at the University of California at Berkeley, this is a deprivation that can cause the children to become discipline problems later.[9]

The Case Against Bilingual Education

Opponents of the bilingual approach generally believe that a well-designed ESL program provides a greater stimulus for learning and results in much more rapid learning. In their view, bilingual education acts to delay the achievement of this objective. Apart from research that they cite in detail showing poor results in comparison with immersion programs (bilingual education advocates cite a comparable package of favorable research findings), opponents of bilingual education tend to focus on what they say is an implicit political agenda of the bilingual education movement. Promoting language and cultural maintenance is posed as damaging to the fabric of society, even threatening "Quebecization" of entire regions of the nation.

Furthermore, bilingual programs are said to reinforce stereotypes, ghettoize immigrant children, and set them apart in programs perceived by students and teachers alike to be of inferior status. Bilingual education is also faulted as a "jobs program" emanating from an entrenched bureaucratic base and as fuel for a political lobby more interested in building a Hispanic constituency than in educating youngsters.

Research Studies and Their Results

Care and due prudence should be watchwords for anyone endeavoring to learn the whole truth about the validity of bilingual education. Much of the research has been accomplished by passionate advocates seeking documentation of preconceived conclusions for or against bilingual education. On both sides, misapplied definitions, selectively presented findings, and generalizations derived from worst-case scenarios abound. Political considerations too often infuse these presentations; spurious "victory celebrations" following various skirmishes cloud the air. Reasonable debate, or even academic challenge, in this atmosphere becomes problematic.

Some recent impartial and relatively well-designed research projects point the way out of this morass. One longitudinal study, ironically cited by both proponents and opponents of bilingual education, has been conducted since 1986 by the staff in the Office for Research and Evaluation of the El Paso Independent School District. LEP students in the district's two major bilingual programs are being tracked. One program incorporates a transitional bilingual approach originally proposed under Texas Senate Bill 477. Students in the beginning levels of this "SB 477" program learn to read in Spanish and (since 1990) are provided with English instruction designed to develop both oral and written language skills. Content areas of mathematics, science, and social studies are also taught in Spanish at beginning levels.

The other is a bilingual immersion program (BIP), a name which has given rise to misinterpretation. This is not solely English language immersion; dual language immersion is a more apt label, as both English and Spanish are used as languages of instruction. The program includes a Spanish component designed to promote literacy and language maintenance for at least four years of instruction. It also focuses on oral and written English instruction through content-area thematic units rather than the traditional ESL approach.

By the end of the sixth year of the study, the researchers concluded that both programs were strong; however, the dual language immersion group appeared to have a slight lead. Test scores indicate that the immersion group acquired a head start in the primary grades, though by the sixth grade the gap between the two groups had narrowed.

Grade averages for the two groups were very close, though again the dual language immersion students had a slightly larger percentage of passing grades in three of the four core courses.

Results of a survey of teachers in the two programs showed that a higher percentage of the dual language immersion teachers believe their program would be successful than was shown for the transitional bilingual education teachers. A sample of students in the two programs were also interviewed; with only two exceptions, there were no discernable differences between the respective groups. The dual language immersion students were perceived to be slightly more fluent in conversational English by the interviewers (although more of the transitional bilingual students claimed such fluency). The dual language immersion students also seemed to have better-defined ideas about going to college, though it was noted that this might be more reflective of home attitudes than of anything having to do with the program.

In reviewing these results (and their earlier iterations), proponents and opponents of bilingual education have each claimed victory. Opponents say that results from standardized tests in reading and language reveal that the dual language immersion students are doing better than students in the transitional bilingual program. This, they say, provides impressive evidence on behalf of this instructional approach.[10] Not so, say bilingual education proponents, who note relatively few differences between the two groups.[11]

Claims of either sort are premature. The most that El Paso district researchers will say at this point is that the dual language immersion program "works well in [immersion] schools and that it must be considered an effective, viable approach to bilingual education."[12] They are not prepared to draw the conclusion that dual language immersion is a superior method. It must also be remembered that both programs in the comparison are bilingual; the amount of Spanish language instruction in each is the variable. A program of solely English language immersion instruction is not part of the study at all.

Another study provides evidence that is positive in its implications for bilingual education. In seeking to drop a requirement in the Bilingual Education Act that native-language instruction be mandated for any federally supported program in the schools, Ronald Reagan's Department of Education claimed that research in the area was inconclusive. Was this indeed the case? In an effort to find out, Representative Augustus Hawkins, then chairman of the House Committee on Education and Labor, asked the General Accounting Office (GAO) to assess the validity of statements being made by Department of Education officials.[13]

The result was a report issued in March 1987 that caused an apoplectic reaction on the part of officials in the department. Experts selected by the GAO came from both sides of the bilingual education controversy; the panel was, however, quite one-sided in its support of native language teaching. Only two of the ten experts agreed with the Department of Education's assertion that there was insufficient evidence to support the law's requirement of the use of native language to the extent necessary to reach the objective of learning English.[14] Seven of ten experts disagreed with the department's conclusion that teaching methods not employing native language show more promise. Few agreed with the department's assertions that long-term school problems experienced by Hispanic youths are associated with native-language instruction. Few also agreed with the department's general interpretation that evidence in this field was too ambiguous to permit conclusions.[15]

The GAO report was generally viewed by bilingual education proponents as a stunning victory for their cause. In their view, the Department of Education should have accepted the report's findings, because six of the members of the GAO panel had either been recommended by the Department of Education or had their work cited by the department in support of its position. A Reagan Department of Education official, however, accused the GAO of everything from failure to "honor the usual canons of scholarship, program evaluation and scientific research" to operating beyond the bounds of its proper legal authority.[16]

In spite of these findings, proponents of continuing the requirement for use of native language in nearly all federal programs funded under the Bilingual Education Act were unsuccessful in maintaining this provision. When reauthorized in 1988, the act included a new provision that enabled nonbilingual ESL programs to receive as much as 25 percent of funds made available under the program;[17] Only 4 percent had been allowed previously.

In February 1991, the U.S. Department of Education released results of a four-year study of three different educational approaches: (1) immersion programs with all or nearly all instruction in English, (2) four-year-exit bilingual programs, and (3) six-year-exit bilingual programs.[18] Some two thousand Spanish-speaking elementary school pupils in five states were the studied group. As ultimately developed, the study did not purport to compare the effectiveness of the three approaches. This idea was scrapped after the researches were unable to find all three approaches within the same school district, and they concluded that they could not control for variations between districts. Some comparisons were drawn, however, between immersion and early-exit programs when found in the same district.[19]

The researchers concluded that children in all three groups not only outpaced other at-risk students but were able to keep up with their counterparts in the norming student population. Bilingual instruction did not impede them from learning English or any other subject. Approximately 40 percent of immersion, 44 percent of early-exit, and 28 percent of late-exit students were reclassified as having fluent English proficiency at the end of three years. Approximately 67 percent of immersion, 72 percent of early-exit, and 51 percent of late-exit students were reclassified by the end of four years. Approximately 79 percent of late-exit students were reclassified by the end of the sixth program year.

Interestingly, most students stayed in both the immersion and early-exit programs for a longer period of time than the models specified, with less than 26 percent in either program being mainstreamed by the end of the third grade. Many teachers clearly believed that many students would benefit by remaining in such programs even after they had been reclassified. This finding suggests that the time frames for either immersion or bilingual instruction may need reexamination.

In releasing these findings, the Department of Education promptly asserted that its position that no one method could be upheld as superior to another appeared to be upheld. The Bush administration moved forward with its intention to change current provisions in the Bilingual Education Act allowing immersion programs to receive no more than 25 percent of federal bilingual education funding. But other views were also heard, and the controversy over bilingual instruction in the nation's public schools was by no means settled. Both sides charged that the study was flawed, because too few sites had been examined. Ronald Saunders, executive director of U.S. English (an organization that opposes bilingual education), noted the study did not compare the relative effectiveness of the program models and labeled the $4.5 million effort as "probably . . . a waste."

Proponents of transitional and maintenance programs accused the Department of Education of downplaying findings showing that long-term instruction in the native language increased the degree of achievement. This is probably a justified complaint. One such finding was that the growth rates of students in the late-exit program accelerated at certain points where deceleration in growth was typical both in the other groups and in the norming student population.[20] James Lyons, executive director of the National Association for Bilingual Education, said the study should have followed students into high school years and recorded dropout rates.[21]

The battle of research findings between pro- and anti-bilingual education forces is likely to go on. But it seems clear that there is a body of recent research findings that provides some support for bilingual education as an appropriate educational *option* for immigrant students who do not speak English. Well-designed bilingual education programs appear to be as effective as other methods in at least some educational settings. There is no unambiguous evidence, however, that they are more effective. On that account, the continuing effort to allow more participation by ESL programs under the Bilingual Education Act appears well advised. The controversy attending bilingual education has more to do with ethnic and social than with pedagogical concerns.

14

The Politics of Language in Education: The Law and the Players

Current federal policy on bilingual education is stated in the still fiercely debated Bilingual Education Act of 1988, which authorizes funds to support bilingual education in the schools, training for teachers and aides, development of instructional materials, and encouragement of parental involvement. Less complicated and controversial political threads define the other significant aspect of language instruction for immigrants, that of English as a second language (ESL). Although there are some in the ESL advocacy community who would like their own bill, this seems hardly necessary. Substantial amounts of federal dollars are already being spent on ESL via existing federal programs; including those in library services, adult education, and bilingual education.

The Bilingual Education Act: A History

Understanding the full dimensions of current controversies about language in education requires some knowledge of the historical context. Bilingual education is by no means a newcomer on the national scene. In the nineteenth century, a period of heavy immigration to the United States, a number of states authorized instruction in languages other than English. By the turn of the century, more than six hundred thousand youngsters in the nation's schools (about 4 percent of the public and parochial elementary school population) were being taught at least some of the time in German.[1]

The Cuban revolution of 1959 was a major trigger for the bilingual education movement of the present era in the United States. Fidel Castro's regime drove to American shores hundreds of thousands of Spanish-speaking refugees who had no intention of giving up their language or culture. Had the influx been small or dispersed, bilingual education would not have found resonance in any national forum. But the U.S. Congress had to take into account the demands of so large and articulate group from what had been Cuba's middle and upper classes. The Cubans found natural allies in the rising tides of Mexican immigrants to states in the Southwest, Puerto Ricans in New York, and among the native-born active in the then-burgeoning civil rights movement.[2]

The first comprehensive bilingual program of the present era was established in the Coral Way Elementary School in Miami in 1963. Aimed at native-born children and their Cuban peers, the Coral Way experiment was partly financed by the Ford Foundation.[3] The Spanish-speaking sector of the target group was children of Cuban refugees, most of them from educationally and socially advantaged families but who nonetheless were experiencing academic difficulty in the city's English language school programs. Admirers of the Coral Way program point to a school district 1966 study showing that in English reading, both language groups did as well or better than counterpart students in English language schools. Social benefits to both groups as observed by teachers are also cited as evidence of success.[4] In succeeding years, many schools in areas heavily impacted by newly arriving immigrants have installed bilingual education programs, most of them featuring Spanish and English. Because of inconsistencies of definition, no record of the number of bilingual programs in U.S. school districts exists. However, the number of such programs has grown rapidly.

The force with which bilingual education hit the U.S. schools can at least in part be explained by the principle of the sway of a pendulum. Bilingual education was not always accepted in U.S. schools. In Texas, for example, it was a crime until 1973 to provide instruction in a public school in any language except English.[5] Immigrant children had often been made to suffer in cruel ways during the days of sink-or-swim instruction, where little or no allowance was made for their language difficulties. Punishment for speaking one's native language was not unusual, and native cultures were most often neglected (if not denigrated) by administrators and teachers insensitive to, and ignorant of, the worlds from which their immigrant students came. The dissatisfaction with this policy was understandably strong, though it lacked political support.

The idea of bilingual language education in the present era began in January of 1967 when Senator Ralph Yarborough (D-Texas) introduced what he called the American Bilingual Education Act as an amendment to the Elementary and Secondary Education Act of 1965. The legislation was designed, he said, to address "the special educational needs of the large numbers of students in the United States whose mother tongue is Spanish and to whom English is a foreign language." Yarborough was from Texas, where the dropout rates of Spanish-speaking school students were depressingly high. Most Texans 14 years of age and older with Spanish surnames spent fewer than five years in school, Senator Yarborough told his Senate colleagues.[6] Part of Senator Yarborough's motivation as he moved forward with the Bilingual Education Act was his sense of the scandal and injustice characterizing the school experiences of immigrant children, as revealed in a National Education Association (NEA) report in 1966.[7]

As eventually enacted during the Nixon administration, the Bilingual Education Act differed from the first bill introduced by Senator Yarborough in several respects. One of these was that the target group was changed from "Spanish-speaking children" to "children of limited English-speaking ability." From the perspective of some bilingual education advocates, this broadening of focus was not entirely desirable in that it emphasized the concept of deficiency in the English language rather than proficiency in another language. Strengthening of the native language was not included.[8] The act's provisions limited financial assistance under the competitive grant program to schools serving high concentrations of children from families with incomes below $3,000 per year or receiving payment under a program of aid to families with dependent children. No specific approaches for this task were specified.[9]

With the act's reauthorization in 1974, however, a more prescriptive approach was taken. Education in the student's native language was to be the method used by districts receiving federal funds. Furthermore, the goal of acquiring proficiency in English was now matched with an emphasis on the importance of "instruction given with appreciation for the cultural heritage of such children." It was this shift that would later bring down the wrath of Ronald Reagan's education secretary, William Bennett.[10]

Interestingly, the Nixon Administration was extremely supportive of bilingual education. Ironically, this very support seems to have been the instrument of some of the program's difficulties today. Federal dollars were made available before schools were equipped to spend them wisely. All too many teachers without appropriate qualifications or training were employed, and grants were not always well conceived or implemented. This was especially true in the early years following enactment of the Bilingual Education Act, when by nearly every account some mistakes were made in launching bilingual education programs. The errors and oversights of the past have remained to haunt bilingual education in its much more sophisticated present-day incarnation.

In 1978, during the Carter administration, the Bilingual Education Act was reauthorized. Congress allowed that a child's native language could be used "to the extent necessary to allow a child to achieve competence in the English language." Language maintenance programs were, however, prohibited; all programs funded under Title VII were to be transitional.[11]

It was during this period that the Carter administration got itself into trouble with Congress when, in an effort to court Hispanic votes, it promulgated rules going beyond the Lau guidelines that would have *mandated* bilingual education in schools where at least twenty-five LEP children of the same language-minority group were enrolled in two consecutive elementary grades (K–8). This plan was enthusiastically endorsed by only two national organizations, the National Education Association and the National Association for Bilingual Education; reaction from other education groups was assertively negative. Some 4,600 public comments, most of them negative, were logged in by the Department of Education. Given these pressures, the proposed new rules were withdrawn. The proposal may have been popular with Hispanic-American voters, but it hurt President Carter with other voting blocs.[12]

Ronald Reagan was no friend of bilingual education, and his administration moved as quickly as possible to cut funding for the Bilingual Education Act. Spending under the act's provisions was reduced by 47 percent between 1980 and 1988. (Real support for all education programs declined by 8 percent during the same time period.[13] Ronald Reagan's first secretary of education, Terrel Bell, was somewhat ambivalent about bilingual education. But the generally pacific Bell was replaced after a relatively short tenure by the generally pugnacious William Bennett. In him, bilingual education advocates acquired a formidable opponent.

Bennett's view of the federal government's assertive role in specifying bilingual instruction was that the government thought that local school districts could not be trusted to devise the best means to teach their students English. Furthermore, bilingual education was no longer seen so much as a means to ensure that students learned English as it was an emblem of cultural pride or means of producing a positive self-image in the student.[14] While pride in one's heritage was "natural and commendable" and to be encouraged, Bennett said, the federal government's responsibility was that of ensuring that "local schools succeed in teaching non-English-speaking students English, so that every American enjoys access to the opportunities of American society."[15]

In a noteworthy 1985 speech in New York City, Secretary Bennett attacked the "intrusiveness and heavy-handedness" of 1975 Department of Health, Education, and Welfare policies that he said "began to require that educational programs for non-English-speaking students be conducted in large part in the student's native language, as virtually the only approved method of remedying discrimination."[16] Although these regulations had never been formally published, they had allegedly served as the basis of about five hundred "compliance agreements" negotiated with school districts across the country between 1975 and 1980. If a school district did not wish to use transitional bilingual education, it had to prove that the proposed alternative was equally effective, which was certainly a questionable demand when the U.S. Office of Education had never proved that bilingual education was effective.[17]

In 1984, despite Reagan administration opposition or inaction, the Bilingual Education Act was again strengthened a bit. The goal was clarified as that of enabling LEP children "to achieve competence in the English language . . . [and] to meet grade-promotion and graduation standards." Two general-purpose programs were authorized: transitional bilingual education (which was to receive 75 percent of instructional grant funds) and developmental bilingual education. Bilingual education proponents were elated at the addition of developmental bilingual programs, even though a relatively small share of instructional grant funds could be used for this purpose. For the first time, the statutes would permit use of federal funds for native-language enhancement. Not only that, the law's language stated that "where possible," developmental bilingual education programs should enroll approximately equal numbers of native English-speaking children "whose native language is the second language of instruction and study in the program."[18]

Reagan administration officials had, of course, opposed this provision. Part of the price for their approval of the final product was the authorization of a third category of general instructional grants for so-called special alternative instructional programs (SAIP)—a euphemism for ESL instruction in districts where "establishment of a bilingual education program may be administratively impractical due to the presence of small numbers of students of a particular native language or because personnel who are qualified to provide bilingual instructional services are unavailable."[19]

The 1988 reauthorization of the Bilingual Education Act as Title VII of the Augustus F. Hawkins–Robert T. Stafford Elementary and Secondary Education Improvement Act resulted in an extremely complex, even tortured, restructuring of the funding formulas for the three types of bilingual education programs authorized. Senator Edward Kennedy, author of this compromise, described it as a way of accommodating the Department of Education's "quest for greater funding flexibility without mandating increased spending for monolingual instructional programs."[20] Before reauthorization, 96 percent of funds granted to local education agencies had to be used for "transitional bilingual education"; the remaining 4 percent of funds were made available to other methods of instruction, including ESL, sheltered English, and structured immersion.[21] In 1988, it was decided to allow 25 percent of the funds for ESL and other English-based methods. This was a decided change in the direction of flexibility, and one not welcomed by the hard-core bilingual lobby.

The Education Department of George Bush's administration was less hostile to developmental bilingual education programs than was its Reagan predecessor. Certainly the jarring and generally unhelpful rhetoric that typified the reign of William Bennett was largely eliminated. Optimism was the prevalent note at the 1992 meeting of the National Association for Bilingual Education (NABE) in Albuquerque. "NABE has had bad years, and those bad years are gone," the organization's president, Paul E. Martinez, told the more than five thousand members in attendance.[22]

Bilingual Education and the States

Some of the states most heavily affected by immigration have enacted bilingual education statutes of their own. The first of these came in 1971 when Massachusetts enacted such a law.[23] California's official support to the bilingual education approach ended when Governor George Deukmejian, by exercising his veto, allowed the state's bilingual education law to expire in 1987. Bilingualism for *all* students, however, is the objective of a new foreign language framework policy adopted by the California State Board of Education in 1988. By the middle of the 1990s, all school districts in the state are to adopt a "communication-based" (not grammar-based) second-language plan from kindergarten through the twelfth grade. A more controversial provision states that all students from homes where the language is other than English must have the chance to develop their native language in public school on a continuous basis from the day of entry.[24]

Under a consent order developed under threat of a suit in 1990, the Florida State Board of Education is implementing a tough new set of "emergency rules" relating to the education of LEP students that have significant implications for nearly all of the Florida's teachers. One key provision specifies that *every* teacher of LEP students (not just those in ESL and bilingual education classes) must have ESL endorsement and certification or endorsement to teach English or be in training programs leading to the completion of the requirements for certification by the beginning of the 1994–95 academic year.[25] This is evidence of the growing political clout of immigrant and LEP student parents in the state.

The Opposing Sides

The national debate over language education continues and has generated a number of issues that need examination. But who are the players? A number of organizations are active in the battle to determine the course of language instruction for immigrants.

Even its fiercest opponents admit that the organization known as U.S. English, the chief source of opposition to the bilingual education movement, has struck a responsive chord with the public. Currently, U.S. English has two stated goals: first, to make English the official language of government, and second, to guarantee the opportunity for all people of the United States to learn English. The organization asserts that "while a heritage of linguistic and cultural diversity has lent strength to the nation and while an individual's knowledge of more than one language is highly desirable, the promotion or maintenance of languages other than English is of secondary importance to the need to ensure fluency in English."

It didn't take U.S. English long to become one of the largest associations in the nation, with more than four hundred thousand members as of July 1992. The well-appointed (though not posh) offices of U.S. English, located just a block from the White House, stand in contrast to the more spartan quarters of most of its opponent organizations. Clearly this is an organization that can hold its own in the capital city.

The increasing use of the Spanish language by new residents of the United States is a source of particular concern to U.S. English. Spanish-language background immigrants are indeed a growing minority in a number of states (figure 14–1).Tapping a kind of linguistic backlash effect, U.S. English and its allies have been successful to date in getting English designated as official, either constitutionally or by law, in nineteen states as of July 1992. Legislation is officially pending in two other states (see figure 14–2).

What happens when a state passes a law or constitutional amendment making English its official language? Even U.S. English admits that not much changes; the impact of the action is psychological. Bilingual education programs do not appear to have been harmed by official English language legislation where it has been enacted. California, which made English official in 1986, still has a very large number of bilingual programs, as does Illinois, which has had an official English laws since 1969.[26]

Although it received its chief impetus from a court case initiated by a Chinese-American, bilingual education is primarily supported by Hispanics. The National Association for Bilingual Education (NABE) is overwhelmingly Hispanic in its governance and orientation. The Ford Foundation took a leading role in founding the Mexican-American Legal Defense and Education Fund (MALDEF) and the National Council of LaRaza in the early 1970s. It is these organiza-

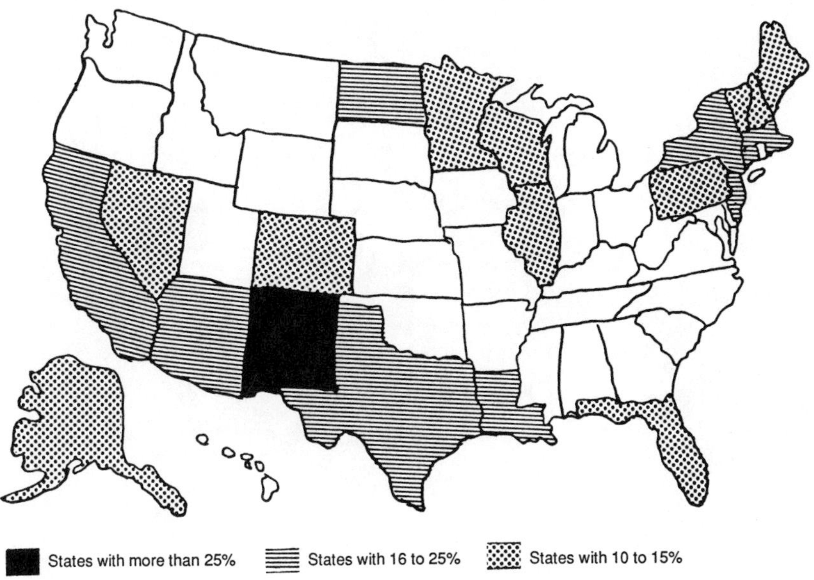

Figure 14–1. Persons of Spanish-Language Background as a Percentage of Total State Population.

Source: National Council of La Raza.

tions that have taken the leading role in developing the bilingual education movement and giving it its distinctly Hispanic tinge.

It is a mistake, however, to assume that Hispanics are unanimous, or nearly so, in their support of the bilingual education approach in their children's schools. There are prominent dissenters. In his autobiography, author Richard Rodriguez asserts his Mexican-American heritage but takes bilingual education proponents to task for saying that "children lose a degree of 'individuality' by becoming assimilated into public society." He describes his own experience: "Only when I was able to think of myself as an American, no longer an alien in *gringo* society, could I seek the rights and opportunities necessary for full public individuality."[27]

Richard Estrada, a syndicated columnist for the *Dallas Morning News* also opposes bilingual education. So does Linda Chavez, former director of the U.S. Commission on Civil Rights in the administration of Ronald Reagan. Chavez is concerned that an undue emphasis on a separate cultural identity for Hispanics will ultimately hinder immigrants in their search for full participation in national life. Language

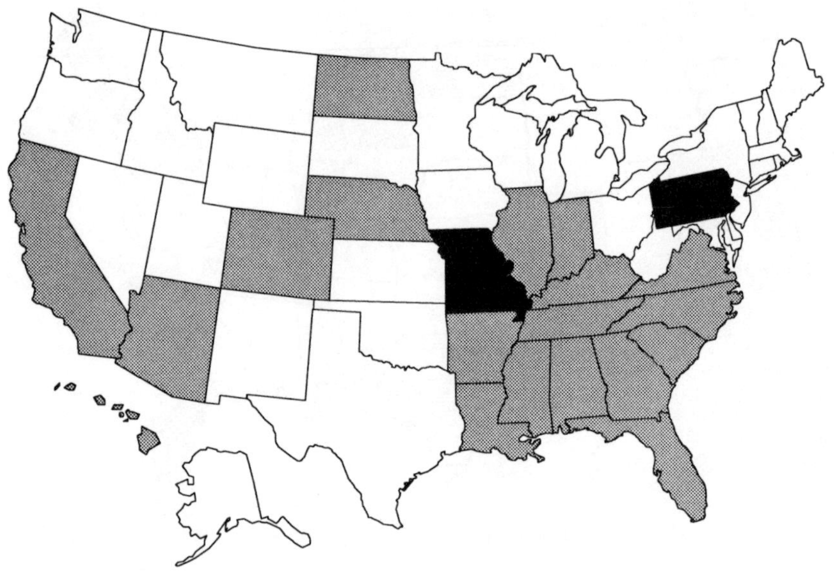

Figure 14–2. Status of Official English Legislation in the United States

Source: U.S. English

and culture may be preserved, and political gains may be made by Hispanic voters living in ethnically defined electoral districts. But, she says, the price will be that "Hispanics must remain in the barrio."[28]

The National Education Association (NEA) is the nation's largest teacher union. As the representative of bilingual education teachers, and conscious also of the role of incoming immigrants in keeping open schools that might otherwise be closed, the organization supports bilingual instruction. It is viewed by U.S. English as the latter's chief opponent.

The English Plus Information Clearinghouse (EPIC) is a coalition established under the auspices of the National Immigration, Refugee, and Citizenship Forum and the Joint National Committee for Languages. Formed as a direct challenge to U.S. English, English Plus holds that the national interest is best served "when all members of our society have full access to effective opportunities to acquire strong English language proficiency plus mastery of a second or multiple languages." English Plus also cites a need for "a vastly expanded network of facilities and programs for comprehensive instruction in English and other languages." The purposes and goals of English Plus were endorsed, as of the summer of 1988, by some forty-five organizations ranging from the American Civil Liberties Union to the "Stop English Only" committee of Hostos Community College in New York.

Teachers and Language Politics

One of the tragic outcomes of the long, drawn-out battle over bilingual education is the deep gulf that has developed in some schools between bilingual and mainstream teachers. Teachers tend to bristle at the suggestion they are "monolingual," although such a statement may be entirely true. Teachers who do not have a second-language skill feel increasingly threatened in an era of immigration from non-English-speaking nations.

Many of the nation's teachers have been caught in cruel dilemmas stemming from the changing needs of the school population. At times, schools have been urged to hire only teachers from the same ethnic background as the students. Teachers born in the United States have been told that they do not qualify for a particular job because they are not of the same cultural group as the students who will be served. Even finer distinctions may be made; instructors from the Dominican Republic, for example, may be labeled as unable to "relate" to students from Puerto Rico.[29]

At its most extreme, this position facilitates development of a teacher-student immigrant subculture within a school. Development of English language ability has not always been high on the practical agendas in some such programs. A former Anglo school board member in a Texas border-area school district told me of a rural school in which the announced objective of a bilingual program was that of moving toward bilingual instruction. "However, when we got into that school we found that the whole program was nothing but Spanish, and that's the way they wanted it to stay," he said. It was undoubtedly his opposition to this situation that helped cause his defeat for reelection by a predominantly Mexican-American electorate.

There is certainly some animosity engendered within school systems when bilingual teachers are paid more than others. With burgeoning immigrant populations, some school districts find it necessary to pay substantially higher salaries to teachers with bilingual qualifications. Such pay incentives for bilingual or ESL teachers, however, exist in only 11.3 percent of all school districts, according to a 1991 survey. The bulk of these (58.5 percent) are in larger districts enrolling between twenty thousand and fifty thousand students.[30]

Faced with a burgeoning number of students with limited English proficiency, California school districts are scurrying to find bilingual teachers. In mid-1991, a task force in that state reported that a shortage of some fourteen thousand bilingual teachers existed, with only 1 bilingual teacher available for every 107 LEP students. Bilingual education teachers in the Southeast Asian languages are in especially short supply.[31]

California school districts may also retrain mainstream teachers in bilingual instruction—a process that is not always voluntary. Oakland Unified School District, for example, requires any teacher with more than ten LEP students ("if you want to say here,") to have a bilingual credential or to sign a waiver stating that he or she will work toward one.[32]

California teachers who pursue bilingual or language development specialist credentials must make a serious commitment to the project (one year of training beyond the regular teaching credential, plus mastery of a second language). The majority of teachers now taking such action in the state are themselves bilingual and so have a head start on language fluency. Those individuals who do not have language fluency, or at least language knowledge, in advance face a far greater and more time-consuming challenge.[33]

A survey of teachers in Los Angeles in 1988 showed that 78 percent of them opposed bilingual education. Nonetheless, the Los Angeles school system proceeded with implementing a master plan that mandates even more instruction in the student's native language. Whether the opposition of so many teachers stems at its roots from concerns about the educational validity of bilingual education or from fears that inability to speak a language other than English may ultimately cost them their jobs is unknown. The truth is that new teachers in most parts of California have virtually no choice except to be bilingual. The openings for them tend to be in the troubled schools—those dealing with large numbers of immigrant students. More experienced teachers often wish to transfer out of such schools.[34]

15

Issues Surrounding Bilingual Education

Apart from pedagogical concerns, a number of questions, not all of them mutually exclusive, lie at the heart of debates about bilingual instruction for immigrants. Among them are these: (1) Does bilingual education have a political agenda, and if so, what are its implications? (2) Is bilingual education the only method of instruction that should be implemented for some categories of students in the public schools? (3) Is bilingual education maintained more for the benefit of its bureaucracy than for the benefit of immigrant and other students with limited English proficiency? (4) Does bilingual instruction encourage or result in segregation in the schools and in society? (5) Are the alternatives to bilingual instruction promoted from a racist or nativist point of view? (6) Is the English language essential for national unity, and therefore should it be made the official language of the United States?

A Political Agenda?

The fight for bilingual education has at its roots something more than arguments over instructional methodology. Opponents, whose views have generally prevailed in the administrations of Ronald Reagan and George Bush, have been nervous about an agenda that carries as many political as educational ramifications. "Yes, there is a political agenda for bilingual education, and it doesn't bother me," says Leonard Britton, former superintendent of schools in Miami and Los Angeles. He considers such education a useful tool for moving the United States toward multicultural education approaches. Such a view is, in fact, de rigueur for most any superintendent with a predominantly Hispanic constituency. The record suggests that the debate about bilingual education does not revolve around the concerns of students who speak Chinese, Vietnamese, or Creole French; it is a debate about the use of Spanish.

The Spanish language, as well as their native cultures, is highly valued by U.S. residents of Mexican heritage. In one nationwide survey of Mexican-Americans, 90 percent expressed the desire that their children maintain Mexican traditions as they grow up. Another large number (75 percent) said that bilingualism was an aspect of Mexican culture they hoped their families would maintain.[1] This value often is fiercely held. Some Hispanic parents interviewed for one study told the interviewer that they sometimes pretended not to understand English so their children would be forced to address them in Spanish. The same group, however, was anxious for their youngsters to learn English, as well as to learn it themselves.[2]

Critics also charge that bilingual education proponents have a shifting and ever-widening mission. The expansionist thrust, if that is what it is, of the bilingual education movement can be seen in the assertion of the National Clearinghouse for Bilingual Education that bilingual education programs should be expanded so that "all American students, regardless of language background, have an opportunity to become bilingual and even multilingual."[3] If this is a call to action, it is being heeded in Dallas, where School Superintendent Marvin Edwards is proposing that Spanish classes be required for all high school graduates. In introducing his plan, Edwards stated that by acquiring a knowledge of Spanish, English-speaking students would gain "the tools to deal with life in their heavily Hispanic city and state."[4] If this controversial proposal succeeds (as it has not as of 1992), Dallas would be the first major school district in the United States to require study in a specific non-English language in order to graduate.

It is certainly true that bilingual education is a political as well as an educational movement. The demand is political in that it is an assertion of cultural and language rights. The proponents of bilingual education have much in common with the advocates of "black power" in the 1960s and 1970s.

A corollary issue surrounds the question of whether it is appropriate for the public schools to assist in the maintenance of immigrant cultures. Some school districts in the United States, most of them heavily populated by Hispanic immigrants, have decided that cultural maintenance *is* their responsibility and have developed bilingual maintenance programs. These actions, often rather pugnaciously advanced by representatives of Hispanic immigrants, have in many cases drawn fierce opposition both locally and at the national level from groups that see maintenance of an immigrant culture as a misuse of public funds.

Perhaps the poles of this arguments are not irreconcilable. Clearly, the United States has an interest in development and maintenance of its own democratic civic culture. Such a mission has been, and should remain, incarnate in the programs of every public school. Intelligent and aggressive pursuit of that mission in the present era necessarily incorporates a study of cultures that make up the whole of the United States. It is possible that well-designed bilingual education programs of every variety might contribute to this goal. It should be noted, however, that not all immigrants look to the public schools for the teaching of native language and culture. Parents often turn to schools of their own making to fulfill this function. In the Washington, D.C., area alone, there are estimated to be more than fifteen Chinese schools and possibly as many as eighteen Korean schools organized for this purpose. Schools teaching Spanish, Czech, Hindi, Vietnamese, Farsi, and other languages are also thriving.[5]

The Only Suitable Method?

Bilingual education advocates believe that native language instruction must be important in—if not the core of—education for immigrant children. There must furthermore be not only respect for but maintenance and even development of the native culture. As the movement gained strength, some (by no means all) proponents proclaimed that bilingual education ought to be the sole method used in the education of the children of non-English-speaking immigrants. President Jimmy Carter, in search of Hispanic votes, saw to it that this position prevailed in the Department of Education during his administration.

It was at this point that the opposing sides crystallized and the battle lines were drawn.[6]

The play of this debate can be seen in congressional hearings over what percentage of funds available under the Bilingual Education Act should be available for instruction that does not employ the student's native language. In the original legislation, only 4 percent of funds could be made available for anything except bilingual education. In the 1988 reauthorization, antibilingual education advocates were successful in getting this figure raised to not more than 25 percent. As the act is debated for reauthorization in 1993, this restriction on ESL and related funding is again under attack.[7]

Advocates of bilingual education as the only suitable method in educational programs aimed at LEP children do not have firm support even within their own constituency for this position. While interviewing family members (almost always in Spanish) as a bilingual teacher, Rosalie Porter found few, if any, who took doctrinaire positions with respect to the kind of instructional program that was most suitable for their children. The parents did want respect for themselves, as well as their children, on the part of school officials and their teachers. They also wanted communication in their home language where this was necessary to effect understanding and decision making on various options. She found this did not necessarily translate into any demand that the language of the home also be the primary language of instruction; some, in fact, were opposed to this option. Most of all, immigrant parents seemed anxious that their offspring learn English and learn it as rapidly as possible.[8]

Bilingual programs are not always viewed positively, even by relatively uneducated illegal immigrants. A substantial number of such persons interviewed in one study indicated that they did not want their children to enroll in such programs. Some even saw bilingual education as a barrier standing in the way of the all-important task of learning English. As for the Spanish instruction incorporated in such programs, these parents tended to see themselves as capable of teaching the Spanish language at home. Admittedly, some of this aversion to bilingual programs was based on inaccurate information as to the aims and nature of bilingual education; results of the poll might have been different if the survey group had been more fully informed.[9]

In St. Paul, where many Hmong refugees have settled, school officials are struggling to work with students who not only do not know English but come from a culture that had no written language until very recently. The city's Hmong community has informed school personnel that they do not wish the schools to help their children maintain their native language; it is only English language instruction that is wanted.[10]

Two educational goals need sorting out as part of any effort to analyze the effectiveness and appropriateness of bilingual maintenance programs in particular settings. Is the primary goal to be that of teaching a non-English speaker to speak English? Or is the primary goal that of enabling a child of whatever language background to be truly bilingual and bicultural? If the primary goal is that of learning English with all possible speed, then one of the English immersion instructional programs may hold the most promise. If, on the other hand, the desired goal is that of true bilingualism and biculturalism, then the bilingual instructional route should certainly be given serious consideration. Possible delays in some students learning English may be compensated for by other educational and social benefits. Among these would be the preservation and indeed the cultivation of an existing advantage the child has, namely, the ability to speak the home language.

Immigrants and other residents of the United States have always been well served when a variety of educational options are available to them. Bilingual education is but one among several that should be available.

A Self-Serving Bureaucracy?

Among the charges frequently hurled against the bilingual education movement are that it is basically a jobs program for bilingual teachers, that it is expensive to administer, that it is backed by a huge bureaucracy anxious to hang on to political power, and that it is characterized by a creeping expansionism in its mission. Are any of these statements true?

Some of bilingual education's proponents, when pressed, will admit that there is a grain of truth in the charge that bilingual education has in some instances been an administrative nightmare. Even today under the best of conditions, installing a bilingual education program means that curricula need to be changed. School timetables have to be altered. New teachers have to be recruited, and others need retraining.[11] Parents of English-speaking children become fearful or even hostile. Teachers who speak only English begin to worry with some justification about whether they will be able to retain their jobs.

From an immigrant community perspective, bilingual education programs are seen to create jobs in the school system of a sort that can be filled by some of their people. Newcomers are enabled to become a part of the bureaucracy and to begin the process of upward mobility.[12] It is only natural that bilingualist "turf" builds up in many school systems populated by large numbers of immigrants; bureaucracies quite naturally wish to hang on to power once it has been acquired. The same can be said of representatives of any educational movement that attains a place for itself in the nation's educational system.

Promotes Segregation?

The massive inflow of immigrant students with limited English proficiency to some neighborhoods and schools districts has created segregation issues akin to those that festered in the nation's cities in the 1960s. Does bilingual education tend to create de facto "separate but equal" classrooms and schools, and by extension promote an unhealthy form of ethnic separatism within U.S. society? The concept of "empowerment pedagogy," as much as English language acquisition, has been seen by some bilingual education proponents as the heart of the argument for this mode of instruction. As "antiracist education," bilingual instruction is intended to function as a means for social and economic advancement of minorities.[13]

Bilingual education classrooms are, by definition and of necessity, "segregated" unless they are of the type that include native English speakers who are engaged in learning another language. One of the purposes of instruction is to develop and nourish the students' home culture; this is a worthwhile objective. School officials and teachers must be aware, however, of the dangers in long-term (and even short-term) segregation of immigrant students in bilingual education classrooms, as in other aspects of student life. Bilingual education teachers have a special responsibility to see that their students are encouraged to move beyond mere ethnic consciousness. Their aspirations to enter and participate in the national civic culture must be encouraged.

Is Opposition to Bilingual Education Racist in Nature?

The charge of "racism" or "nativism" is frequently hurled at opponents of bilingual education, particularly U.S. English. Is this true? In some instances the answer clearly is yes. There are plenty of nasty stories to go around, but these worst cases ought not to be set forth to define the field on either side.

U.S. English has been dogged by the legacy of its former board chairman, Dr. John Tanton, who resigned in October 1988 after authoring a memo warning that in the absence of border controls, Hispanics might take political control over the United States via high rates of immigration and high birthrates. "Perhaps this is the first instance in which those with their pants up are going to get caught by those with their pants down" was Tanton's most inflammatory remark.[14] That was too much for U.S. English's Hispanic-heritage president, Linda Chavez, who resigned—and not quietly. She had this to say: "I have renounced all formal ties with U.S. English as a matter of principle. This is not a personal dispute but reflects my own sense of outrage at statements by the founder of U.S. English . . . [that] were not taken out of context. They reflect a deep-seated and long-term animosity toward Hispanics and Catholic immigrants that I don't share, and I felt compelled to resign."[15] Walter Cronkite, then a member of the board of advisors to U.S. English, also resigned in protest.[16] Chavez still supports the U.S. English goal of a common language and believes such programs as bilingual education may "slow down assimilation." But she now rejects the idea of mandating official use of English.[17]

If evidence of racism among opponents of bilingual education can be cited, so can evidence of reverse racism on the other side. "Baloney" is the response of a U.S. English official when asked about the charge that her organization is blindly nationalist or even racist. "It's an easy charge to make. The people who are racists are those who are saying that Hispanics or Asians or whatever can't learn English. Of course they can. They are also saying let's have separate schools—keep people separate. Well, if anything is racist, that's racist . . . You can't have separate but equal.

The political armor of some of the more militant members of the bilingual education movement is evident in their unfortunate tendency to label as "racist" or worse anyone who questions their preferred educational methods. This stance is shortsighted at best and is one of the reasons why some members of the public are at least suspicious of the bilingual education movement. Not all of these persons hold nativist, hostile, or otherwise insensitive views of the needs and aspirations of immigrants to this country. Where racism exists, it should be named and condemned. But racism should not be assumed as implicit in all opposition to bilingual education.

English: Should It Be the Official U.S. Language?

The late S. I. Hayakawa—a linguist, U.S. senator from California, and honorary chairman of U.S. English—was not enchanted with the "salad bowl" concept of the United States in which the various ethnic elements do not melt but mingle. He was assertively a product of, and advocate for, the traditional melting-pot metaphor. Hayakawa noted that in the era of heavy immigration, "strong resistance to the melting pot idea has arisen—especially among those who claim to speak for our Hispanic-American citizens."[18] As a nonwhite immigrant (he was of Japanese ancestry), Hayakawa was an effective voice for U.S. English when it was labeled, as it frequently was, as an organization of xenophobes and racists. "We are concerned about the future unity of our nation," he said. "We are convinced Americans must share a common language. And that language must be English."[19]

Hayakawa conceded that using the native language might help advance a child's education under some circumstances but with two provisos. First, bilingual education should be chosen freely by local school authorities, not imposed by federal or state governments. Second, the program must be "truly transitional, preparing the student for transfer into a standard-English classroom after one or not more than two years."[20]

Is primacy of English in the United States in any serious way threatened by the current wave of non-English-speaking immigration? It is certainly a fact that foreign language enclaves have developed, especially in the barrios of Los Angeles and along the Mexican border.[21] A number of inhabitants of these areas do not need English in order to survive and thus make no effort to learn it. Most residents of the United States would agree that such "English avoidance" subcultures are not an encouraging development.

Some immigrant schoolchildren needing experience at using English get little opportunity to practice at home. In interviews conducted by the National Coalition of Advocates for Students (NCAS), only 15 percent reported speaking any English to their children, and 82 percent reported speaking no English to them at all. Of immigrant children interviewed, 32 percent said they spoke English to each other occasionally when at home; only 9 percent of the children said they spoke English frequently to each other at home.[22]

Still, the pull of English language learning is very strong within most immigrant communities. The fears of U.S. English do not appear to be confirmed by the NCAS survey, which showed that the parents of immigrant children were unanimous in desiring that their children learn English. This implies no rejection of the primary language, which more than 80 percent of them wanted their children to retain. A study of immigrant students in California showed that 78 percent of them also wished to retain their first language.[23] A study issued in 1988 indicates that Hispanics are more likely than other minority groups to retain their native language. After they have been in the United States for fifteen years, however, "some 75 percent of all Hispanic immigrants are speaking English on regular daily basis. . . . Seven out of ten children of Hispanic immigrant parents become English speakers for all practical purposes, and their children—the third generation—have English as their mother tongue."[24]

Given the fears of the U.S. English proponents, there is a certain irony in the report that Mexican-born teenagers now living in California are criticized for their poor Spanish when they return to their home villages in Mexico. In one such town, the local operator of a raffle game for children doesn't accept the response of a child who gives his winning number in English. He insists that any winner repeat the winning number over and over in Spanish.[25]

Knowledge of English has been shown by nearly every study to be the most important factor leading to successful adaptation to life in the United States. Most immigrants themselves are well aware of this and flock to English language classes. Those who themselves feel unable to learn English are anxious for their children to learn it.

A great strength of the United States in the eyes of most of the world is its single national language. This country has managed to avoid the language warfare that drains the energies of too many nations. Most members of the public firmly believe that permanent residents of this country should learn English. Yet, in our democracy, the approach taken by U.S. English to make English the nation's official language seems out of place. It is persuasion, not force, that ought to be the governing principle. We don't need English-only laws, or rigid laws governing use of English in any educational setting. We do need a national ethic (and financial commitment) that supports English instruction in schools, homes, workplaces, on television and in other media—wherever immigrants need it. A more assertive outreach program of language instruction at all levels ought to be the centerpiece of national policy on adult immigrant education.

No problem of English language instruction should, however, convey even implicitly the suggestion that the native language is somehow a handicap. On the contrary, the native language should be valued as the asset that it is, and its development encouraged where desired. Bilingual education is not un-American.*

---

*Readers desiring more comprehensive analysis of the bilingual education controversy may wish to consult at least two other sources. A well-researched and quite elegant statement of the case for bilingual education is represented by James Crawford's book *Bilingual Education: History, Politics, Theory, and Practice*. An arresting critique by a former bilingual education teacher is Rosalie Pedalino Porter's *Forked Tongue: The Politics of Bilingual Education.*

16

Immigrant Student Performance

How well are immigrant children doing in the nation's schools? There are some notable exceptions, but many groups of immigrant children are experiencing major difficulties.

A report from the Council of Chief State School Officers notes that immigrant children are more likely to be retained in grades and placed in low academic tracks on the basis of insufficient English language skills and low academic progress. Regardless of their degree of English proficiency, language-minority students tend to perform less well at all grade levels than do students from homes where English is the predominant language. Such students are also more likely to be enrolled in vocational courses than in courses on the academic track.[1] A research effort published in 1988 by the immigrant advocacy group California Tomorrow revealed that the academic achievements of the majority of immigrant students in that state do not equal those of their native-born counterparts. This pattern persists even after such children are long enrolled in school and are officially designed as proficient in the English language.[2]

More optimistic findings are reported in a 1990 study, also in California, of four recently arrived immigrant and refugee groups of widely different sociocultural origins. This evidence suggests that most of the children studied were making a "rapid and positive adjustment" and in many instances were outperforming native-born whites in such basic indicators as grades and graduation rates.[3]

The Wave Theory

The wave theory of immigration has special relevance for predicting the success of immigrant children in the schools. First-wave children will tend to be the offspring of the better educated, urban, and socially advantaged classes. In the succeeding wave will be children of somewhat lower level, but still relatively well-educated classes. The final wave will include the rural poor, the least educated, those least favored in the native country. The proportion of persons having English language skills and educational attainment will decrease within each succeeding wave of immigration.[4]

This phenomenon prevails in the patterns of immigration from Cuba since the Castro takeover. It is already evident in the inflow from Asia; school officials cannot necessarily assume that Asian immigrant children will become some of their best students. A number of present entrants from Asia, many of them from the nations of Indochina, have languished for years in refugee camps. Their parents, many of whom are on welfare, often do not value education or push their children to succeed as middle-class parents in earlier waves do.

The Dropout Dilemma

Dropout rates for many categories of immigrant students are very high. For some very troubled groups, a dropout rate approaching 70 percent is reported.[5]

The dropout rate among Hispanics born outside the United States is 43 percent. This rate is more than five times that of the non-Hispanic population born elsewhere.[6]

What has been called "defensive nonlearning" has been identified as a characteristic in schoolchildren in some Hispanic and other minority groups with a substantial immigrant component. School is not seen as a way up but rather as a tool of the white oppressor.[7]

Hispanic young people, many of them immigrants, currently drop out at the alarming rate of 35 percent, which is more than double the national rate of 13 percent. The dropout rate in some heavily Hispanic communities is as high as 68 percent. But the dropout factor for other immigrant groups, even the highly touted Asians, can be high in urban districts where poverty levels are high.[8] Demographer Kevin McCarthy of the RAND Corporation has noted that the completion rate for Mexican-born students in California schools begins to diverge sharply from that of all California students until "by the end of high school it is only half that of the state total." McCarthy also believes it will be at least two generations before the *grandchildren* of the Mexican immigrants in California will achieve the U.S. average dropout rate. Even then, though, these children are unlikely to attend college at the same rate as the U.S. average.[9]

Certain subgroups of Asian refugee immigrants also have very high dropout rates. A study of dropout rates in California schools showed that the highest dropout rate (48 percent) was for schools with high concentrations of Southeast Asians. Similarly high attrition was reported in Lowell, Massachusetts, public schools, where approximately 33 percent of students are native to Southeast Asia.[10]

Immigrant students drop out of school for all of the same reasons native-born students do, but there are some added dimensions to their difficulties. Dropouts of immigrant students are heavily correlated with factors associated with refugee or illegal immigrant status. The parents in many such families have very little education, which is itself a factor linked with school dropouts generally. Family transience is also a factor that is particularly associated with immigrant student difficulties. So is enrollment in overcrowded, resource-poor, and otherwise troubled schools. Parents in some immigrant communities have relatively low expectations for their children's academic success in school. Students from many poor immigrant families often carry full-time jobs, the demands of which impinge upon their time in school.

Low Levels of Prior Schooling

Few have a more difficult time with the educational aspects of adjusting to life in the United States than teenage refugees who arrive with little previous education. A study of refugees in the San Diego area, among others, documented the extreme frustration of Southeast Asian refugees faced with this dilemma. Too often the task of learning English and other academic subjects is found too daunting, and dropping out of school is the result. Students illiterate in their own language are especially prone to this outcome.[11]

Even students in the most troubled groups and in overtaxed

schools, however, can be helped to persist. A survey by the Center for Applied Linguistics of programs serving seventeen- to nineteen-year-old Amerasian immigrants found dropout rates as high as 50 percent. Nevertheless, it was also learned that a strong advocate within the educational program can make a difference. Such persons, often a single teacher or administrator, sensitized other staff members and found ways to assist a student who might otherwise have dropped out.[12]

Family Transience

Very high turnover (the percentage of students who leave school during an academic year) is characteristic at schools having high levels of enrollment of immigrant students from low-income families. In Lennox, California, for example, the rate runs between 30 and 40 percent annually. Teachers find it almost impossible to keep track of students, much less provide a quality learning experience for them. Transience has a negative effect upon academic performance; with unsettled lives, the parents have little time to assist children with homework. The principal at the Whelan Elementary School in Lennox notes a high incidence of child abuse in families undergoing this kind of stress. He set up child abuse clinics and worked with parents to help them find acceptable ways to discipline their children.[13]

The California Tomorrow researchers found a high degree of correlation between undocumented immigrants who tend to be highly mobile and those who drop out or do not enroll. Such students also experienced more problems in completing homework and have more physical and mental health difficulties.[14] One way to add stability to the education of mobile immigrants is to enroll them in newcomer schools. Although frequent moves within the district are a reality for many such children, those enrolled in the newcomer school do not need to change schools when they move to a new neighborhood.

Parental Influence

The high rate of dropouts of students of Mexican heritage in California schools is attributed to the generally low levels of education and limited English proficiency of parents, as well as the demands of large families. Good performance in school is directly related to the assistance that parents can give to children, and academic assistance is something that too many Mexican-born parents cannot provide. Large families mean pressure for more family income, the result being that older children often tend to leave school to get a job. Also, the cramped quarters occupied by large families offer less than ideal space or privacy for doing homework. In Los Angeles, for example, approximately two hundred thousand people in poor immigrant neighborhoods are living illegally in converted garages.[15]

Education is by no means a universally held value among immigrants. In Central America and other regions where people have endured generations of poverty, school is generally not viewed as important in the scheme of life. This attitude does not disappear overnight when persons imbued with this culture arrive in the United States. Lauro Cavazos, the first Hispanic ever to serve in a president's Cabinet, took note of the difficulties of Hispanic young people and urged their parents to work harder at encouraging their children to do well in school.[16]

Job Demands

Work is a common denominator for many Hispanic young people in U.S. high schools. For example, Elmer Rosales, a seventeen-year-old immigrant to Washington, D.C., from El Salvador, is out of bed by seven in the morning and is soon off to Cardozo High School. He's there until three in the afternoon, when he leaves for his job as a busboy, which lasts until midnight. Only then is there time for homework. How much mental energy is left under these circumstances?[17]

In 1992, the INS began a stepped up plan of searching for Central American immigrants employed illegally by Washington-area employers. As a result, teachers of English as a second language in area schools began noticing increased absenteeism and decrease in performance by students as young as eleven years of age. The reason was that immigrant parents, fearing to be employed themselves, were sending their children into the job market. These youngsters, who now often slept during class, were often providing the sole financial support for the families. Their employment, though often illegal under child labor as well as immigration laws, was apparently harder to detect than is employment in jobs typically performed by adults.

Asian Immigrants: Some Reasons for Stellar Performance

It is ironic that the racist immigration policies of the nineteenth and early twentieth centuries may in the long run have strengthened the position of Asian minorities in the United States. With immigration of Asians limited to a trickle, it was only those with higher educational attainments who could manage to enter. In many instances, the educational levels of these immigrants exceeded those of the white population of the country. These individuals, once established, tended to prosper economically and expected their children to extend themselves in acquiring an education; this pattern can be traced at least in outline for the Japanese, Chinese, and Filipino communities. More subtle factors may also have been at work. With restrictive immigration policies in effect, resident communities of Asians were less burdened with responsibilities for supporting new arrivals. It is possible that some of the resources thus saved were applied to the education of their children.[18]

In the years between passage of the 1965 Immigration Act and the new law in 1990, it became relatively easy for immigrants with low educational attainment from Mexico to enter the United States. The relatively short distance involved lessened the costs of transportation; also, the law facilitated entry of certain agricultural and other low-skilled workers from Mexico. Asians, on the other hand, were faced with much greater distances and fewer legal routes to use in entering the country. Consequently, it was the more highly educated and skilled classes who tended to come to the United States.[19]

A study of the educational attainment of men and women who immigrated to this country from the Philippines and Korea provides some clues as to the reasons for the impressive educational performance of Asian-Americans (including immigrants). It shows that all of these immigrants were far better educated than those in the same age group who did not immigrate. Those who left between 1975 and 1980 at age twenty or older, after their high school years, generally had nearly as high a proportion who had completed high school as did Filipinos or Koreans who immigrated before age twenty or those who were U.S.-born.[20]

It wasn't long before the outstanding achievements of some

Southeast Asian refugee students in U.S. schools became evident. A survey of San Diego's County high school graduating classes in 1986 was among the first to be noted. In San Diego, almost one-fourth of the valedictorians and salutatorians among students graduating in 1986 were Vietnamese, even though only about 7 percent of the graduating seniors in those high schools were Vietnamese. Vietnamese were also found to have very high grade point averages, math achievement scores in the top quintile nationally, improving language proficiency scores, a high rate of admissions to colleges and universities, and high visibility at the graduate and professional school level. The researchers attributed this success to

> their families' continuing belief in and support of education as a vehicle for upward mobility, their sophistication in dealing with educational institutions and, most impressively, their ability to develop collective strategies of resource-pooling and general support networks based on tightly knit extended-family organizations.[21]

Also, the San Diego study noted that among Southeast Asian students the Vietnamese had the highest GPAs, followed by the Chinese-Vietnamese, Hmong, Khmer, and Lao. The Vietnamese, Chinese-Vietnamese, and (remarkably) the Hmong students had GPAs above the white majority student average. The Khymer and Lao students had GPA averages below the GPA average for white students. Interestingly, the study revealed that the children of Southeast Asian refugees who strongly maintained ethnic pride and cultural identity performed better in school than those students whose parents were more "Americanized."[22]

Strong parental controls over children are generally a given in much of the Asian community. Korean parents, for example, are much more likely than the parents of white native-born students to instruct their children in reading, writing, and arithmetic before school entry.[23]

Performance as Perceived by Communities

The spectacular success stories of some students—those from certain Asian nations in particular—are held up as a point of pride by school districts. Communities react adversely, however, when they perceive that incoming immigrant students are lowering overall test scores within a school district.

Albert Cortez, research director for the Texas-based Intercultural Development Research Association, notes that school districts where composite test scores fall below state minimum standards are publicly cited for their "failure" by the state board of education. When districts with high enrollments of immigrant students fall into this category, the immigrants tend to be singled out as the reason for the district's unsatisfactory rating. "It is not uncommon," Cortez reports, "for general community reaction to include pressure on school boards to 'keep out' immigrant children who are 'taking up space and costing us money.'"[24]

Motivation and Performance of Immigrant Adults

As one would expect, the parents who press their children to do well tend to do very well themselves at educational ventures. One experienced adult program director notes that Asian refugees in particular in her programs typically have a "burning desire" to learn. A theme running through many accounts of work with many groups of immigrants is their higher degree of motivation relative to native-born clients in the same programs. One who notes this is Jane Jones, volunteer coordinator of Project Literacy U.S. (PLUS) in Kittitas County in the state of Washington, which got its start under the auspices of Yakima Valley Community College.

The program was originally designed for illiterate U.S. citizens or area residents anxious to improve their language skills. But local officials decided that no one should be turned away, and as things developed, the classes tended to fill with immigrants newly relocating to the area (Romanians, Cambodians, Japanese, Chinese, Peruvians, Mexicans, Poles, and Hondurans), most of whom were transferring from courses in English as a second language. Mrs. Jones observes that the immigrants tend to outperform the native-born. "They have a reason to want to improve themselves," she says. "And it's positive for us as far as their futures are concerned. Foreigners are seeking more for themselves than the Americans are."[25]

Adults enrolled in ESL programs have reasonably good persistence rates, according to a U.S. Department of Education study. Some

21 percent completed the instructional level in which they were originally enrolled, and another 53 percent continued to progress in the same instructional level. Only 26 percent left the program before completing an instructional level or meeting their objectives.[26]

Two adult learning success stories—one Laotian, the other Nicaraguan—provide the heroic outlines of many such accounts.[27] Somchay Sisauyhoat's story is horrifying and dramatic, yet not atypical among those recounted by refugees from Southeast Asia. This refugee immigrant to the United States grew up in a family of simple farmers in Laos. Through her husband, she learned to read and write in her native language. In 1978, after the United States pulled out of Laos, communist soldiers broke into the couple's home and took Sisauyhoat's husband away to prison. It took her eleven years to learn that he had died in a work camp in 1984.

In 1981, the soldiers again appeared and forcibly removed the oldest child for enrollment in a boarding school. At that point, Sisauyhoat began making plans to escape from Laos. After a harrowing series of trips down the Mekong River, she was able to bring her four children to safety in Thailand. Sisauyhoat and her family eventually arrived in Iowa, where she enrolled in ESL classes at North High School in Des Moines. Initially, she walked a distance of four miles through a dangerous part of town to attend the nighttime classes. Later, she was able to enroll in ESL classes at the Hawthorn Hill School where transportation was provided. When classes at Hawthorn Hill were expanded from two to four days a week, she did not hesitate to double her hours of attendance.

But Somchay Sisauyhoat is not just a taker of education at Hawthorn Hill. She is also a giver and leader and advocate among the students. She volunteers to take other refugees to doctors' offices, housing offices, utility companies, and other places or service or business. Each morning, she calls several dozen other students, reminding them to be ready for the bus. One of Somchay's principal methods for advancing her own knowledge is to insist that anyone using a word that is new to her write it down so that she can later look it up in a dictionary or encyclopedia. Many a doctor or nurse has had to pause in order to do this for her. At home, the family learning scheme includes educational television, but also game shows, with the quiz program "Jeopardy" being a particular favorite. It is small wonder that Somchay's own children have become model students in the school system; two of them have completed high school with outstanding grades and are enrolled in college. Armed with new skills herself, their mother is looking for a job.

Mauricio Arrieta is one of Somchay's Hispanic counterparts. He is achieving success in this country against tremendous odds. An illegal immigrant from Nicaragua, Arrieta had worked for his uncle, an accountant, in Managua before arriving in Hyattsville, Maryland, where he lived with relatives and began work as a janitor in an office building in nearby Bethesda. Living in the undocumented "shadow world," he subsequently worked as a cleaner, dishwasher, busboy, and waiter. But life wasn't easy. At one point, he gave up and moved to Miami with the intention of making enough money to move back to Nicaragua. It was a library across from the hotel where he worked as a busboy that helped keep him in the United States. He spent his spare time reading; he also noticed that there was room for advancement at his job. The energetic busboy could become a waiter, even a supervisor in time. Eventually, the idea of going back to Nicaragua became unthinkable.

Back in the Washington area after applying for amnesty, Arrieta made education for work in the United States his primary goal. Continuing to work full time, he also enrolled in English classes at the Gordon Adult School in Washington. He achieved a GED high school diploma and (with a boost from a $150 scholarship from the D.C. Office of Latino Affairs) he entered Montgomery County Community College in suburban Maryland. It hasn't been easy; he has been forced to drop out of school a number of times because of financial or scheduling difficulties. But Mauricio is determined to acquire an associate degree, and one suspects he will do so.

Improving Performance

Improved performance by immigrant adults as well as children results from specialized attention by the institutions expected to serve their needs. Well-conceived programs of ESL instruction or bilingual education are essential, as are specially tailored institutional and programmatic arrangements of the type described for children in chapter 8.

17
Higher Education: The Immigrant Challenge

The new immigration touches colleges and universities in a number of ways—some dramatic, others more subtle.[1] Immigration is one of the driving forces creating a much more diverse student body, which in turn is creating pressures for fundamental curricular and social change. But more than just national concerns are at stake, as the drawing power of higher education institutions in the United States fuels a significant "brain drain" from less favored nations.

U.S. Colleges and the Brain Drain

The worldwide pressure in the direction of immigration to the United States is clearly (though not always explicitly) felt in college and university admissions offices. Many young people from foreign nations enter U.S. higher education hoping to use their educational credentials to secure work and permanent residence in this country.

When they acquired access to catalogues of United States colleges and universities in 1989, young people in the Soviet Union began a massive letter-writing campaign to request admission. It is evident from a reading of many of these letters that getting an education is not all that is on their minds. Immigration to this country is the ultimate goal. Consider this letter (reproduced with original syntax and spelling) from a student in Leningrad that was received in June 1990 at the American Council on Education, an association of U.S. colleges and universities in Washington:

> I'm Andrew [last name omitted], 19 year old and I live in USSR. I'm study the Political Science. I like the history, philosophy, leterature, economic science and so on. I want take education of this science. In USSR no very good education in this science. And your known, what in USSR not need expert in Political and Economic science. That is why, I no need in USSR too. I want give my ability and future knowledge American Society. Anybody man want be Liberty. Soviet perestroika no give Liberty.
>
> I want went in U.S. I want take American education. I want live in United States. But I don't known what is me allowance?
>
> I write in many American organization. Help me, please. What is alloweance for me? This question I appeal in your organization. I want go in USA and take American education. Help me, please!
>
> Sorry, thank you. Good bie.

There are more Andrews in the former Soviet Union and eastern Europe. Since the fall of the Berlin Wall, eastern European enrollments in U.S. colleges and universities have shot upward from only 2,000 in the 1987–88 academic year to 4,780 in 1990–91.[2]

One measure of the importance of higher education as a port of entry for many immigrants is the number of foreign students who ultimately seek adjustment of their visas from student to permanent resident (i.e., immigrant) status. The rate of such adjustments has steadily increased since 1987. In 1990, the number of conversions jumped by 14 percent over the previous year.[3]

Of the more than 300,000 foreign students admitted to U.S. colleges and universities each year, most remain for at least one or two years after graduation. During this period, many seek employment as a means of enhancing their chances for permanent residency. Still others marry U.S. citizens and immediately qualify for immigrant status in that way.[4] A survey of foreign students receiving U.S. doctoral degrees by the National Science Foundation, released in 1990, reinforces this pattern. Some 57 percent of those who had made definite plans wanted to stay in the United States. Of those who wanted to stay, 33 percent planned to extend their student visas by pursuing further studies. The remaining 24 percent were looking for jobs.[5]

Colleges and universities may also be backed into roles as facilitators of immigration for students who find themselves cut off after actions of totalitarian governments in their home countries. Many of the nearly 40,000 Chinese students and scholars in this country have virtually assured themselves of a long (if not permanent) stay by their public statements of opposition to the communist regime in Beijing. Under an executive order issued by President Bush, they are permitted to stay in the United States until at least January 1, 1994. In spite of 1989 regulations intended to restrict study abroad, which include a requirement that applicants work for five years in China first, a record number of Chinese students are enrolling at colleges and universities in the United States. The number of arrivals increased by more than 18 percent in the 1990–91 academic year. And not only are more coming; they are staying longer.[6] Similarly, individuals from other nations with repressive governments (such as Iran and Ethiopia) have gained asylum and subsequent permanent residence status in this country while enrolled as students at U.S. colleges and universities.

Immigration of Faculty

The higher education community gets nervous about any attempt to alter immigration law in ways that would make it difficult for colleges and universities to hire foreign scholars. Prior to enactment of the Immigration Act of 1990, the higher education community criticized lengthy labor certification procedures and delays in immigration visa processing that made it difficult for institutions to attract talented personnel from overseas.[7] Some accommodation was made to this concern: The 1990 immigration Law specifies that "outstanding professors and researchers" who are "recognized internationally" may be admitted under the first employment-based category for "priority workers." The new implementing regulations are not unduly bothersome, and a number of academics have already arrived or are in the pipeline.[8]

If ex-Soviet students in significant numbers are seeking entry to the United States, so are some of their teachers at universities in Russia and the other former Soviet Republics. These are mostly top scholars in mathematics and the sciences, people the former USSR can hardly afford to lose.[9] Five of six permanent positions at a newly formed theoretical physics institute at the University of Minnesota were recently filled by Russian scientists. Other universities, including Michigan State, Pennsylvania State, Princeton, Rutgers, Yale, and the Massachusetts Institute of Technology, have been successful in recruiting Russian mathematicians and scientists for their faculties. In the view of some academic observers, these Russian emigres are an infusion of talent that is comparable to that which came to U.S. university physics departments following World War II.[10]

It is not only the former Second World that is supplying new faculty talent to colleges and universities in the United States. Approximately one thousand British faculty have been moving to the United States each year in order to acquire higher salaries and superior research facilities.[11] The Third World is also a significant supplier of talent in some fields. More than half of all new engineering faculty members at institutions of higher education in the United States are foreign-born, with Asians being in the majority.[12]

The net effect of immigration upon U.S. colleges and universities is certainly positive, as measured by the quality of the majority of students and faculty who are attracted to this country. Among the best and brightest students at U.S. universities these days are immigrants or would-be immigrants. But a global perspective illuminates the dark side of this picture. From China, the former Soviet Union, eastern Europe, Latin America, Southeast Asia, and Africa comes a stream of talented people who are desperately needed in the struggle to build or rebuild the troubled or impoverished nations from which they come. Emerita S. Quito, chair of the department of philosophy at De La Salle University in Manila, put it this way: "The most pernicious evil that can beset a country is the mass exodus of its professionals, and in a Third World country like the Philippines, the loss of its professionals is irreparable."[13]

The U.S. higher education community has yet to face the ethical dimensions of its role in facilitating the continuing hemorrhage of talent from less fortunate countries. Discussion of this issue should be placed on the agendas of higher education associations and organizations. One option that should have more higher-level discussion than it has been given is that of a post-graduation home-country residency requirement for most students entering the United States on nonimmigrant visas. Such a provision would need to be accompanied by programs designed to facilitate home-country employment and reentry. Returning the practical training for international students that now tends to serve as a stepping stone to permanent U.S. residence to its original purpose of preparation for home country employment would be one way to do this.

Ethnic Separatism on Campuses

Immigration has brought much more diverse student bodies to higher institutions. A troubling result of this is the spread of on-campus ethnic separatism of a sort not anticipated by the college and university presidents who rather too quickly authorized the creation of ethnic dormitories and corridors in the 1970s. A study in 1990 by the Carnegie Corporation for the Advancement of Teaching found that at nearly every campus examined, Hispanic, Jewish, Polish, Italian, Muslim, Arab, Vietnamese, and Haitian students had organized separate groups.[14]

Unaligned college and university students often find themselves pressed to acquire an ethnic identity. At the University of California at Berkeley, even "European-Americans" are receiving attention as ethnics, using a term that one white faculty member called "bizarre." "I'm not a European-American. . . . I have never met a European-American," he snorted.[15] At the university's sister campus in Los Angeles, every major student ethnic group has its own newspaper.[16]

As in the public schools, there is too often very little productive engagement between groups. At times, tensions spill over into hostility; by most standards, there has been a significant loss of a sense of campus community. This is a condition that does not bode well for the future of democratic higher education. College and university presidents, in consultation with faculty and students, need to find ways in which groups of students can seek common ground and learn from each other. Given the sensitivities involved, this will be a difficult task—one that will need to be accomplished incrementally.

Multicultural Curricula

In contemporary institutions of higher education in the United States, students from many cultures encounter each other, often for the first time. Heightened cultural consciousness is an inevitable development in such a situation, and one key dimension of this condition has been a press for curricular alterations that give more attention to non-

European history and cultures. No immigration-driven issue so rocks U.S. college campuses as does this one.

Defenders of the traditional curriculum typically begin their case by asserting that mainstream life and institutions undeniably are rooted in western European culture and historical tradition. It is necessary for any educated person to understand this, and to that degree, they assert, a Eurocentric curriculum is defensible. They point out that the precepts of Western tradition need not be accepted by all those who study it, and neither does such study rule out the study of other traditions and cultures. Some traditionalists express concern that multicultural approaches can damage the fabric of the nation's civic life by emphasizing differences and underlining separateness. At its worst, they reason, this approach results in self-segregation of ethnic groups on campuses and constitutes a violation of traditional U.S. ideas about community.

Advocates of a multicultural curriculum argue that a Eurocentric curriculum is insufficient (some say even damaging) for any student in today's extremely diverse student body. For some, consciousness of cultural separateness is a desirable goal, rather than a hazard to be avoided. A multiculturalist approach at its best is not, however, divisive in spirit. Rather, it can be the means for facilitating understanding, appreciation, and accommodation.

Multiculturalism, in any event, is well established. More than one-third of all U.S. colleges and universities now have a multicultural general education requirement, and more than half have added multicultural components to their departmental course offerings. More than 60 percent of colleges and universities have multicultural advising programs, and more than a third have multicultural institutes or centers.[17] But such proposals are not always victorious. In March of 1992, faculty at the University of Texas at Austin overwhelmingly rejected a plan that would have required all undergraduates to take a three-hour course on U.S. minority groups or Third World culture.[18]

In the present volatile atmosphere, ethnic studies once considered exotic are flourishing. Asian-American studies, once largely confined to West Coast campuses, are now expanding across the country. African studies, Chicano studies, Caribbean studies, and even Hungarian studies are among the new additions at institutions that did not previously have them.[19]

Traditional educators and some students are sometimes uneasy about the potential for cultural hubris in courses that emphasize a particular ethnic heritage. Too often, in the view of some, the curriculum becomes a kind of "oppression studies."[20] It is natural for instructors in such courses to present their subjects with vigor and assertiveness, but such action is not by definition narrow and propagandistic. Given the openness of this nation's society, there is room for optimism about the ultimate result.

Immigration and Teacher Training

Teacher training institutions are changing curricula to accommodate new demands being imposed on their graduates by the flood of immigrant students in many of the nation's schools. Some have instituted urban concentrations that explicitly address the environment in which teachers in urban settings will work. But the results of these efforts have yet to penetrate some existing classrooms. The National Coalition of Advocates for Students is quite critical of the performance of some teacher education institutions; citing survey findings, it charges them with failing to understand the "profound and permanent changes" represented by the new immigration.[21]

A group of thirty-six teachers consulted by the California Tomorrow Immigrant Students Project was not especially sanguine about the quality of teacher training preparation for their work with immigrant students. "I don't think teachers are trained with the reality of the situation at all," reported one. She reported that she had received no instruction relevant for dealing with "ethnic groups, gangs, kids who don't speak English, cultural differences." Another echoes many of these complaints, adding, "We don't feel that the universities really know what's going on. The realities are that it's not just academics anymore—it's the whole child, and that means what *their* home is like, and *their* culture and their language."

The same group recommended that faculty members in teacher training work to gain a better understanding of the implications of the new immigration for K–12 classrooms in California. Its members were unanimous in recommending that *all* teacher trainees be required to have at least minimal exposure to second-language acquisition theory and techniques. The feedback on teacher training, however, was not all bad. The teachers interviewed praised some approaches, including that of San Francisco State University, which requires teacher training professors to spend a semester teaching in K–12.[22]

States are beginning to require teachers to acquire more training in multiculturalism. Accrediting agencies are also looking more closely at this aspect of teacher training; however, change in this direction appears to be slow. The National Council for Accreditation of Teacher Education (NCATE) reported in 1991 that more than half of the 132 universities it has evaluated since adopting guidelines on cultural diversity were found deficient in this sector. The NCATE guidelines specify that multicultural perspectives must appear throughout a teacher education program, not just in a course or two.[23] A recent study by the National Association of State Boards of Education included a recommendation that accreditation for teacher training institutions "should be linked to a comprehensive infusion of multiculturalism in teacher education programs, including course work in linguistics, cross-cultural communication, and diverse learning styles."[24]

The political wars involving curriculum have often found intense focus in the area of teacher training. Assertive, even jingoist Chicano studies departments in some teacher training institutions have produced equally assertive and jingoist young Hispanic teachers imbued with what one observer describes as "a bias against non-Hispanics" as teachers of Hispanics. In the view of one seasoned teacher of Hispanic background who spoke with me, "it takes a while for these kids to figure out that older teachers aren't racist." Political pressures by Hispanic advocacy groups produced a controversial, though temporary result at the University of Massachusetts at Amherst when the university dropped a requirement that candidates for degrees as bilingual teachers needed to demonstrate competency in both Spanish and English. For a time, testing was done only in Spanish; students could graduate and begin teaching without ever having their skills in the English language assessed.[25]

Language and Access

In court and elsewhere, immigrants with limited English proficiency are arguing for the right to enter colleges and universities and to receive specialized help in bettering their language skills. Phieu Bui, a refugee from Vietnam, was valedictorian at Hope High School in South Providence, Rhode Island, but this was not enough to gain him admission to the University of Rhode Island. The reason, according to university officials, was that his English skills were insufficient. Bui could have enrolled in a college readiness program, but did not do so because he did not want to add another year to his college program.

Bui, however, gained an important ally in Governor Edward D. DiPrete, who made the matter very public as he demanded that the state's Commission of Higher Education review not only Bui's application but the admission policies of the state's college system. Ultimately, the storm died down when Bui was persuaded to enroll at a community college. Although his high school grades had been high, the university's admissions office maintained that Bui's English skills were not good enough to enable him to succeed at the university.[26]

The same difficulty is shared by many immigrant students throughout the country. Some have organized to demand a response by colleges and universities. In California, Hispanic groups were successful in pressuring the state's 107 community colleges to end placement practices that allegedly made it harder for students with English language difficulties to enter universities. An agreement made in mid-1991 ended a pending lawsuit; it specified that the colleges would de-emphasize assessment tests in favor of interviews, high school transcripts, and other achievement records in placing students. A spokesperson for the Mexican-American Legal Defense and Educational Fund charged that some of the testing systems being used were out of date and did not meet "the modern requirements of national education testing institutes." She added that community colleges were "a key instrument for entry of Latinos into the education system"—an important consideration in a state where only about 13.3 percent of Latino high school graduates are eligible for the California state university system and only about 5 percent for the University of California.[27]

Another immigration-related boom is occurring in college and university programs to prepare teachers of English as a second language. The number of such programs nearly tripled during the 1980s. As of 1992, more than 304 degree programs in either ESL or bilingual education exist in some 171 institutions; this includes 33 doctoral programs, 178 master's degree programs, and 29 bachelor's degree programs, along with programs leading to certificates, state endorsement or validation, or an undergraduate minor.[28] With increasing numbers of immigrant students on college campuses, more such courses are being offered.

Most academics will endorse arrangements for ESL instruction, but agreement ends there. There are those who say that a college course in ESL is a contradiction in terms; shouldn't anyone entering college be fluent in English already? In their view, institutions of higher education should not be in the business of providing instruction in what is essentially a skill, not a discipline.[29] Even given an acceptance of ESL instruction, a further question arises: should academic credit for such courses be given? At some institutions, all ESL courses are considered remedial. At others, full academic credit is given, the rationale being that the courses are equivalent to high-level foreign language courses for English-speaking students. Still others will give credit, but not of the sort that will count toward graduation.

ESL instructors at the college level tend to share the ambiguous state of their discipline in the K–12 sector. Most of them are part-time, adjunct faculty. This is not a status that is comfortable for many of them. It is notable that the opening article in the very first issue (March 1991) of the journal *College ESL* focuses on the "marginalization" of ESL at the postsecondary education level.[30]

In the 1990s, few institutions of higher education can afford to ignore the need for ESL instruction, though the form and substance of such programs will necessarily vary, depending upon an institution's mission. In any event, all programs should be staffed by teachers who have been professionally prepared to teach ESL and who have an understanding of its application in postsecondary educational settings.

Not only students but faculty members may need ESL instruction. If immigrant faculty are sometimes extremely well qualified academically, their English language skills may leave something to be desired. After receiving numerous complaints from college students about their difficulties in understanding instructors whose native language was not English, a number of state legislatures have enacted laws that address the problem. Pennsylvania, for example, requires all public and private colleges to evaluate new faculty members and to certify their fluency in English; the only exceptions are visiting faculty and instructors in continuing-education programs. Institutions failing to meet their requirement are subject to a fine of $10,000 for every course taught by a faculty member not so certified.[31]

Most individuals affected by the law are graduate students who serve as teaching assistants at research universities. At one of these, The Pennsylvania State University, many departments are sending their international teaching assistants to a training program operated by the Center for English as a Second Language. Fewer complaints are now being reported. Problems where they exist tend to lie more in the realm of cultural differences and unfamiliar accents than with English competency. Also, some students have been known to use international teaching assistants as scapegoats for their own academic difficulties.[32]

Pre-Entry Programs for Immigrants

Increasingly, specialized preparation of immigrants is taking place prior to college entry. One of the best known of these is that of the International High School, which opened on the campus of Fiorello H. LaGuardia Community College in New York City in September 1985. Here, intensive study of English is combined with a high school program designed to facilitate entry to college; entry to LaGuardia Community College is in fact guaranteed to each graduate.[33]

Results at LaGuardia, as measured in the areas of student retention and academic achievement, have been impressive. The annual average daily attendance rates have exceeded 90 percent. In contrast, the New York public school attendance rate was 78 percent for the same period. The dropout rate has been 3.9 percent, as compared with a New York City school dropout rate of almost 30 percent.[34]

At Mission High School in San Francisco, students may enroll in after-school courses for college credit at San Francisco State University as part of the "Step to College" program. This is one of the largest of sixteen such programs at the California State University (CSU) campuses. The programs began in 1985 in response to a state university chancellor's initiative asking campuses to develop programs that would encourage the enrollment of Latino high school students in the CSU system.[35]

Implications of Illegal Immigration for Higher Education

Colleges and universities have no legal decision that compares to *Plyler v. Doe* to simplify their decision with respect to admitting illegal immigrants or charging them resident tuition; neither do they have firm guidelines that have wide acceptance. The result has been a confusing tangle. Beginning in the fall of 1989, New York City began allowing undocumented immigrants who could prove they had lived in the state of New York for one year to enroll in any of the twenty-one institutions of the City University of New York at the same rate of tuition paid by other state residents. Public institutions in the states of Illinois and Arizona more recently followed suit.[36]

But this practice is by no means common. In California, Governor Pete Wilson vetoed a bill in June 1991 that would have granted illegal immigrants in-state tuition at public colleges and universities. In a letter to the California Assembly, the governor said that the state has "a legitimate interest in not subsidizing the education of those who may be deported and in maintaining respect for government by not subsidizing those who are illegal in this country."[37]

Federal law prohibits any illegal immigrants from receiving student financial aid under Title IV of the Higher Education Act. The federal government admits, however, that present enforcement procedures are insufficient guards against use of fraudulent documents presented to institutions of higher education in support of claims of legal immigration statues.

Financial Concerns

The Higher Education Act specifically enables immigrants to qualify for student financial aid provided that they are able to produce evidence from the Immigration and Naturalization Service of intent to become a permanent resident. Remedial (including remedial language) study is also authorized, a provision that enables many colleges and universities to serve immigrant students who are not proficient in English. Full-time students pursuing a graduate degree in areas related to programs for LEP students may receive financial assistance from the federal government.[38]

Sometimes higher education institutions have taken on more than they bargained for in admitting students from nations undergoing political turmoil. As a result of conditions in China, as well as U.S. foreign policy, the number of Chinese students and scholars in the U.S. climbed from zero to about forty thousand in 1989. The Chinese government's share of financial support for these individuals dropped from 54 percent in 1980 to 17 percent in 1985. By 1988, institutions of higher education in the United States were footing between 60 and 70 percent of the bill for their Chinese enrollees, most of whom may never return to China.[39] These students currently remain in the United States under a Presidential executive order.

Transfer of Credentials

The longtime problem of effecting transfer of educational credentials across national boundaries gains new emphasis in the era of high immigration. The difficulties acquire sharpest focus in degrees defining the professions; refugee physicians and medical personnel have been particularly disadvantaged. One way out of this dilemma is being pioneered by the New York Association of New Americans, which is sponsoring a program to retrain refugee doctors in related health fields.[40]

Another innovative program is that in which the University of Lowell and the state of Massachusetts are helping Southeast Asian refugees document their previous education and employment. Persons with teaching credentials in their home countries are intensively interviewed by an academic credentials committee consisting of prominent Southeast Asians who are intimately familiar with the education systems of their native countries. If certified by the committee, a candidate is exempt from repeating educational programs that the committee determines were already completed in the home country. The state accepts the committee's findings in determining whether a candidate has met the requirements for becoming a teacher. The program was prompted by a court order requiring Lowell to improve the education of language-minority students and by a critical shortage of persons qualified to instruct students from Southeast Asia.[41]

The European community is ahead of the United States in its efforts to come to terms with this problem as it affects intra-Europe personnel movements, and so is Canada. In 1989, the Ontario Ministry of Citizenship published a detailed report of transfer of credentials issues facing trades and professions. Included are plans for developing a prior learning assessment network.[42] Colleges and universities in the United States would be well advised to initiate, or involve themselves in, similar efforts in this country.

18

Financing Immigrant Education

Some difficult issues involving finance have arisen as educational institutions and agencies in the United States strive to provide services to immigrants. How should the added costs of educating immigrants be generated? Should immigrant education programs by separately authorized from comparable programs serving the native-born? Finally, do immigrants "pay their way" by contributing in taxes an amount sufficient to meet their additional educational costs? These basic issues are being debated at the national and local levels, but such discussion is not always enlightened to the extent possible by knowledge of how much immigrant education actually costs or of the values that are at stake; nor are the issues always stated explicitly.

Categories of Costs

Immigration, in common with all generators of population growth, imposes costs upon state and local governments. These include public health and welfare, infrastructure (water, transportation, energy), and most importantly, education. Of these services, the states have the least degree of control over education costs, as they are legally mandated to educate *all* children, including the children of refugees and illegal immigrants. Immigrant children typically cost more to educate adequately than do the children of citizens, because they tend to require more special services. Immigrants also tend to have larger families than their citizen counterparts, a factor that increases per-household educational costs.

Immigrant adults also require special educational services. In the present era, basic literacy education and ESL instruction are primary among these. Others include citizenship or amnesty education and vocational education. All well-designed educational programs for adult immigrants require appropriate outreach efforts and counseling services.

Language

English language education for immigrant children is obviously a major item when calculating the educational costs of immigration. ESL and bilingual instruction can be expensive; personnel costs are the largest factor involved. Bilingual teachers are in very short supply, which enables them to command salaries not available to other teachers. Los Angeles pays its two thousand bilingual teachers a bonus of $5,000, yet still has trouble finding enough of them. With its two hundred thousand non-English-speaking students, the city could use twice the number of bilingual teachers now on the payroll.[1]

Los Angeles, at least, has the money; some cities are not as well fixed. Chicago Public School Superintendent Charles Almo says his district doesn't have adequate funding for its schools, a fact that rules out bonus payments to include bilingual teachers.[2] The personnel director of the Houston Independent School District indicated in 1990 that his employer needed fifteen hundred more teachers to instruct LEP students. Teachers were being lost to California, where an annual bonus that was $2,500 higher than Houston's was being paid.[3] Similarly, at a forum sponsored by the U.S. Department of Education in January 1990, administrators from small districts reported they were finding it difficult to compete with the higher pay and other incentives offered to bilingual educators by some large districts.[4]

With the shortage of qualified bilingual education teachers, aides who speak the languages required are vital. Traditionally, they are hired and paid on a part-time basis and are paid a minimum wage; however, this era may be ending. In Los Angeles, teacher aides unionized in 1990 and won for themselves a fringe benefits package of

$4,000 per aide. With about ten thousand aides, the district now finds itself with skyrocketing expenses. The Stockton Unified School District in California, meanwhile, is using some of its federal bilingual education funds to subsidize the tuition and books of bilingual aides who enter college or university teacher preparation program.[5]

Construction

A school district may also have to build new schools, rent space, or acquire relocatable classrooms for students who cannot be housed in existing facilities. For example, with its enrollments swelled by huge numbers of immigrants, the Dade County, Florida, school district is beginning a massive construction and renovation program. Within the next five to seven years, forty-nine schools are slated for construction. The voters passed a $980 million referendum in 1988, but this did not take into account a very substantial increase in immigration from Nicaragua. The district reports that its present student space is 20 percent less than what is needed for just its current enrollments. To accommodate the overflow, class size has increased, space is being rented, and rooms intended for other purposes are being converted to classrooms.[6]

Immigration-related school construction needs are not limited to larger cities. LaCrosse, Wisconsin, a city that had virtually no minority population ten years ago, now has an enrollment of 12 percent minorities in its public schools,[7] mostly Hmong refugees from Laos. A citizens' long-range planning committee in LaCrosse has recommended nearly $18 million in immediate school construction and another $2 million by no later than 1995. As it considers its options, the LaCrosse school board is considering year-round sessions, split shifts, increased class size, two-teacher classrooms, short-term leasing of private-school space, portable classrooms, and reduced programs.[8]

Special Services

Schools in which immigrants are enrolled require a number of special services. Assessment and intake centers require trained personnel, and counselors and psychologists need special training in work with the problems of immigrant students. Immigrant students often need transportation to special centers or newcomer schools. A "late bus" in the afternoon may be required to transport students who stay after school for special tutoring classes. Clothing and free breakfasts and lunches are provided to immigrant students who require them, as quite a number do—especially the children of refugees and illegal immigrants.

One source of higher costs for immigrant students is the smaller class size aimed for in some school districts. At the Newcomer School in Sacramento, for example, the average class size is 23.4, as compared with a district norm of 29.1 students. In addition, most such programs employ aides for primary language support and provide one-on-one academic assistance. Teachers are also able to divide their classes into small groups.[9]

Other Cost Factors

Beyond the measurable costs of the massive influx of immigrant students is a more subtle one mentioned by one administrator: the time spent in just thinking about the problems. How many immigrant students are to be expected this year? What languages will they speak? What special needs will they have? Can they be accommodated within presently available physical facilities, or will more space be needed? What special staff training will be involved? This administrator, while optimistic about what the schools are capable of doing with immigrant students, acknowledged that the need for creative work with immigrant students drastically cut into his time for equally creative work with often disadvantaged U.S.-born students.

Total Costs

What are the true educational costs of immigration of the present kind and levels? No one knows. The difficulty in isolating immigrants from others in the population also using educational services is one reason for this information gap; another is that a fairly large number of immigrants are provided with educational services without such activity being reported. Even obtaining a reliable estimate of total national spending for English language education for immigrants is problematic. LEP students receive support from a variety of federal programs in the realm of migrant, special, compensatory, and vocational education. But in a number of states, these federal funds serve only a fraction of the immigrant students in need.[10]

In the absence of a reliable and comprehensive study, bits and fragments of information suggest mere outlines of the total picture. Several studies of this kind have focused on the costs of educating the children of illegal immigrants.

Education is by far the largest tax-supported service used by illegal immigrants, according to a study in 1984 by the Lyndon B. Johnson School of Public Affairs at the University of Texas.[11] At a Senate hearing that same year, Raul Besteiro, superintendent of schools in hard-hit Brownsville, Texas, outlined the high costs to his system of accommodating the large numbers of illegal immigrant children. Among these costs was $2,160,000 for rapid construction of classroom space. Some 50 percent of the elementary school classrooms in Brownsville during this period were un-airconditioned portable units.[12] Elsewhere, the Los Angeles Unified School District spends $500 million a year in educating the children of illegal immigrants and is currently planning for a 20 percent annual increase in this expenditure.[13]

The Center for Immigration Studies in 1991 estimated that the total cost of federal and state services to illegal aliens in 1990 was $5.4 billion. Of this, the largest sector was that for K–12 public education, which at $2.1 billion represented 39 percent of the total; approximately 93 percent of this amount was expended by state and local sources. These figures are based on an estimated illegally resident population of 4.2 million and do not include expenses for those previously illegal aliens redefined as legal under amnesty provisions of the Immigration Reform and Control Act.[14]

In a study of estimated costs of public assistance and education during the first year for a proposed cohort of 1.6 million immigrants in 1991, the Center for Immigration Studies determined that primary and secondary education would be by far the largest such cost. Their projection was $1.5 billion for an estimated school population of 289,000, with an average per-student expenditure of $2,243. No estimates for the costs of illegal immigrants during the same period were part of this study.[15]

As with the federal government, there is only incomplete information on state expenditures for immigrant education. One of the earliest studies, a 1980 examination of the fiscal impact of Mexican immigration upon California, showed that the state spent an average of $2,128 for all types of education per Mexican immigrant household in Los Angeles County. This was $859 above the average for all households in the county. A major contributing reason for this was that each Mexican immigrant household enrolled an average of 2.25 times the number of children in K–12 schools as the average household in Los Angeles County (1.06 versus 0.47 children per household).[16]

What these fragmentary data suggest is that the nation actually does not know what it spends on the education of immigrants. This is an inexcusable gap in knowledge in an era when immigration is having massive economic and social effects on the U.S. educational system.

The federal government has responded to the educational needs of immigrants in a rather haphazard way. Only one federal program, the Emergency Immigrant Education Act, addresses immigrant education concerns exclusively. Two other federal programs, the Refugee Act and the State Legalization Impact Assistance Grants of the Immigration Reform and Control Act, address education among other immigrant concerns.

In addition, immigrants are often heavily served by legislation that authorizes education and training programs not specifically targeted to them. Immigrants are the major beneficiaries of the Bilingual Education Act. Immigrants are served as well under the bilingual vocational provisions of the Carl D. Perkins Vocational and Applied Technology Act and by the Job Training Partnership Act. The National Literacy Education Act also is extensively used in support of programs for immigrants.

Emergency Immigrant Education Act

In introducing the Emergency Immigrant Education Act (EIEA) on the Senate floor in 1984, Senator Lloyd Bentsen (D-Texas) cited the need for a response to a financial crisis that was facing school districts in which large numbers of immigrant children were enrolled.[17] Although the bill was triggered by an influx of illegal immigrants, the ultimate bill takes into account enrollments of both legal and illegal immigrants. Funds may be used for a wide variety of educational services, including even the costs of providing additional buildings and transportation.

To qualify for EIEA funding, a school district must have at least 500 immigrant students, or these students must represent at least 3 percent of its total enrollment. Only immigrant students who have been in one of the nation's schools for less than three complete academic years can be considered in determining a district's eligibility. A maximum annual appropriate of $500 for each such student is then authorized.[18]

School districts receiving funds under the Emergency Immigrant Education Act program may apply these funds to bilingual or ESL instruction, and many do. Of school districts qualifying for EIEA support about 81 percent have used some such funds for English language programs.[19] The majority of EIEA funds are applied to academic instructional programs—about 80 percent in the 1989–90 school year. The balance of 20 percent of funds were used for such purposes as student testing and counseling, parental involvement activities, and administrative services.

In a study of expenditures during the 1989–90 school year, the U.S. Government Accounting Office estimated that 700,000 immigrant students met EIEA program eligibility criteria. Of these, about 564,000 (85 percent) were in the 529 school districts that received EIEA funds. The remaining 136,000 immigrant children were dispersed among roughly 4,000 school districts that were either ineligible for EIEA funding or did not apply for it.[20]

Funding for the Emergency Immigrant Education Act has remained relatively constant at around $30 million per year since its inception date in 1884. The number of students served, however, has increased, which has resulted in a progressive drop in the average dollar amount spent per student. In 1984–85, the dollar-per-student amount was $86; in 1989–90, it was only $62.[21] This is a mere pittance in relation to the need in many school districts.

A review of proposals accepted for funding in 1992 reveals that 39 states or U.S. territories submitted acceptable proposals, requesting support for the school needs of eligible 795,080 immigrant students. States reporting the largest numbers of students were California (348,142), New York (139,626), Florida (49,847), Texas (41,332), Illinois (39,074), and New Jersey (23,592). Increasing numbers of immigrant students, however, are being reported in other states as well. North Dakota reported a "crisis situation" as a result of an inflow of Southeast Asians, eastern Europeans, and Kurds. The Vermont State Education Agency noted that it "is perhaps a landmark moment in the history of Vermont's largely homogenous population that qualification for the Emergency Immigrant Education Act is even an option." Although only Burlington, the state's largest city, qualified for the grant with 3 percent of its enrollment as eligible immigrants, many other areas of the state are nearing that mark.[22]

Refugee Act

Admission to the United States as a refugee brings with it advantages that do not accrue to those admitted as immigrants. Designated refugees qualify for a wide array of social services, including English language training, support in preparing for employment, medical treatment, and cash allocations.

One provision of the Refugee Act established the Office of Refugee Resettlement and a program under which new arrivals could receive assistance. Under this program, as currently authorized under the Refugee Assistance Extension Act of 1986, federal funds are provided for the special educational needs of refugee children who are enrolled in public and nonprofit private elementary and secondary schools. It authorizes instruction designed to improve English language skills, bilingual education, remedial programs, school counseling and guidance services, in-service retraining for educational personnel, and training for parents. Even school construction costs, rental of space, and transportation costs directly attributable to additional basic instructional services are authorized.[23]

Appropriations for the Office of Refugee Settlement for programs including refugee education have been rising steadily since 1987 and reached $411 million in fiscal year 1991.[24] A portion of these funds may be spent on ESL instruction for adults. In 1991, just over $11 million in refugee funds were used in support of some forty thousand ESL enrollments.

Refugee funds may also be used for vocational education and preemployment training. The U.S. Department of Health and Human Services does not separate out these expenditures, but a knowledgeable federal official has estimated that the amounts expended are approximately equal to those for ESL.[25]

Immigration Reform and Control Act

As was seen in chapter 6, the federal government provided State Legalization Impact Assistance Grants (SLIAG) to states and localities hard-hit by the inflow of illegal immigrants. These monies, as authorized under the Immigration Reform and Control Act, could be used for education, health, and public assistance for newly legalized aliens. At least 10 percent of each state's allocation, however, had to be spent on education.

States were quite disparate in their decisions about how much of their IRCA-generated federal dollars to spend on education. In 1989, for example, Illinois spent 71 percent of its share on education; Florida spent only 23 percent. Other state figures were New York, 41 percent; Texas, 58 percent; and California, 28 percent. California's expenditures on education during the first five years of the program amounted to about $300 per person.[26]

The total federal allocations for such grants as of September 1992 were about $2.1 billion. Seven states (Georgia, Indiana, Kansas, Missouri, Nebraska, Oklahoma, and Pennsylvania) spent the majority of their federal funds on education.[27]

Bilingual Education Act

The Bilingual Education Act addresses the special needs of children of limited English proficiency. Bilingual as well as ESL programs are authorized for support. The bulk of such funds go to programs serving children in K–12 levels; however, a Family English Literacy Program in the act also offers services to adults and out-of-school youths. Appropriations for the Bilingual Education Act grew steadily during the 1970s and 1980s and stood at $195 million in 1992.[28]

National Literacy Education Act

Signed by President Bush on July 25, 1991, the National Literacy Act extended the Adult Education Act and gave new emphasis to the nation's struggle with the problem of illiteracy. Very large numbers of immigrants are served under its provisions.[29] Funds allocated to states under this statute may be applied to a wide variety of literacy education, high school diploma, and ESL programs. Workplace literacy programs are also included.

Included in this legislation is a program, the National English Literacy Demonstration Program for Adults of Limited English Proficiency, that primarily serves immigrants. This is, however, a very small program, carrying an appropriation of just under $700,000 in fiscal year 1991.[30]

Almost half of the 2.2 million adults enrolled in basic education programs under the National Literacy Education Act are of limited English proficiency. Almost all of these are in the prominent immigrant-receiving states of California, Florida, New York, Texas, and Illinois.[31] In the 1990 program year, some $140 million in federal funds were expended under the National Literacy Act. A substantial share of enrollees were immigrants served in ESL classes.[32]

Carl Perkins Act/Job Training Partnership Act

Some immigrants are serviced by certain provisions of the new Carl D. Perkins Vocational and Applied Technology Education Act of 1990, which targets federal funds for vocational education to the poorest schools. Some 75 percent of federal grants are set aside for schools with large numbers of students who are handicapped, poor, or who have limited English proficiency. The Bilingual Vocational Training Program, funded under the Carl Perkins Act, has been and continues to be very small and has often been proposed for elimination. Between fiscal years 1986 and 1988, only about 1,800 persons received training under funds provided by this program.[33] In 1992, the U.S. Department of Education announced that it was accepting applications for ten grants of $200,000–$300,000 each for $2.2 million in bilingual vocational training grants.[34]

Immigrant Demonstration Projects are conducted under a special program of the Job Training Partnership Act. Grants go to private industry councils that have cooperative working relationships with community organizations that serve immigrant populations.[35]

A response to alleged displacement of native-born workers by immigrant labor is represented by a provision in the Immigration Act of 1990 that authorizes the secretary of labor (in consultation with the secretary of education) to provide grants to states for educational assistance and training for U.S. workers, taking into account "location of alien workers admitted to the United States," among other factors. This was a much watered-down version of an earlier bill that would have extracted for this purpose fees of $1,000 per immigrant fees from employers who imported immigrants.[36] But authorization does not equal appropriations, and Congress has not to date funded this provision.[37]

Miscellaneous Federal Programs

In addition, certain federal programs have provisions that to some degree aid sponsors in implementing educational programs for immigrants. Among these are Chapter I of the Educational Improvement and Consolidation Act (EICA), which primarily supports compensatory elementary education for poor children; migrant education programs of the Elementary and Secondary Education Act and the Higher Education Act; the Even Start program (family-centered education projects) of the Elementary and Secondary Education Act; the magnet-schools assistance program of the Elementary and Secondary Education Act; the School Breakfast Program of the Child Nutrition Act; the National School Lunch Act; the Star Schools Program, which was recently expanded to support distance-education technologies that support improved instruction for LEP students in rural areas;[38] and the Cooperative Extension Service Programs under the Smith-Lever Act.

Issues

Three issues either explicitly or, more often, implicitly pervade discussions of finances for immigrant education. These have to do with the appropriate sources for funding, whether funding for immigrants should be separated out from other authorizations, and whether the educational and other expenses attending immigration are offset by taxes paid by immigrants.

Federal versus State Funding

A basic fiscal issue is whether the states or the federal government should pay the educational costs that accrue from federal immigration policy. Education is, of course, a state responsibility in the United States, but immigration adds a distinctive consideration. Substantial front-end educational costs are incurred, or should be incurred, to facilitate the entrance of the new immigrants to the larger society. At present, the federal government shifts the majority of these costs (except for some termed "emergency" and generally related to refugees and illegal immigrants) to state and local governments. This is an unfair and shortsighted policy.

By any rational standard, it is unconscionable to pass on to school districts—poor ones in particular—the responsibility for the start-up educational costs of newcomers to the United States. Too many school administrators must choose between buying computers or hiring bilingual teachers; U.S. citizens already disadvantaged educationally are being disadvantaged even more. Congress has allocated "emergency" funds designed to cover the admittedly high educational costs associated with refugees and illegal immigrants, but has made no comparable commitment to those admitted under the legal numerical quotas. These costs tend to be less but remain relatively high when ESL services are taken into account. The lion's share of costs for immigrant education is now being assumed by the relatively few states most heavily affected by the new immigration. In many instances, the true start-up expenses are not being adequately covered.[39]

Congress should face up to its responsibilities in this arena by increasing its appropriations for the Emergency Immigrant Education Act (EIEA), which provides support for immigrant-heavy school districts. The structures of funding under this legislation also needs attention. In its present form, eligibility is limited to immigrant children born outside of any state and who have attended school in any one or more states for fewer than three complete academic years. This unduly narrow definition does not take into account real costs incurred in educating children born on U.S. soil to immigrant families. Neither does it accommodate higher costs that in many instances extend beyond three years in work with children with limited English proficiency, low prior levels of education, and families in poverty.

The federal government is the sole decision maker in setting immigration law and immigration regulations. Whenever Congress admits a legal immigrant (or fails to exclude an illegal immigrant), it passes along to some state a financial obligation to educate that person. Because of the numbers of immigrants being admitted and the special educational needs they pose, many school systems are facing a serious financial crisis or even the prospect of bankruptcy. In its position as the nation's gatekeeper, the federal government has responsibilities that accompany its decisions about how many and whom to admit. One such responsibility is that of providing funding that will to a greater extent than at present support the resulting educational costs.

Separate Out Immigrant Education Costs?

A very touchy issue, not often discussed openly, is that of whether funds for immigrant education should be set aside within authorizing and appropriations legislation. The educational and training costs associated with immigration are substantial, and in some instances have the effect of diminishing funds available to serve the comparable needs of citizens. Yet such costs are seldom brought to the fore and discussed in their full implications at the federal level unless Congress is accommodating a situation of dire emergency.

One bureaucratic reason is that it is the judiciary committees of Congress, rather than their education and labor counterparts, that develop immigration legislation. The minds of these members are not tuned to education issues. Furthermore, no one in Congress in these days of fiscal crisis is working overtime to discover problems that need money spent on them. If there is one that can safely be ignored, so much the better.

Another is the absence of information as to the exact total of immigration-related education costs. Groups advocating high levels of immigration do not wish such information to be circulated, in the fear that it would hurt their cause. These groups are wary of requesting funds to assist in immigrant education because they believe it will play into the hands of their opponents, who cite the costs of immigration in opposing higher levels of permitted entry. It is not good politics for proponents to encourage any linking of the needs for funds with the immigration policy that produced such a need.

The costs of educating immigrants, adults as well as children, are well-known to urban school districts. Privately, school officials will admit to major, even overwhelming problems associated with the immigrant inflow. But they are hardly in a position to advocate that immigration be cut back. In most large cities a significant (if not majority) share of a district's constituency is made up of immigrants or their ethnic colleagues; to oppose further admissions would amount to political suicide.

Still, an unquestioning acceptance of increasing immigration also poses political hazards to local officials. In some areas, a backlash mentality is developing as a result of resource shortages and school overcrowding. No one is very happy when schools need to add portable classrooms, for example, even though their cost pales in comparison with those required to make permanent additions to schools. It is inevitable that providing effective services to immigrant children requires tapping resources that might otherwise be used for other purposes.

In the long run, cover-ups are always a mistake in a democracy. If no funds are explicitly appropriated for immigrant education, the costs inevitably come from programs that serve the native-born—usually the poorest sectors of society. Immigrant students, their native-born counterparts, and indeed the entire community all suffer, and resentment toward immigrants is likely to grow. Relevant financial matters attending immigrant education should be addressed at the time decisions about immigration policy are made. The nation should make an informed determination about how it wishes to spend its resources for education. Costs related to immigration should, where possible, be identified and adequately funded at the federal level, where policy decisions about immigration are also made.

To date, it has not been possible for Congress to enact any sort of pay-as-you go plan for the costs of educating immigrants. No one knows this better than Representatives Lamar Smith (R-Texas), Tom Lewis (D-Florida), and Ron Packard (R-California), who introduced amendments to what became the 1990 immigration act that were designed to identify and address the education, health care, and infrastructure costs incurred by communities as a result of immigration. All of the amendments were soundly defeated either in the Judiciary Committee or on the House floor. The cost-conscious amendments failed principally because most members of Congress do not represent districts that are greatly affected by immigration. In many of the districts where such costs are incurred, the political pressures favoring immigration outweigh the pressures for giving visibility to the associated costs.

Do Immigrants Pay Their Share of Education-Related Taxes?

One question that cannot be answered with certainty is whether expenditures for the costs of immigrant education are balanced out by the taxes they pay. On the national level, some studies suggest that immigrants do not, in most economic sectors, cause a negative cash flow for taxpayers.[40] But educational costs constitute a special case.

At the local level in communities affected heavily by immigration, the tax burden to support education can be very substantial, at least at the outset. A recent study of Mexican immigration to the United States suggests that these new residents probably receive more in educational and certain other tax-supported services than they pay; their relatively low incomes and large families contribute to this result.[41] Other studies also show that state and local expenditures for education substantially exceeding tax revenues derived from immigrants.[42]

A narrow or short-term view of educational expenditures, however, ignores the investment dimension of education. Immediate financial return should not be the measure that is applied in these instances. Few actions are more costly to society than failure to provide appropriate educational opportunities for *all* of society's members. Dollars invested in education for immigrants and their children now will be repaid many times over in the future. The task at hand is to arrange financing of immigrant education that does not unduly burden state and local governments in areas where immigrants are disproportionately located.

19
The Politics of Immigration and Education

Subtle, even byzantine political currents run through the process by which the United States makes its immigration laws. Alliances are eccentric. The real objectives of the various players are not always those officially announced. As with so much of the nation's legislation, the version that emerges reflects interest-group involvement and does not necessarily represent the best interests of immigrants or the general public.

Political Environment

What environmental factors affect decision making about education of immigrants and refugees? Nearly every survey over the past several decades indicates that the majority of the public does not endorse an increase in legal levels of immigration. A national poll conducted by the Roper Organization and released in June 1990 showed that 77 percent of all those surveyed held this opinion; Hispanic-Americans (74 percent) and black Americans (78 percent) shared the majority view. Some 67 percent of those polled stated that they believed the level of legal immigration should be reduced.[1]

A January 1992 Gallup poll found that 64 percent of the survey group would be more likely to vote for a presidential candidate who favored tougher laws on immigration.[2] Very similar results were obtained in polls conducted during the 1980s for the *New York Times*, *U.S. News and World Report*, and the Rockefeller Foundation. One finding of the *New York Times* poll was that some 83 percent of immigrants themselves (those arriving since 1941) want to keep immigration at current levels or reduce it.[3]

Given these attitudes, how has it been possible for Congress in 1965 and again in 1990 to increase substantially the number of persons to be granted admission? A corollary finding of the Rockefeller Foundation survey provides the answer. The Foundation found that refugee and immigration issues are not viewed as especially important when compared with other topics on the national agenda. Few of the surveyed group (only one in eleven) even described themselves as very knowledgeable about these issues.[4] In short, most people do not want higher levels of immigration, but the issue is not considered by most of them to be important enough to engage their political energies. Consequently, Congress is free to respond to the much greater pressures exerted by immigration advocates without undue worry about a constituent backlash.

The "More Immigration" Lobby

The forces in favor of increased admission of immigrants are far stronger than those that oppose such increases. Assertive representations on behalf of increased immigration and immigrant concerns are expressed by representatives of ethnic communities; by far the strongest of these are the Hispanic or Latino organizations. The National Council of La Raza is an umbrella organization currently representing 116 affiliate organizations in the Hispanic community. The Spanish term *la raza* technically means "the race," as some of the organization's opponents like to point out. When used colloquially, however, the term means simply someone who is Hispanic, particularly in the Mexican-American community.

The Mexican-American Legal Defense and Educational Fund (MALDEF) is another effective lobby on Capitol Hill, as are two other Hispanic organizations, the League of United Latin American Citizens (LULAC) and the American G.I. Forum. The National Association of Latino Elected and Appointed Officials (NALEO) asserts that it is "very carefully nonpartisan" on Capital Hill, but it is viewed as an effective lobby by some of its opponents.

Southeast Asia refugees who have been resettled in this country have lost no time in acquiring the political skills needed to lobby Congress. Congressional mailboxes fill quickly when refugee ceilings are discussed, and veterans' groups have also supported Southeast Asians in their efforts. The Bush administration has also looked kindly upon their interests; Southeast Asians voted for George Bush in large numbers in the 1988 election.[5]

The awesome political advocacy of the nation's Jewish community has earned a number of Soviet Jewish refugees places on the admissions list.[6] Their chief organizational representatives for this purpose have been the American Jewish Committee and the Hebrew Immigrant Aid Society. The Irish Immigration Reform Movement was actively involved in development of the Immigration Act of 1990 and was successful in getting a special treatment for their nationals in the new law. A prime objective of pro-Haitian advocates, such as the Haitian Refugee Center, is to get more Haitians who are leaving their troubled isle designated as political (rather than economic) refugees.[7] Only if this designation is obtained in individual cases may remain in the United States under provisions of the Refugee Act.

Also heavily backing the more generous provisions of the immigration Act of 1990 were employer groups interested in acquiring new sources of skilled workers. A comparable coalition of agricultural and other employers of unskilled labor had earlier opposed sanctions on employers who hired illegal aliens. Conversely, labor unions in earlier years have opposed high levels of immigration, seeing immigrants as competitors in the labor market. But teachers' unions are well aware that immigration means jobs for them. Were it not for the increasing flow of immigrants to cities, many schools would now be closed, and their teachers would be out of work.

Some church groups, especially the National Catholic Conference, actively support more generous levels of immigration. So do the American Bar Association and the American Immigration Lawyer Association, many of whose members assist immigrants or would-be immigrants through the intricacies of U.S. immigration law.

The "Less Immigration" Lobby

Opposing high levels of immigration is a far less aggressive lobby; only the Federation for American Immigration Reform (FAIR) is counted as a major factor on this side. Various environmental groups, notably Zero Population Growth (ZPG) and Population/Environment Balance, are also involved, if somewhat tepidly. This was a very weak aggregation when it came to influencing development of the 1990 immigration act.

FAIR, like some of its environmental-organization allies, finds links between uncontrolled immigration and such problems as skyrocketing crime, epidemic drug use, unfair job competition, soaring housing prices, rising pollution, traffic jams, water shortages, overcrowded classrooms, higher taxes for overstretched public services, and loss of prime farmland and open spaces. The organization charges that "powerful, special-interest lobbies that benefit from illegal immigration are spending increasing amounts of money and are working hard to obstruct the will of the people." It is possible, FAIR asserts, to reduce illegal immigration by "humane measures consistent with our democratic ideals" and to bring legal immigration "to a reasonable, sustainable number."[8]

The essence of FAIR's recommendations are as follows: (1) ensure border security, (2) strengthen the Immigration and Naturalization Service (particularly its ability to detect identification fraud and abuse of visitor visas), (3) set a ceiling on immigration with no loopholes, and (4) grant equal opportunity for legal immigration to America based on "merit, not race, family or political connections."

FAIR currently has about forty-thousand members, most of them concentrated in California, Texas, Florida, New York, and Illinois—the states most noticeably affected by immigration. This numerical power, however, does not necessarily translate into political clout. Because of the very powerful influence of immigrant groups in those states, elected officials are generally cautious about adopting any position that could be perceived as anti-immigrant. "What we need," the group's executive director, Daniel Stein, said in an interview with me "is more members in Kansas" or in some other state where a position on the FAIR agenda could more easily be adopted by an elected official. Contrary to popular notion, FAIR does not oppose all immigration. It does advocate a legal limit of about three-hundred thousand persons, a figure that it considers consistent with historic averages.

Although FAIR is undoubtedly right in claiming that a majority of the public would support its proposals, it suffers from the same handicap afflicting all who would speak for large, latent groups. Political muscle in such a group is hard to muster. Representatives of ethnic groups, on the other hand, can tap more immediate wellsprings of support. Many of the latter's constituents have a direct interest in getting relatives to this country and are willing to work to create or preserve these opportunities. This translates into more direct and intense pressures on the political decision making structure.

African-Americans and Immigration

No one wants it, but it is nonetheless there—a collision of interests between African-Americans and immigrants, especially Hispanic immigrants. Many blacks perceive that their share of the national social services pie has gotten smaller because of higher levels of immigration. The concerns of the various groups are palpable, and they are being played out in a number of cities.

In the last months of 1991, leaders of Denver's Hispanic and African-American communities found themselves at odds over how scarce education dollars should be spent. "Within the Hispanic community, there certainly is an agreement that there ought to be less busing," said one Hispanic coalition leader. "We are not able to hire the number of bilingual teachers that we need," said another, who added that if there were a reduction in busing, "then maybe there would be a budget for that." Some black leaders were not so sure busing should end, given the inequities they still perceive to exist within the district.[9]

Other potentially more serious flash points include New York, Los Angeles, Chicago, and Miami, all cities with large Hispanic and African-American populations. Raul Yzaguirre, president of the National Council of La Raza, is one of those most worried about the possibility of open conflict between blacks and Hispanics. He predicts that the chances are "80 percent that within two to three years we're going to have an earthquake in one of the four [cities]."[10] This forecast was realized, though with a different twist, in 1992 when riots erupted in Los Angeles. Among the tensions that surfaced were those between the African-American and immigrant Korean communities. In the world of education, the issues between the two groups focus on resource allocations, appointments to teaching and administrative jobs, and even planning time. Low income African-Americans whose children attend school in areas of heavy immigration often perceive themselves faced with a cruel dilemma. With a history of racial persecution by the predominant white community, how can they justify ill feelings themselves against newcomers with Asian, Latin American, European, or even African origins? On the other hand, does the inflow of immigrants mean that resources that might otherwise be applied to the unique educational needs of low-income (and often black) students will be applied to the needs of these newcomers instead?

When large numbers of immigrants enter a school system, does this in fact take resources that would otherwise be applied to meet the needs of native-born children? When I posed this question to school administrators and teachers, the answer, always explicitly or implicitly not for attribution, was almost invariably yes. Poor districts, especially when faced with still-new demands, too often respond with watered-down services for everyone or fail to respond at all to the newest dimension of need. What would be done with these monies if there were no concurrent demand from immigrant students? Mentioned as requiring urgent attention in this category are programs for dropout prevention, basic skills development, sex education, and anti-gang activities.

These concerns were addressed by Frank Morris, dean of graduate studies and urban research at Morgan State University (a predominantly black institution in Baltimore, Maryland) in testimony submitted to an immigration subcommittee in Congress. Morris noted that black children, many of whom have severe unmet educational needs, are a major presence in Los Angeles, Dade County, Chicago, San Francisco, New York, and Houston—the major urban districts most affected by LEP students and other foreign-born persons requiring special assistance to adjust to a new society. The scarcity of federal and state resources to meet their needs plus "lack of commitment to quality public education for all" in the nation's cities have "ill served black children, even in well-intentioned school districts," Dr. Morris stated.[11]

Morris concluded that all of the various immigration bills then being considered by the House of Representatives in 1990 would in varying degrees worsen all of the problems being experienced by African-American children in the public schools. In essence, the problem was that they would introduce competitors for scarce education and training funds, a conclusion echoed at the same hearing in testimony by Vernon M. Briggs, Jr., a professor of labor economics at Cornell University.[12]

There are other dimensions to the troubling tensions between blacks and immigrants. These relate to the age-old political issue of whose values will prevail in the schools. In the last several decades, African-American teachers and administrators have, at great cost, won places for themselves in many urban schools. In the era of immigration, however, dramatic shifts in population have changed the political equation in ways that threaten these gains.

In Arlington, Virginia, for example, the job of director of school and community relations was created by the local school board during the civil rights turmoil of the 1960s. The job was created as a link with the black community, and it has always been filled by a black. But times are not what they were. Arlington County in recent years has experienced a population explosion of immigrants—the majority of them Hispanic, from such nations as El Salvador, Bolivia, and Peru. In the 1980s, the proportion of Hispanics in the county's school system rose from 7 percent to more than 23 percent. During the same period, the percentage of blacks in the system rose by a much smaller amount, from 16 percent to 17.3 percent. White students account for a bit more than 48 percent of the student population; Asians for 10.6 percent.

When the Arlington school superintendent in 1990 selected a black as director of community relations, he encountered a storm of protest from Hispanics who felt that one of their number should have been chosen. Noting the absence of any Hispanic person in the superintendent's office or on the school board, one Hispanic spokesperson stated the community's position straightforwardly: "Because of our larger numbers, we should have a say in the decision-making positions."

Black parents, on the other hand, pointed to the continuing academic problems being experienced by many black children. They viewed the appointment of a black as evidence that the district had a continuing commitment to work with them in the direction of improved opportunities for black students. They feared that programs designed for use by black children were being shortchanged or overburdened by demands coming from the new arrivals. Both black and Hispanic parents were uneasy, to say the least, about the effects of budget cuts being made by the district. Would minority achievement and ESL programs be diminished by this action?[13]

In Miami at about the same time, a more serious rupture occurred between the local black and Hispanic (largely Cuban-American) community when a Cuban candidate edged out a black candidate for the position as Dade County school superintendent. A black boycott not only of schools but of local businesses not owned by blacks was launched in protest. The Dade County school system was then 46 percent Hispanic, 33 percent black, and 20 percent white.[14] Meanwhile, in Chicago, tensions rose when a black superintendent of schools was fired by a board chaired by a Hispanic. Hispanics cited a high dropout rate and overcrowding in schools in Hispanic districts, but blacks interpreted the action as an effort to deprive them of hard-won power.[15]

In racially diverse Los Angeles, trouble simmers between the immigrant and black communities, particularly in schools that were once predominantly black but more recently have served large numbers of immigrant students. In most such schools, the majority of administrative, teaching, counseling, and support staff are black; in many, however, the predominant ethnic group is now Hispanic. The parents of these children exert pressure on the school district to replace black staff with Spanish-speaking Hispanics, whom they believe can better serve their children. The blacks often resist transferring, and the district cannot force them to do so. In the ensuing standoff, tensions rise.

When the Los Angeles Unified School District announced that it planned to create two schools for immigrant students, black parents objected to the one proposed in the largely black Crenshaw area. It would, they reasoned, divert already scarce resources from their own children.[16] In Crenshaw High School, where black enrollments were declining, the district created one of its special programs for newly arriving immigrant students in grades nine through eleven. In the view of some black parents, they were not adequately consulted before this significant change was made in the mission for the school. Nor were they enthusiastic at the amount of money being spent for special language programs, bilingual education, and field trips for immigrant children—many of whom were from families illegally in the United States—when, in their view, comparable resources were not being directed to meet the needs of their own children. The school board held firm, however, and the special program for immigrants remained at Crenshaw.

Similar tensions relating to the politics of immigration and education were partially responsible for the resignation and early contract buy-out in July 1990 of the Los Angeles school superintendent, Leonard M. Britton. One-third of the students in the huge system are of limited English proficiency; 62 percent are Hispanic. Britton, who is white, frequently had been criticized for failing to provide them with appropriate special services, a task made especially difficult in the race of immense budget deficits and overcrowding.[17] There were two leading candidates to replace Britton: one black and the other Hispanic, each with excellent qualifications. William Anton, the Hispanic candidate, was selected, reflecting in part a need to satisfy what is now largely a Hispanic constituency. In commenting on the change, the school board's only Hispanic member, Leticia Quezada, said, "We felt that with all the problems that we faced, we needed someone who had the confidence of the teachers, the administrators, and particularly the community."[18]

The New York City schools are also headed by a Hispanic, Chancellor Joseph A. Fernandez. He is not, however, the system's first Hispanic chief executive. Since 1983, when Anthony Alvarado became chancellor, the system has had both black and Hispanic chancellors, reflecting a continuing ethnic tug of war.[19]

Immigration and Congress

Immigration is a quirky issue in U.S. politics. One cannot, by using the usual conservative and liberal labels, determine in advance just which side someone will come down on. Pro-and anti-immigration forces alike are filled with both liberal and conservative members of Congress. Liberals, for example, may be strong on civil rights, but they do not always support high levels of immigration. Not all conservatives, meanwhile, agree with the Republican businessmen who favor increasing the immigration flow. Senator Alan Simpson, a Wyoming conservative, is the strongest opponent in Congress of proposals advanced by high-immigration advocacy groups. Having a large Hispanic constituency does not guarantee that a congressman will support a high level of immigration. Lamar Smith, a Republican, represents a Texas district that includes the city of San Antonio, which is 24 percent Hispanic. Many of his constituents are Hispanics with long-term roots in the United States who see large numbers of new immigrants as presenting problems for school systems and other institutions in their communities. Smith was reelected 1992 with 75 percent of the vote.

Pro-immigration members of Congress include not only the very liberal Senators Ted Kennedy (D-Massachusetts) and Paul Simon (D-Illinois), but the ultraconservative Senator Orrin Hatch (R-Utah). The chief advocate for high levels of immigration on the House side is Representative Howard L. Berman (D-California), whose district is heavily populated by immigrants. If liberals and conservatives do not sort themselves out neatly on immigration issues, it is the Democrats who more often tend to be on the side of legislation that would admit larger numbers of immigrants.

The political alliance forged by the black and Hispanic caucuses in Congress and the associated lobbying groups rests on an agreement under which Hispanics support blacks on their primary issue of civil rights. In return, blacks support or do not oppose Hispanics in their quest for higher levels of immigration and opposition to government-imposed sanctions on employers who hire illegal aliens.

In July 1991, the Congressional Hispanic Caucus developed and introduced the Hispanic Access to Higher Education Act, its first piece of legislation since it was formed fifteen years earlier.[20] The sponsors feared a negative reaction if immigrant concerns were explicitly addressed. Consequently no such provisions were included though much of the content of this bill found its way successfully into the reauthorized Higher Education Act of 1992.

Numbers

What are the issues that drive immigration policy-making and that affect the education of immigrants? A prime concern whenever Congress considers the matter is how many immigrants or refugees shall be admitted. In recent times, Congress has been very generous in setting numerical limits. Self-validation is a factor in this point of view. "My grandfather was an immigrant" is a phrase often used by many advocates of higher levels of immigration. Also acting in favor of larger immigrant numbers is the long-standing national love affair with bigness. Frequently implicit is the assumption that bigger is better, that more immigrants of the right kind will improve the nation's economy. Here in the United States, there is always room for more—many more, as this reasoning goes. When tapping this lode in the national psyche, forces favoring higher levels of immigration are prone to prescribe immigrants as the solution to a wide range of national problems.

Environmentalists, who constitute the core of opposition to high levels of immigration, find themselves on the other side of that idea. Nothing that acts to increase the nation's population finds favor with them. They point to population pressure as a root cause of the appalling conditions that are triggering immigration (especially illegal immigration) from desperately poor countries. "The United States no longer needs an increasing population," the executive director of the organization Population-Environment Balance told an audience at a congressional hearing. "Indeed, more people will only threaten our environment and quality of life."[21]

But even environmental groups have a hard time proposing restrictions on immigration. Anxious to recruit new members among the growing Hispanic population, many such groups stay away from the population issue altogether, believing it would alienate them from present or potential members. They fear being accused of racism as well.

Ethnic Makeup

No issue is more sensitive than that of designating the ethnic makeup of immigrants coming to the United States, as even the most casual study of history will show. Profound (though generally unexpressed) unease currently exists among many citizens of European and African ancestry about the unbalanced ethnic makeup of the present immigrant stream. With some 85 percent of newcomers coming from just two regions, Latin America and Asia, rapid and sometimes unsettling population shifts are taking place.

Residents in areas along the southern border that are experiencing the accelerated flow of illegal immigration from Mexico fear being overwhelmed by newcomers quite different from themselves. Is Mexico quietly reconquering the territories it lost to the United States after the Mexican-American War? Given these emotions, there is a certain irony in recalling a statement made in 1848 by the last Mexican governor of California, who said, "We find ourselves suddenly threatened by hordes of Yankee emigrants . . . whose progress we cannot arrest."[22] These "hordes," of course, eventually did take over, and what was a Mexican province became a territory of the United States.

A major motivation behind the Immigration Act of 1990 was that of changing the asymmetrical patterns of inflow and encouraging a more balanced ethnic mix. Concerned about possible charges of racism, however, Congress treaded lightly on ethnic sensitivities in developing the 1990 law and did nothing to lessen the flow from Latin and Asian sources. Instead, it simply arranged to encourage an increase the number of immigrants from other nations, especially those in Europe and Africa. This made it possible for members of Congress to live amicably with all ethnic groups in their districts; the unpleasant and politically threatening controversy that would have attended efforts to reduce the total flow was avoided.

Education/Skills

Another basic issue confronting Congress as it considered new immigration legislation was as follows: Should the United States continue to emphasize family reunification, or should more attention be given to encouraging the admission of highly skilled personnel needed by industry? Should both goals be emphasized? The Immigration Act of 1965 had the effect of discouraging immigration by skilled persons because of its emphasis on encouraging family reunification. In 1987, for example, 75 percent of legal immigrants gained entry because they were related to an U.S. citizen or resident, whereas only 4 percent gained admission because of a useful skill.[23] Family members tend to have less education and fewer skills than an original immigrant.

The 1990 immigration bill, with its emphasis on admission of more skilled immigrants, represents an effort to recruit a larger number of better-educated or skilled immigrants. In the view of some members of Congress, this was partially a response to the inadequacies of the nation's education system. Under this reasoning, U.S. schools are not turning out enough persons who have the skills and competence to fill key jobs. The solution thus is to import workers who do have such skills.

One skills concern that has never been applied in the nation's immigration policy is that of ability to speak English, which is not to say that efforts haven't been made to add such a qualification. In July 1989, Senator Alan Simpson introduced an amendment to the immigration bill (S. 358) that would have rewarded through the bill's "point system" an immigrant's ability to speak English (the bill specified a certain number of points to individuals who had a higher education, a job or job offer, or a critically needed skills, among other items). By a vote of 56 to 43, the Senate voted down Simpson's amendment. Among the key arguments instrumental in defeating it was that the United States had never before given preference to those with English ability.[24]

Given the condition of the educational enterprise in the United States in the present era, was this a wise decision? Should educational background be a criterion for immigrant admissions? The United States has traditionally and with pride adopted egalitarian values in developing its immigration policies. Humanitarian concerns have rightly been considered. The world's poor and even uneducated peoples have been made welcome, and many have established themselves to become good citizens and leaders. The United States has not been, and should not be, a refuge just for the world's elite. Still, it is an undisputed fact that relatively uneducated immigrants are much more costly to the nation in terms of services required than are more highly educated individuals. It also takes them much longer to make the adjustment to this country and to enter its national life.

Policies governing refugees, illegal immigrants, and family members of the initial immigrant—groups that tend to have large numbers of poorly educated people—need to take into account the greater educational expenses that must be incurred to ensure successful integration into the national life. Comparable policies covering legal immigrants should, on the other hand, take into account of the status of a U.S. immigration visa as one of the hottest tickets in the world. This makes it possible to be more selective. Lawmakers could take some of the present burden off the U.S. education system while still endorsing egalitarian values by incorporating *incentives* (not requirements) for would-be immigrants in all categories to acquire at least a high school education and, if possible, basic English language skills before entry to the United States.

Resource Competition

Competition for education resources is one of the hidden, but real, issues involving immigration and education. Immigration policy can cruelly, if unintentionally, impair the educational and training climate for the native-born. Native-born schoolchildren suffer if the school district decides to cut out art, music, or mediated instruction in order to employ bilingual teachers or aides.

Once special programs for immigrant children are installed, hardship attends attenuation of those programs in an era of fiscal stringency. In 1992, the immigrant parents of children in the Fairfax, Virginia, public schools protested school budget proposals that would result in larger classes for students with limited English proficiency. The amount to be spent was scheduled to be increased, but not to a degree sufficient to keep up with the continuing inflow of immigrant students.[25]

Minority and low-income adult citizens see their opportunities diminished if federal funds that would otherwise support their literacy education are coopted for comparable programs in ESL instruction. And in the workplace, it is too easy for immigration to serve as a kind of escape hatch for employers unwilling to take on the vexing problems of productivity, or to improve wages and working conditions. The immediate needs of an employer may be taken care of by immigrants imported to do jobs that could otherwise be filled by native minority workers whose skills are upgraded by suitable programs of education and training.

A redirection of funds away from literacy programs primarily used by English-speaking citizens under the Adult Education Act is producing tensions in some locations. Nonnative speakers of English are in fact the most rapidly growing group of clients in federally funded programs for adult literacy. In the state of Washington, for example, more than 37 percent of students enrolled in adult literacy courses during the 1989–90 academic year were enrolled in ESL classes. In addition, nonnative speakers who had completed advanced ESL classes accounted for approximately 10 percent of enrollees in ABE basic skills and GED preparation classes. About one-third of the state's enrollees in Project Even Start are nonnative speakers.[26]

At times, native-born populations (primarily Hispanic) in need of literacy, ESL, or vocational training are disadvantaged in relation to immigrant students with comparable needs. In California, for example, the state funds a limited number of ESL classes; when the limit is reached, waiting lists develop. Hispanics who are U.S. citizens have blamed immigrants for overcrowding.

School districts in rural areas have seen their vocational education funds under the Carl D. Perkins Vocational and Applied Technology Act diminish or disappear as allocations are being shifted to fewer (but needier) schools. In most instances, the intent is to serve "special populations," often immigrants in urban areas. This translates into "bitterness that funding was ripped away without any type of warning," according to Bret Lovejoy, director of government relations for the American Vocational Association.[27] Similarly, the fact of free vocational training for refugees is a sore point with many Hispanic immigrants in Los Angeles. Not classified as refugees, they are not eligible for these funds and at times resent the more generous allocation of resources to the Asians who constitute the bulk of the nation's refugee population.

Financing education for immigrants by directly or indirectly reducing educational expenditures for the native-born is a serious mistake. It is also an error to provide immigrants with services that the native-born need but cannot have. The policy (or absence of policy) in such cases is sure to result in an acrimonious clash of interests.

Immigrants should be well educated and trained within a system that enriches, rather than damages, comparable educational opportunities for all residents of the United States. One approach of this type was represented in the House of Representatives version of the bill that eventually became the Immigration Act of 1990. Under this portion of the measure (which was removed from the final statute), employers would have been required to deposit fees of up to $1,000 for each "imported" immigrant hired. The U.S. secretary of labor would then have put up these monies as grants to states to provide educational assistance and training for native-born workers.[28] This idea should be revisited by lawmakers.

Long-term damage is done when employers and governments lose the incentive to train and retrain. The nation's periodic labor shortages are not a shortage of available personnel; rather, they are shortages of people who productively engage themselves in education. The solution lies less in importing people from overseas than in meeting the educational and training needs of people already here.

Governing Principles for Immigration and Education Policy-Making

The United States has always looked to immigrants as a revitalizing force, as an important key to the nation's energy. But like all sources of energy, immigration needs control and channeling so that it can be accommodated at a manageable pace. The national and local dimensions of immigration and education need to be brought into better balance.

Immigration control in a democracy is extremely difficult to achieve because it puts into question a lot of other values that the people of the nation feel very strongly about. Citizens of the United States don't much like restrictions on freedom of movement, even for foreigners. When polled, they do not endorse immigration at its present high level; nonetheless, history suggests they will accept without undue backlash a fairly generous level of immigration if they have some assurance that immigration policy is at least fair and not disruptive to important national interests.

Immigration policy at present is not being made under ground rules that are likely to enhance the quality of immigrant education (or the education of the native-born). Key decisions are being made almost unilaterally without adequate attention to significant educational concerns. For example, the Immigration Act of 1965 was enacted with hardly a nod to the nation's education system. Yet this piece of legislation has probably had more effect on all sectors of the national educational enterprise than almost any statute explicitly labeled as related to education. The Immigration Reform and Control Act of 1986, with its amnesty education requirement, brought out a need for crowd control in many adult education centers. But few, if any, key educators were advised, much less consulted, in advance. Who knows what long-term educational effects the 1990 immigration Act will have? The social (and especially the educational) aspects of immigration were given relatively short shrift during the congressional hearings preceding this legislation.

Under the present arrangements, immigration functions as a kind of wild card in the game of education policy-making. When it is played, it can seriously disrupt the strategies of other players. The consequences of such careless political gamesmanship are evident in many of the nation's educational institutions and agencies. By most accounts, public schools in the United States, especially those in urban locations, are a mess. Nearly one-fourth of their students (about half of all minorities in some cities) drop out before finishing high school. Already troubled, these schools are in a tinderbox state as they attempt to serve an unplanned inflow of immigrant children, many of whom arrive in need of specialized educational and support services.

Sam Husk, executive director of the Council of Great City Schools, observes that immigration in this environment poses challenges even greater than those presented by poverty and homelessness.[29] Adult education centers, most operating on soft money and in a stepchild relationship with the parent school systems, are too often overcrowded and underfunded. Heroic efforts on the part of administrators, teachers, and their immigrant clients cannot always compensate for the absence of coordinated planning at the highest levels of the national government.

All of this adds up to "social dynamite," a term used by James Bryant Conant in reference to the problems of ill-educated urban youths just before the civil rights explosions of the 1960s.[30] The situation today is somewhat different, but the ultimate result may be the same—conflict that can tear at the fabric of our nation's democracy. What can be done to head off such events? Two principles ought to govern policymakers as they make or implement immigration policy. First, educators need to be consulted and their advice considered as immigration policy is made. Second, funding sufficient to support the education and training of immigrants at a sufficiently high level should be appropriated in advance.

The issues of immigration and education are inextricably entwined and should not be divorced in policy-making. In making immigration policy, Congress needs more consultation with the nation's educators. Educational policymakers need to be more assertive in giving comparable attention to immigration policy. This must be a shared responsibility. Immigration law should not be made in the absence of information that could be provided via a kind of "impact statement" that should include attention to education concerns along with those of housing, social welfare, employment, and the environment.

The executive branch of the federal government, which develops administrative regulations, should also improve its communication. In 1992, a senior official from the U.S. Department of Education's Office of Bilingual Education and Minority-Language Affairs, speaking on conditions of anonymity, said that federal policies governing the office effectively prevent it from anticipating the needs of new immigrants. Instead, it must wait until being notified of actual enrollments—a policy that results in a yearlong delay in accounting for and funding services to children. This difficulty could be alleviated if the Department of Education had better links with the U.S. Immigration and Naturalization Service.[31]

In addition, Congress explicitly ought to fund education costs that are attributable to its decisions on admitting immigrants. This is not the sort of cost that ought to be passed along to states and localities that have no role in the decision to admit immigrants. Furthermore, legislation under which immigrants now receive educational benefits should be reviewed to be certain that the effect is not that of diminishing the assignment of resources to the native-born. The objective throughout should be that of assuring adequate educational resources for all recipients.

Congress, with its control over immigration policy, must change its modus operandi. The question is not whether immigration is desirable, but how it can be better managed. Immigrants would be the beneficiaries of a more rational process of developing immigration policy as it applies to education, and so would the public.

Some Warning Signals

Some warning signals suggest that the nation had better act quickly if it is to head off some real difficulties. In the face of frustration, the political stresses discussed in this chapter can result in unpleasantness. One such episode occurred in January 1992 in a school board meeting in Dinuba, California, that was disrupted by eighty Hispanic activists protesting the lack of Hispanic representation on the district boards. The incident, which involved chanting and egg throwing, was unusual but reflects tensions that are quite common in California school districts, according to state Hispanic leaders.[32]

To date, however, immigrants to the United States have generally not been disruptive in pressing demands for more spending to meet their needs in education. Their citizen counterparts, too, have been relatively quiescent about crowding and resource shortages. This state of passivity may be short-lived if the French experience is an indication.

The streets of Paris were filled on November 12, 1990, by more than one-hundred-thousand French high school students demanding more government spending on schools. Although most demonstrators were peaceful, a few broke out to go on a two-hour rampage of smashing windows, looting stores, setting fire to cars, and attacking police with rocks and bottles. This rebellion was largely that of young people from the lower classes, often from Arab immigrant families. They were protesting increasingly crowded classrooms, a shortage of teachers, and poor security in the face of rising levels of physical violence in the public schools.

By most standards, the French government has not been stingy in allocating funds for education. Just prior to the demonstration, Prime Minister Michel Rocard had announced a 9 percent increase in education spending, to an amount exceeding the nation's defense budget. Student leaders, however, asserted that the results of the proposed spending increases would not be evident for years. They demanded fast action in the direction of improved instruction in safer classrooms. The students got a hearing with President Francois Mitterrand and Education Minister Lionel Jospin. Nasser Ramdan, one of the organizers of the demonstration, reported that Mitterand expressed his support.[34] Given the appalling condition of many schools in which immigrants are enrolled in large numbers, similar uprisings in this country are not unlikely in the near future.

20
Diversity, Unity, Opportunity

If the situation concerning immigration and education in the United States is as herein outlined, what are the chances that the nation will solve the problems and realize the opportunities? Is it actually possible to achieve unity through diversity? The hazards to success are real and perilous, but there is reason for optimism. We have at our disposal several basic and important building blocks.

The first of these is the commitment to the values of democracy that is one of the most significant characteristics of newly arrived immigrants to the United States. This is a priceless asset that should be recognized and cultivated. We can rejoice that Thomas Jefferson's fears that legislative democracy in the United States would be warped by immigrants and rendered "a heterogeneous, incoherent, distracted mass" have not come to pass.[1]

The second great asset is a national reservoir of goodwill toward immigrants. Neither racism nor mindless nativism has been stamped out, and the numbers and velocity of the present wave at times overwhelm. Most citizens of the United States, however, want newcomers to find their way and are willing to make some accommodations that will help.

The ability to synthesize is a third vital asset in these times. Successful synthesis has always been one of our country's long suits. We may be racially, ethnically, and religiously diverse, but we compromise and adapt—probably with skills unmatched by any other people. It is this national talent that must be called into play by the nation's educators in the years ahead when debate over some educational issues is likely to be more confrontational than in the immediate past.

Eduard Lindeman, the late adult education philosopher, had it right when he asserted that "democratic experience appears to have demonstrated the fact that diversity is superior to uniformity." It was *e pluribus unum* (from many, one) that brought results. The unity promised by democracy would never be achieved through uniformity; there should instead be movement toward unity brought about through the creative use of diversity.[2] Acceptance of this principle with all of its inherent problems, contradictions, and tensions is a basic step that needs to be taken by the nation's educators in the present era. Diversity must not in the end be considered as a problem (though it may present problems). It must instead be considered as a positive value, a rich resource to be mined in the process of education, a force that is productive rather than destructive.

What must not be lost in the great sea of diversity is the essential goal of unity, a sense of national community. This larger democratic civic culture holds the nation together. It values diversity and, indeed, guarantees the right of individuals and communities to be ethnic. The nation's democratic values, its English language, its shared sense of purpose—all of these vital ingredients of the national consciousness need attention at every level of education. What is done in the name of diversity should at all times take into account this larger dimension of community, just as what is done in the name of national community must accommodate the diversity that is the United States.

There are some subtle dimensions to this task. It is not the lowest common denominator, mere tolerance or sullen acceptance, that should be sought after. Rather, the goal should be what Frank F. Wong, vice president for academic affairs at the University of Redlands, has called "intercultural community," a highest common denominator where differences help lead to a "fuller understanding of what is universally true."[3]

Residents of the United States will have much to show the world if they can demonstrate that people from very diverse ethnic and cultural backgrounds can live together in peace, valuing their constituent cultures and yet building, over time, an equally valued and shared national culture. If this is to happen, educators must come to terms with the problems and opportunities inherent in these themes and work toward creative and enlightened practice.

Notes

Chapter 1

1. Passel and Edmonston, *Immigration and Race*, Table 1 (no page).
2. Population Crisis Committee, *Population Pressures*, 4.
3. Edmonston and Passel, *Future Immigration Population*, 38.
4. Population Crisis Committee, *Population Pressures*, 6.
5. U.S. Senate hearings, 23 October and 11 December 1987, 183.
6. U.S. Senate hearings, 23 October and 11 December 1987, 189.
7. Beards, *Basic History*, 34.
8. Bell, "Making of 'Good' Americans," 7.
9. Bouvier and Gardner, "Immigration to the U.S.", 9.
10. U.S. Senate hearings, 23 October and 11 December 1987, 183.
11. U.S. Senate hearings, 23 October and 11 December 1987, 183.
12. U.S. Senate hearings, 23 October and 11 December 1987, 183.
13. Fuchs, *American Kaleidoscope*, 58.
14. Higham, *Strangers in the Land*, 163–64.
15. Higham, *Strangers in the Land*, 104–105.
16. Higham, *Strangers in the Land*, 191–193.
17. Higham, *Strangers in the Land*, 203.
18. Higham, *Strangers in the Land*, 308.
19. Archdeacon, *Becoming American*, 163.
20. U.S. Senate hearings, 23 October and 11 December 1987, 183.
21. U.S. Senate hearings, 23 October and 11 December 1987, 189–90.
22. Quoted in Borjas, *Friends and Strangers*, 29; Higham, *Strangers in the Land*, 318.
23. Bouvier and Gardner, *Immigration to the U.S.*, 13.
24. U.S. Senate hearings, 23 October and 11 December 1987, 183.

25. U.S. Senate hearings, 23 October and 11 December 1987, 184.
26. U.S. Senate hearings, 23 October and 11 December 1987, 184.
27. Bouvier and Gardner, *Immigration to the U.S.*, 13.
28. U.S. Senate hearings, 23 October and 11 December 1987, 184.
29. Rockett, "American Immigration Policy," 14–15.
30. Passel and Edmonston, *Immigration and Race*, May 1992, 2.
31. Rockett, "American Immigration Policy," 16.
32. Borjas, *International Differences*, 10–11.
33. Burns, *Two Essays* ("Whiz Kids" essay), 3.
34. Fuchs, *American Kaleidoscope*, 279–280.
35. U.S. Department of Health and Human Services report, 31 January 1989, 4–5.
36. Fix and Passel, *Door Remains Open*, 16, 17.
37. Carlson, *Americanization Syndrome*, 2, 29–30.
38. Carlson, *Americanization Syndrome*, 60–62.
39. Higham, *Strangers in the Land*, 237.
40. Higham, *Strangers in the Land*, 239–242.
41. Archdeacon, *Becoming American*, 184.
42. Bell, "Making of 'Good' Americans," 10.
43. Patrick, "Immigration in the Curriculum," 172.
44. Carlson, *Americanization Syndrome*, 5.
45. Dewey, "School as a Means," 515.
46. Thompson, *Schooling of the Immigrant*, 11–12, 15.
47. Ravitch, *Great School Wars*, xxix.
48. Ravitch, *Great School Wars*, 263.

Chapter 2

1. Fletcher and Taylor, "Village Apart," 9.
2. Golini, paper, 24 October 1991.
3. Aguayo and Fagen, *Central Americans*, 78–79.
4. *Washington Post*, 27 May 1992.
5. U.S. Department of Labor, *The Effects of Immigration*, 1989, 88–89.
6. Fletcher and Taylor, "Village Apart," 13.
7. *Washington Post*, 17 June 1991.
8. *New York Times*, 12 September 1990.
9. *Washington Post*, 9 December 1990.
10. Pereira, "Education of Juan Tipsuda," 11.
11. Center for Immigration Studies, *Scope*, Summer 1992, 6.
12. Yale-Loehr, *Immigration Act of 1990*, 4–1.
13. *Interpreter Releases*, 21 October 1991, 1479–80; Cose, *Nation of Strangers*, 197.
14. Center for Immigration Studies, *Scope*, Spring 1992.
15. *Refugee Reports*, 31 July 1991, 11.
16. Center for Immigration Studies, *Scope*, Summer 1991, 9.

17. GED Testing Service, American Council on Education.

18. Passel and Edmonston, *Immigration and Race*, Table 1; estimate of illegal immigration from U.S. Census Bureau.

19. Riche, "We're All Minorities," 28.

20. Edmonston and Passel, *Future Immigrant Population*, 18.

21. *Education Week*, 20 March 1991.

22. Riche, "We're All Minorities," 28.

23. Riche, "We're All Minorities," 28.

24. *Education Week*, 20 March 1991.

25. Woodrow et al., "Recent Immigration," 10.

26. National Coalition, *New Voices*, 10.

27. Passel and Edmonston, *Immigration and Race*, Table 2.

28. U.S. Bureau of the Census.

29. Center for Immigration Studies, *Scope*, Fall/Winter 1991, 14.

30. Chang, *Newcomer Programs*, 5.

31. Azores, "Educational Attainment," 49.

32. Bouvier, *Fifty Million Californians*, 5–6.

33. Population Crisis Committee, *Population Pressures*, 24.

34. *Washington Post*, 14 December 1990.

35. Bachu, "Profile of the Foreign Born Population", Table C.

36. U.S. Department of Education, *Update on Adult Illiteracy*, as cited in Maine Litecary Coalition, *Handbook*, July 1988.

37. U.S. Department of Education, "Basic Data on Literacy," January 1990.

38. *Hispanic Education Report*, June 1991, 3; "Hispanic Education: A Statistical Portrait," 1990.

39. U.S. House of Representatives hearing, 28 September 1988, 18.

40. U.S. House of Representatives hearing, 28 September 1987, 19.

41. *Washington Post*, 16 June 1992.

42. *Washington Post*, 6 July 1992.

Chapter 3

1. President's statement on signing Immigration Act of 1990, 29 November 1990.

2. This and all subsequent references in this chapter are to the Immigration Act of 1990, Public Law 101–649, 29 November 1990.

3. *Washington Post*, 28 October 1990.

4. Yale-Loehr, *Immigration Act of 1990*, 2–3.

5. Center for Immigration Studies, "United States."

6. *Refugee Reports*, 31 July 1991.

7. *Washington Post*, 17 June 1991.

8. *Esquire*, July 1990, 33; *Washington Post*, 31 July 1990.

9. U.S. Postal Inspection Service report, 8.

10. Fletcher and Taylor, "Village Apart," 13.

11. Fletcher and Taylor, "Village Apart," 13.

12. Texas, *Governor's Task Force*, 40.
13. Edmonston and Passel, *Future Immigrant Population*, 24.
14. Center for Immigration Studies, *Scope*, Summer 1991.

Chapter 4

1. Cose, *Nation of Strangers*, 70.
2. McCarthy, "Right to an Education," 283–5.
3. Carrera, *Immigrant Students*, 4–5.
4. Orum, *New Immigration Act*, 8–9.
5. Carrera, *Immigrant Students*, 5.
6. Olivas, "*Plyler v. Doe*," 27–29.
7. Govan and Taylor, *One Nation, Indivisible*, 113.
8. Crawford, *Bilingual Education*, 35.
9. 414 U.S. 563, 566.
10. 414, U.S. 563, 565.
11. Govan and Taylor, *One Nation, Indivisible*, 114–115.
12. U.S. Commission on Civil Rights, *Civil Rights Issues Facing Asian Americans*, February 1992, 83.
13. Govan and Taylor, *One Nation, Indivisible*, 115; U.S. Commission on Civil Rights, *Civil Rights Issues Facing Asian Americans*, February 1992, 83.
14. Crawford, *Bilingual Education*, 42.
15. U.S. Commission on Civil Rights, *Civil Rights Issues Facing Asian Americans*, 83.
16. U.S. English, "Backgrounder" (undated).
17. *San Francisco Examiner*, 27 February 1989.
18. Fineman in Samuda and Woods, *Perspectives*, 201.
19. *Education Daily*, 6 August 1990.
20. *Education Daily*, 20 December 1990.
21. *Education Daily*, 11 January 1991.
22. Chang, *Newcomer Programs*, 26.
23. *Education Week*, 8 May 1991.

Chapter 5

1. *World Refugee Survey*, U.S. Committee for Refugees, 1992, 32–36.
2. U.S. Department of Health and Human Services report, 31 January 1989, 6.
3. U.S. Department of Labor, *Effects of Immigration on the U.S. Economy*, 155–56.
4. Center for Immigration Studies, "United States."
5. Rockett, "American Immigration Policy," 16.
6. U.S. Senate hearing, 28 October 1983, 63.
7. U.S. Senate hearing, 28 October and 1983, 78.
8. U.S. Senate hearing, 28 October 1983, 101.

9. U.S. Senate hearing, 28 October 1983, 66.
10. U.S. Senate hearing, 28 October 1983, 66.
11. Chuong, "Working with Vietnamese," 2.
12. Chuong, "Working with Vietnamese," 2.
13. Chuong, "Working with Vietnamese," 2.
14. Chuong, "Working with Vietnamese," 2.
15. U.S. Commission on Civil Rights, *Civil Rights Issues Facing Asian Americans*, 67.
16. Ranard, "The Hmong," 8.
17. *Newsweek*, 9 October 1989, 45.
18. U.S. Department of Health and Human Services report, 31 January 1989, iv.
19. U.S. Department of Health and Human Services report, 31 January 1989, iv.
20. U.S. Department of State, Bureau for Refugee Programs, 30 September 1989.
21. U.S. Department of Health and Human Services final report, January 1985, 6–7.
22. U.S. Department of Health and Human Services report, 31 January 1989, 139.
23. Bliss, "Providing Adult Basic Education," 16.
24. U.S. Department of Health and Human Services final report, January 1985, 87.
25. *Federal Register*, 13 April 1990, 13976.
26. *Federal Register*, 13 April 1990, 13978.
27. *Federal Register*, 13 April 1990, 13978.
28. *Federal Register*, 13 April 1990, 13976.
29. de la Puente, "Employment and Training Programs," 104.
30. Gozdziak and Martin, *Refugee Early Employment*, 1.
31. Ranard, "From There To Here," 2.
32. Ranard, "From There To Here," 2.
33. Tollefson, *Alien Winds*, 57.
34. Tollefson, "Economics and Ideology of Overseas Refugee Education," 545.
35. U.S. Department of Labor, Employment and Training Administration, "Notification of Award," F-3967–2–00–80–60.
36. U.S. Department of Education, *America 2000*, 29.
37. U.S. Department of Health and Human Services final report, January 1985, 242.
38. U.S. Department of Health and Human Services final report, January 1985; 68.
39. Ranard, "The Hmong," 9.
40. Ranard, "The Hmong," 6–7.

Chapter 6

1. *Washington Post*, 17 June 1991.
2. *Washington Post*, 6 October 1990.

3. Center for Immigration Studies, "United States."
4. U.S. Immigration and Naturalization Service.
5. Hesburgh, *God, Country*, 276.
6. Orum, *New Immigration Act*, 5.
7. Orum, *New Immigration Act*, 6.
8. Orum, *New Immigration Act*, 7.
9. Terdy and Spener, *English Language* (unpaged).
10. Terdy and Spener, *English Language* (unpaged).
11. National Association of Latino Elected and Appointed Officials, *Legalization's Second Step*, 21–25.
12. Leon (Florida) County Schools, "Immigration Stress," FCS-1.
13. Bliss, "Amnesty and Adult Education," 18 November 1988.
14. U.S. House of Representatives hearing, 28 September 1987, 16.
15. U.S. House of Representatives hearing, 28 September 1987, 86.
16. U.S. House of Representatives hearing, 28 September 1987, 13.
17. *Los Angeles Times*, (undated clipping in "News Clippings" file in office of *Interpreter Releases*, Washington, D.C.).
18. U.S. House of Representatives hearing, 28 September 1987, 35–38.
19. *Chronicle of Higher Education*, 6 June 1990.
20. U.S. House of Representatives hearing, 28 September 1987, 224–25.
21. U.S. Senate hearing, 3 March 1989, 153.
22. North and Portz, *U.S. Alien Legalization Program*, 15.
23. *Washington Post*, 8 November 1990.
24. Terdy and Spener, *English Language* (unpaged).
25. North and Portz, *U.S. Alien Legalization Program*, 76.
26. New York status report, 30 June 1991, 6.
27. U.S. Department of Justice, *Immigration Reform and Control Act*, 5.
28. U.S. Department of Justice, *Immigration Reform and Control Act*, x.
29. U.S. Department of Justice, *Immigration Reform and Control Act*, x.
30. U.S. Department of Justice, *Immigration Reform and Control Act*, ix.
31. U.S. Department of Justice, *Immigration Reform and Control Act*, x.
32. U.S. Department of Justice. *Immigration Reform and Control Act*, 27.
33. California State Department of Education, "Fact Sheet: Amnesty Education."
34. New York State Education Department status report, 30 June 1991, 5.
35. *Washington Post*, 9 July 1992.
36. Center for Immigration Studies, *Scope*, Spring 1992.
37. Skerry (citing research by Wayne Cornelius), "Borders and Quotes," 86.
38. *Washington Post*, 6 October 1990.
39. James, *Illegal Immigration*, 128.
40. *Time*, 19 November 1990, 16.
41. James, *Illegal Immigration*, 45.
42. James, *Illegal Immigration*, 103.

Chapter 7

1. Texas Education Agency, *Case Study*, 21.
2. Texas Education Agency, *Case Study*, 108.
3. Texas Education Agency, *Case Study*, 41–42.
4. Texas Education Agency, *Case Study*, 42.
5. Texas Education Agency, *Case Study*, 64.
6. Texas Education Agency, *Case Study*, 44, 50.
7. Texas Education Agency, *Case Study*, 68.
8. Texas Education Agency, *Case Study*, 99.
9. Texas Education Agency, *Case Study*, 50–51.
10. Texas Education Agency, *Case Study*, 81.
11. U.S. House of Representatives hearing, 21 February 1990, 514.
12. Minicucci and Olsen, "Programs for Secondary Limited English Proficient Students", 3.
13. Olsen, *Schoolhouse Border*, 6.
14. *New York Times*, 8 October 1989.
15. Olsen, *Schoolhouse Border*, 5.
16. Olsen and Dowell, *Bridges*, 5.
17. Olsen, *Schoolhouse Border*, 14.
18. U.S. General Accounting Office *Immigrant Education*, March 1991, 18.
19. Bennett, "Welcome to L.A.," 14.
20. U.S. House of Representatives hearings, 21 February 1990, 647.
21. Muller and Espenshade, *Fourth Wave*, 80.
22. National Coalition, *New Voices*, 42.
23. *Education Daily*, 22 March 1991.
24. Olsen, *Schoolhouse Border*, 15.
25. *Education Week*, 17 April 1991; *Washington Post*, 16 April 1992.
26. *New York Times*, 21 November 1989.
27. *New York Times*, 30 March 1991.
28. *Washington Post* 16 April 1992.
29. *Education Week*, 17 April 1991.
30. Fernandez, *Directory of Languages*.
31. Marshall and Bouvier, *Population Change* (summary, unpaged).
32. *Education Week*, 18 September 1991.
33. Cutler, "Welcome," 48.
34. *Washington Post*, 3 September 1990.
35. *Edinburg [Texas] Daily Review*, 5 November 1985.
36. U.S. House of Representatives hearing, 21 February 1990, 508.
37. *Congressional Record*, 3 October 1990, H8714.
38. National Coalition, *New Voices*, 12.
39. National Coalition, *New Voices*, 56.
40. Kiang, "Southeast Asian Parent Empowerment," 10.
41. *Education Week*, 29 November 1989.

42. Ellingson, "Problems of the 1980's," 5–6.
43. *Washington Post*, 21 October 1989.
44. *Washington Post*, 23 January 1991.
45. National Coalition, *New Voices*, 11.
46. National Coalition, *New Voices*, xiii.
47. *Education Week*, 17 January 1990.

Chapter 8

1. Fillmore in Cabello, *California Perspectives*, 30.
2. Olsen and Dowell, *Bridges*, 14.
3. Olsen, *Schoolhouse Border*, 50.
4. Olsen, *Schoolhouse Border*, 52.
5. Olsen, *Schoolhouse Border*, 52.
6. National Coalition, *New Voices*, 29; Minicucci and Olsen, "Programs for Secondary Limited English Proficient Students," 5.
7. Minicucci and Olsen, "Programs for Secondary Limited English Proficient Students," 5.
8. Govan and Taylor, *One Nation, Indivisible*, 108.
9. Govan and Taylor, *One Nation, Indivisible*, 109.
10. Council of Chief State School Officers, *School Success*, 12.
11. "New Faces," 3.
12. U.S. House of Representatives hearings, 21 February 1990, 647.
13. Federation for American Immigration Reform, "Immigration and the California Education System."
14. *New York Times*, 18 August 1991.
15. *Education Week*, 29 November 1989.
16. Bischoff and Koop, *Guide for Understanding*, 20.
17. National Coalition, *New Voices*, 21.
18. *Education Week*, 1 August 1990.
19. Olsen, *Schoolhouse Border*, 80.
20. Cuban American National Council, *Challenge of Education*, 9.
21. Olsen, *Schoolhouse Border*, 80.
22. Gonzalez, "Schools and Language Minority Parents," 15.
23. Yao, "Working Effectively with Asian Immigrant Parents," 225.
24. *Washington Post*, 20 February 1992.
25. Kiang, "Southeast Asian Parent Empowerment," 12.
26. Rist, "This Immigrant Wave," 15.
27. U.S. Department of Education, "Exemplary Programs" news release, 1992.

Chapter 9

1. Cummings, "Children of the Caribbean," 492.
2. West, "New Arrivals," 84, 86.

3. West, "New Arrivals," 86.
4. National Coalition, *New Voices*, 20.
5. Sue, "Challenge of Multiculturalism," 7–8.
6. Roop, *The Hmong*, 1990.
7. Chang, *Newcomer Programs*, 14.
8. *ERIC Digest*, September 1984.
9. *ERIC Digest*, September 1984.
10. Minicucci and Olsen, "Programs for Secondary Limited English Proficient Students," 13.
11. Bliss, "Providing Adult Basic Education," 30–31.
12. U.S. Department of Education, Fact Sheet #3, 19 June 1989.
13. *TESOL Matters*, April/May 1992.
14. *New York Times*, 16 April 1992.
15. Rist, "This Immigrant Wave," 17.
16. U.S. Commission on Civil Rights, *Civil Rights*, 102.
17. Olsen and Dowell, *Bridges*, 89.
18. Wolfgang, "Intercultural Counseling," in Samuda and Woods, *Perspectives*, 212.
19. Sue, "Challenge of Multiculturalism," 12–13.
20. Esquivel and Keitel, "Counseling Immigrant Children," 216.
21. Sue, "Challenge of Multiculturalism," 12.
22. Chuong, "Working with Vietnamese High School Students," New Faces of Liberty, Berkeley, California, 12 (unpublished).
23. Rist, "This Immigrant Wave," 17.
24. Ravitch, "Diversity and Democracy," 20.
25. *Chronicle of Higher Education*, 6 February 1991.
26. Dewey, "Nationalizing Education," 140.

Chapter 10

1. National Coalition, *New Voices*, xiii.
2. Minicucci and Olsen, *Programs for Secondary Limited English Proficient Students*, 5.
3. *New Voices*, newsletter, Spring/Summer 1992.
4. Olsen, *Schoolhouse Border*, 7, 30–31.
5. Olsen, *Schoolhouse Border*, 35.
6. Olsen, *Schoolhouse Border*, 36.
7. U.S. Department of Health and Human Services, *The Adaptation of Southeast Asian Refugee Youth*, January 1988, 59.
8. U.S. Department of Health and Human Services, *The Adaptation of Southeast Asian Refugee Youth*, January 1988, 60.
9. Chang, *Newcomer Programs*, 9.
10. Bischoff and Koop, *Guide for Understanding*, 13, 44.
11. *Washington Post*, September 1991.
12. National Coalition, *New Voices*, 25.

13. National Coalition, *New Voices*, 22–23.
14. *Washington Post*, 1 May 1990.
15. U.S. Commission on Civil Rights, *Civil Rights*, 30–31.
16. U.S. Commission on Civil Rights, *Civil Rights*, 93.
17. Gibson and Bhachu in Gibson and Obgu, *Minority Status and Schooling*, 77.
18. *Washington Post*, 24 October 1991.
19. *San Francisco Chronicle*, 20 May 1991.
20. *San Francisco Chronicle*, 20 May 1991.
21. *San Francisco Chronicle*, 20 May 1991.
22. *Washington Post*, 14 March 1991.
23. *Education Week*, 15 January 1992.
24. *Washington Post*, 19 July 1992.

Chapter 11

1. Nielsen, "An Evaluation," 25–26.
2. *Washington Post*, 3 April 1990.
3. Nielsen, "An Evaluation," 26.
4. Bell, "'Good' Americans," 4.
5. Nielsen, "An Evaluation," 1, 23.
6. Nielsen, "An Evaluation," 23.
7. U.S. Senate hearing, 3 March 1989, 128
8. Bliss, "Providing Adult Basic Education," 16.
9. Campbell and Blain, "Community Education," 18, 25.
10. Lopez-Valadez et al., *Immigrant Workers*, 24.
11. U.S. House of Representative hearings, 21 February 1990, 242.
12. "Myth #13," 2.
13. U.S. House of Representatives hearing, 28 September 1987.
14. "Myth #13," 4.
15. Ranard, "The Hmong," 3.
16. Bliss, "Providing Adult Basic Education," 15–16.
17. Ranard, "Family Literacy," 1–2.
18. Ranard, "Family Literacy," 2, 4.
19. *Education Daily*, 28 January 1991.
20. U.S. Department of Education, *Descriptive Study of the Family English Literacy Program*, 15.
21. Vargas, *Literacy*, 25–26.
22. *Education Week*, 16 October 1991.
23. GED Testing Service staff memo, August 1990.
24. Bliss, "Providing Adult Basic Education," 23–24.
25. Lopez-Valadez et al., *Immigrant Workers*, 30–31.
26. Bliss, "Providing Adult Basic Education," 17.
27. de la Puente and Bendick, "Employment and Training Programs," 97.
28. Lopez-Valadez et al., *Immigrant Workers*, 23.

29. *Washington Post*, 21 March 1991.
30. U.S. House of Representatives hearings, 21 February 1990, 606–7.
31. "Myth # 13, " 5.
32. Lopez-Valadez et al., *Immigrant Workers*, 32.
33. *Washington Post*, 29 January 1990.
34. U.S. Department of Labor, Employment and Training Administration, "Notification of Award," F-3968-2-00-80-60.
35. U.S. Department of Justice, El Paso, "Citizenship Awareness."
36. Kirschten, "Speaking English," 1157.
37. Bliss, "Providing Adult Basic Education," 17.
38. Thompson, *Schooling the Immigrant*, 58–59.
39. U.S. House of Representatives hearing, 28 September 1987, 88.
40. *Washington Post*, 21 September 1989.

Chapter 12

1. Bailey and Görlach, *English as a World Language*, vii.
2. Telephone call, Marie Pees, U.S. Bureau of Census.
3. U.S. Department of Education, "Teaching Adults with Limited English Skills," 10.
4. "Myth # 13, 2."
5. Bliss, "Providing Adult Basic Education," 4.
6. Chang, *Newcomer Programs*, 5.
7. Council of Chief State School Officers, *School Success*, 15.
8. Crawford, *Bilingual Education*, 76.
9. Crawford, *Bilingual Education*, 76–77.
10. U.S. Department of Education, *Condition of Bilingual Education*, 8, 47.
11. Govan and Taylor, *One* Nation, Indivisible, 107.
12. "New Faces," 6.
13. Olsen, *Schoolhouse Border*, 13–14.
14. *Education Week*, 6 December 1989.
15. Council of Chief State School Officers, *Recommendations for Improving the Assessment,* (Summary).
16. Letter to author, Ronald Pugsley, U.S. Department of Education, 17 August 1992.
17. U.S. Department of Education, Clearinghouse on Adult Education and Literacy, Fact Sheet.
18. *ERIC Digest*, December 1987.
19. Bliss, "Providing Adult Basic Education," 15–16.
20. Bliss, "Providing Adult Basic Education," 16–17.
21. Grognet, "Winds of Change," 5.
22. Mostek, "Exploring the Definition," 18.
23. Judith McGaughey, panelist on PBS/College Board closed-circuit television presentation, 1992.
24. *TESOL Newsletter*, June 1989.

25. Snow, *Common Terms*, 10–11.
26. U.S. Department of Health and Human Services, *Guidelines for ELT Programs*, E-1, E-2.
27. *TESOL Matters*, April/May 1992.

Chapter 13

1. U.S. General Accounting Office, *Bilingual Education*, March 1987, 76.
2. Imhoff, "Position of U.S. English," 16.
3. U.S. General Accounting Office, *Bilingual Education*, March 1987, 76.
4. Snow, *Common Terms*, 4–5.
5. Snow, *Common Terms*, 4.
6. Snow, *Common Terms*, 9.
7. Crawford, *Bilingual Education*, 107.
8. Crawford, *Bilingual Education*, 104.
9. Fillmore, "A Question," 32–33.
10. Porter, *Forked Tongue*, 68–69.
11. Crawford, *Bilingual Education*, 119.
12. El Paso, *Bilingual Education Evaluation*, 47.
13. U.S. General Accounting Office, *Bilingual Education*, March 1987, 1.
14. U.S. General Accounting Office, *Bilingual Education*, March 1987, 3.
15. U.S. General Accounting Office, *Bilingual Education*, March 1987, 3–4.
16. U.S. General Accounting Office, *Bilingual Education*, March 1987, 63.
17. *Federal Register*, 4 February 1992, 4327–28.
18. Aguirre International, "Final Report: Longitudinal Study."
19. *Education Week*, 20 February 1991.
20. Aguirre, "Longitudinal Study" (Executive Summary), 22.
21. *Education Week*, 20 February 1991.

Chapter 14

1. Crawford, *Bilingual Education*, 20.
2. Govan and Taylor, *One Nation, Indivisible*, 110.
3. Crawford, *Bilingual Education*, 28.
4. Lyons, "Past and Future," 68; Crawford, *Bilingual Education*, 28.
5. Crawford, *Bilingual Education*, 26.
6. Lyons, "Past and Future," 67.
7. Crawford, "Educating Language Minority," 62.
8. Lyons, "Past and Future," 68.
9. Govan and Taylor, *One Nation, Indivisible*, 110.
10. Bennett, "Toward a Common Language," 4.
11. Crawford, *Bilingual Education*, 41.
12. Crawford, *Bilingual Education*, 42; Crewdson, *Tarnished Door*, 305.
13. Lyons, "Past and Future," 74.

14. Bennett, "Toward a Common Language," 3.
15. Bennett, "Toward a Common Language," 3–4.
16. Bennett, "Toward a Common Language," 3.
17. Rossell and Ross, "Social Science," 388.
18. Lyons, "Past and Future," 75–76.
19. Lyons, "Past and Future," 76.
20. Lyons, "Past and Future," 77.
21. Porter, *Forked Tongue*, 224.
22. *Education Week*, 12 February 1992.
23. Porter, *Forked Tongue*, 27.
24. Cortés, E Pluribus Unum," in Cabello, *California Perspectives*, 15–16; Ovando, "Politics and Pedagogy," 354.
25. National Council for Bilingual Education, *Forum*, November 1990.
26. Porter, *Forked Tongue*, 218.
27. Rodriguez, *Hunger of Memory*, 26–27.
28. Chavez, *Out of the Barrio*, 40.
29. *Washington Post*, 22 April 1990.
30. Pelavin Associates, "Revised Analysis," 10.
31. *Education Week*, 19 June 1991.
32. Olsen and Mullen, *Embracing Diversity*, 65.
33. Olsen and Mullen, *Embracing Diversity*, 63–64.
34. Crawford, *Bilingual Education*, 158.

Chapter 15

1. Diáz-Lefebvre in Cassara, *Adult Education*, 217.
2. Delgado-Gaitan and Trueba, *Crossing Cultural Borders*, 132–33.
3. National Association for Bilingual Education, *Forum*, March/April 1990.
4. *U.S. English Update*, November/December 1989.
5. *Washington Post*, 3 November 1991; *Washington Post*, 10 July 1992.
6. Porter, *Forked Tongue*, 4.
7. *Federal Register*, 4 February 1992, 4327–28.
8. Porter, *Forked Tongue*, 33.
9. Cornelius, "Future of Mexican Immigrants," 51.
10. Rist, "This Immigrant Wave," 15.
11. Crawford, *Bilingual Education*, 14.
12. Ovando and Collier, *Bilingual and ESL*, 40.
13. Cummins, *Empowering Minority Students*, Chapter 5.
14. Crawford, *Bilingual Education*, 57.
15. *La Raza Education Network News*, May/June 1989.
16. Padilla et al., "The English-Only Movement," 122.
17. *La Raza Education Network News*, May/June 1989.
18. Hayakawa, "Make English Official," 36.
19. Hayakawa, "Make English Official," 39.
20. Hayakawa, "Make English Official," 39.

21. Bikales and Imhof, "Kind of Discordant Harmony," in D. Simcox (ed.), *Immigration in the 1980s*, 1988 (as cited in James, *Illegal Immigration*, 100).
22. National Coalition of Advocates for Students, *New Voices*, 17.
23. National Coalition of Advocates for Students, *New Voices*, 20.
24. Crawford, *Bilingual Education*, 60 (citing work of Calvin J. Veltman.)
25. Fletcher and Taylor, "Village Apart," 15.

Chapter 16

1. Council of Chief State School Officers, *School Success*, 10, 14.
2. Olsen, *Schoolhouse Border*, 84.
3. Rumbaut, "Immigrant Students in California Public Schools," 27–28.
4. Stein, "Understanding the Refugee."
5. Olsen and Dowell, *Bridges*, 4.
6. National Center for Education Statistics, "Hispanic Dropout Rates," Issue Brief.
7. Suarez-Orozco, "Immigrant Adaptation," in Gibson and Ogbu, *Minority Status and Schooling*, 42.
8. Council of Chief State School Officers, *School Success*, 5.
9. U.S. House of Representatives hearing, 21 February 1990, 535–536.
10. U.S. Commission on Civil Rights, *Civil Rights*, 73.
11. U.S. Department of Health and Human Services, *The Adaptation of Southeast Asian Refugee Youth*, January 1988, xiv.
12. Gilzow and Ranard, *The Amerasians*, 7–8.
13. Rist, "This Immigrant Wave," 17.
14. Olsen, *Schoolhouse Border*, 27.
15. James, *Illegal Immigration*, 3.
16. Chavez, *Out of the Barrio*, 168.
17. *Washington Post*, 28 February 1991.
18. Hirschman and Wong, "Immigration, Education," 26, 35.
19. Burns, *Two Essays* ("Whiz Kids" essay), 4.
20. Gardner et al., "Asian Americans," 25–26.
21. U.S. Department of Health and Human Services, *The Adaptation of Southeast Asian Refugee Youth*, January 1988, xvii.
22. U.S. Department of Health and Human Services, *The Adaptation of Southeast Asian Refugee Youth*, January 1988, xiii, xiv.
23. Lee, "Koreans," in Gibson and Obgu, *Minority Status and Schooling*, 157.
24. National Coalition of Advocates for Students, *New Voices*, 45.
25. *The Daily Record*, Ellensburg, Washington, 24 February 1990.
26. U.S. Department of Education, *Teaching Adults with Limited English Skills*, October 1991, 17–18.
27. American Association for Adult and Continuing Education, Outstanding Adult Learner Awards, 1990.

Chapter 17

1. Much of the content in this chapter first appeared as an article by the author entitled "Immigration and Higher Education: The Crisis and the Opportunities," *Educational Record*, 72 (Fall 1991) 20–25.

2. Institute of International Education, *Open Doors: Report on International Educational Exchange*, 1985/86–1990/91.

3. U.S. Immigration and Naturalization Service, *Statistical Yearbook. 1987–88 through 1990–91.*

4. Fuchs, *Americans Kaleidoscope*, 280.

5. *New York Times*, 29 November 1990.

6. *Chronicle of Higher Education*, 15 January 1992.

7. *Higher Education and National Affairs*, 23 July 1990.

8. Yale-Loehr, *Understanding the Immigration Act*, 3–2, 3–3.

9. *New York Times*, 8 May 1990.

10. *Chronicle of Higher Education*, 3 June 1992.

11. Schieffer, "Mapping the Migration of Talent," 21.

12. Ong, Cheng, and Evans, "Brian Drain Boomerang," 28.

13. Swinerton, *Philippine Higher Education*, 83.

14. Carnegie Foundation, *Campus Life*, 29.

15. *Washington Post*, 27 May 1991.

16. Wong, "Diversity and Community," 51.

17. Levine and Cureton, "The Quiet Revolution," 25–27.

18. *Chronicle of Higher Education*, 11 March 1992.

19. *Chronicle of Higher Education*, 10 April 1991; *Higher Education and National Affairs*, 3 June 1991.

20. *Chronicle of Higher Education*, 11 March 1992.

21. National Coalition of Advocates for Students, *New Voices*, 114.

22. Olsen and Mullen, *Embracing Diversity*, 76–77.

23. *Chronicle of Higher Education*, 27 November 1991.

24. National Association of State Boards of Education, *The American Tapestry*, 15.

25. Porter, *Forked Tongue*, 27.

26. *Chronicle of Higher Education*, 5 July 1990.

27. *Executive News Service*, 3 June 1991.

28. *TESOL Directory* and staff interview.

29. Auerbach, "Politics, Pedagogy," 1.

30. Auerbach, "Politics, Pedagogy," 1–9.

31. *Chronicle of Higher Education*, 11 July 1990.

32. Telephone call Karen Johnson, Center for ESL, The Pennsylvania State University; *The Daily Collegian*, 23 September 1991; *Centre Daily Times*, 3 September, 1990.

33. Nadelstern, "International High School," March 3–8, 1986.

34. Lieberman et al., "After Three Years," 22.

35. Olsen and Dowell, *Bridges*, 90.
36. *Chronicle of Higher Education*, 6 August 1989.
37. Federation for Immigration Reform, *Immigration Report*, August 1991.
38. *Federal Register*, 4 January 1990, 351.
39. U.S. House of Representatives hearing, 21 February 1990, 125.
40. *Refugee Reports*, 22 January 1988.
41. U.S. Commission on Civil Rights, *Civil Rights*, 99–100.
42. Ontario Ministry of Citizenship, *Access! Task Force on Access To Professions and Trades in Ontario*, 1989.

Chapter 18

1. *Education Daily*, 16 January 1990.
2. *Education Daily*, 16 January 1990.
3. *Education Week*, 17 January 1990.
4. *Education Week*, 17 January 1990.
5. "New Faces," 2.
6. U.S. General Accounting Office, *Political Asylum Applicants*, 4–5.
7. School District of LaCrosse, "Facility Needs Analysis," 9.
8. U.S. House of Representatives hearing, 21 February 1990, 657–658.
9. Chang, *Newcomer Programs*, 18.
10. Council of Chief State School Offices, *School Success*, 11–12.
11. U.S. Senate hearing, 21 June 1989, 200.
12. U.S. House of Representatives hearing, 29 March 1984, 25, 27.
13. *Washington Times*, 21 May 1990 (as cited in James, *Illegal Immigration*, 41).
14. Center for Immigration Studies, "Estimate of Annual Cost," February 1991.
15. Center for Immigration Studies, "Estimated First Year Public Assistance and Education Costs," 7 September 1990.
16. Muller and Espenshade, *Fourth Wave*, 130, 143.
17. *Congressional Record*, 27 June 1984, 19380.
18. U.S. General Accounting Office, *Immigrant Education*, March 1991, 2.
19. U.S. General Accounting Office Report, *Immigrant Education*, 6.
20. U.S. General Accounting Office Report, *Immigrant Education*, 3.
21. U.S. Department of Education, Office of the Secretary, *Biennial Report to Congress on the Emergency Immigrant Education Program*, 29 June 1992, 4.
22. U.S. Department of Education, Office of Bilingual Education and Minority Languages Affairs, Emergency Immigrant Education Act Proposals, 1992.
23. U.S. House of Representatives, *Immigration and Nationality Act*, April 1989.
24. *Refugee Reports*, 31 July 1991.
25. Telephone conversation with Carmel Thompson, U.S. Department of Health and Human Services, 28 August 1992.
26. U.S. House of Representatives, *Immigration Reform and Control Act*, 30 November 1988, 305.

27. David B. Smith, U.S. Department of Health and Human Services, Administration for Children and Families.

28. U.S. Department of Education, *Program Profiles*, 6; Appropriations data from U.S. Department of Education, Office of the Secretary.

29. Irwin, "National Literacy Act of 1991."

30. U.S. Department of Education, "1992 Resource Guide for Discretionary National Vocational-Technical and Adult Literacy Education Programs," January 1992.

31. U.S. Department of Education, Division of Adult Education and Literacy, "Adult Education for Limited English Proficient Adults: An Update," January 1991.

32. National Adult Education Professional Development Consortium, *The Adult Education Program Annual Report*, program year 1990, 31.

33. Vargas, *Literacy*, 25.

34. *Education Daily*, 23 June 1992.

35. *Federal Register*, 4 March 1992, 7799.

36. U.S. House of Representatives, *Family Unity and Employment Opportunity Act*, 19 September 1990, 86.

37. Telephone conversation with Emory Biro, U.S. Department of Labor.

38. U.S. Department of Education, Program Memorandum 92–19, 23 April 1992.

39. U.S. House of Representatives, *Family Unity and Employment Opportunity Act*, 19 September 1990, 138.

40. For example, Simon, *The Economic Consequences of Immigration* and "What Immigrants Take From, and Give To"; a recent critique of Simon's analysis is offered in North, "The Missing Tallies in Julian Simon's Work," 13–15.

41. Vernez and Ronfeldt, "Current Situation," 1192.

42. McCarthy, and Valdez, *Current and Future Effects of Mexican Immigration*, 24.

Chapter 19

1. U.S. House of Representatives, *Family Unity and Employment Opportunity Act*, 19 September 1990, 137.
2. Center for Immigration Studies, *Scope*, Spring 1992, 5.
3. U.S. House of Representatives hearing, 21 February 1990, 71.
4. Kane, *A Survey of Public Attitudes*, 7.
5. *Newsweek*, 9 October 1989, 45.
6. *Newsweek*, 9 October 1989, 45.
7. Allen, "America: Restricted Territory," 10.
8. Federation for Immigration Reform. *An Introduction to FAIR*, brochure.
9. *Education Week*, 11 December 1991.
10. *Hispanic Education Report*, June 1991, 17.
11. U.S. House of Representatives hearing, 21 February 1990, 827.
12. U.S. House of Representatives hearing, 21 February 1990, 827.
13. *Washington Post*, 10 December 1990.

14. *Education Week*, 14 November 1990.
15. Fuchs, *American Kaleidoscope*, 374.
16. U.S. House of Representatives hearing, 21 February 1990, 657.
17. *Education Week*, 1 August 1990; *Washington Post*, 18 July 1990.
18. *Education Week*, 1 August 1990; *Washington Post*, 18 July 1990.
19. Ravitch, *Great School Wars*, xvi–xxi.
20. *Washington Post*, 20 July 1991.
21. U.S. House of Representatives hearing, 21 February 1990, 658.
22. *Time*, 13 June 1983.
23. *Wall Street Journal*, 5 April 1990.
24. *English First Members' Report*, Summer 1989.
25. Fairfax County Public Schools (Virginia).
26. *Developments*, Spring 1991, 2.
27. *Education Daily Special Supplement*, 15 July 1992.
28. U.S. House of Representatives, *Family Unity and Employment Opportunity Act*, 19 September 1990, 19.
29. *Education Daily*, 22 March 1991.
30. Conant, *Slums and Suburbs*, 146.
31. *Education Week*, 12 February 1992.
32. *Education Week*, 15 January 1992.
33. *Washington Post*, 13 November 1990.

Chapter 20

1. Gordon, *Assimilation in American Life '91.*
2. Stewart, *Adult Learning in America*, 185.
3. Wong, "Diversity and Community," 53.

References

Aguayo, Sergio; and Patricia Weiss Fagen. *Central Americans in Mexico and the United States: Unilateral, Bilateral, and Regional Perspectives.* Hemispheric Migration Project, Center for Immigration Policy and Refugee Assistance, Georgetown University, 1988.

Aquirre International. Final Report: "Longitudinal Study of Structural English Immersion Strategy, Early-Exit and Late-Exit Transitional Bilingual Education Programs for Language-Minority Children." U.S. Dept. of Education Contract No. 300-87-0156. San Mateo, Calif.: Aguirre International, February 1991.

Allen, Charlotte. "America: Restricted Territory." *Insight* (16 March 1992): 6–11, 34–37.

Archdeacon, Thomas J. *Becoming American: An Ethnic History.* New York: The Free Press/Macmillan, Inc., 1983.

Auerbach, Elsa Roberts. "Politics, Pedagogy, and Professionalism: Challenging Marginalism in ESL." *College ESL* 1 (Spring 1991): 1–9.

Azores, Tania. "Educational Attainment and Upward Mobility: Prospects for Filipino Americans." *Amerasia Journal* 13 (1986–87): 39–52.

Bachu, Amara. "Profile of the Foreign Born Population in the United States." *Studies in American Fertility.* Series P-23, No. 176, U.S. Government Printing Office, Washington, D.C., 1991.

Bailey, Richard W., and Manfred Görlach, eds. *English as a World Language.* Ann Arbor: University of Michigan Press, 1982.

Beard, Charles A., and Mary R. Beard. *The Beards' Basic History of the United States.* New York: Doubleday, Doran & Co., 1944.

Bell, Samuel R. "The Making of 'Good' Americans: Civic Education of Immigrants." Paper presented at the 64th Annual Meeting of the National Council for the Social Studies, Washington, 15–19 November 1984.

Bennett, Philip. "Welcome to L.A." *The Boston Globe Magazine* (13 October 1991): 14–17, 50–54.

Bennett, William J. "Toward a Common Language: One Nation, One People." Speech reprint, 1985.

Bikales, Gerda, and Gary Imhof. "A Kind of of Discordant Harmony: Issues in Assimilation." In *Immigration in the 1980s: Reappraisal and Reform*, edited by David E. Simcox. Boulder, Colo.: Westview, 1988.

Bischoff, Henry, and Kathryn Koop. *Guide for Understanding Students and Families of the New Immigration*. Mahwah, N.J.: Ramapo College of New Jersey, Center for the Study of Pluralism, 1989.

Bliss, William B. "Amnesty and Adult Education." Speech at meeting of Connecticut Association of Adult and Continuing Education, 18 November 1988.

———. "Providing Adult Basic Education Services to Adults with Limited English Proficiency." Background paper prepared for Project on Adult Literacy of the Southport Institute for Policy Analysis, December 1988.

Borjas, George. *International Differences in the Labor Market Performance of Immigrants*. Kalamazoo, Mich.: W. E. Upjohn Institute for Employment Research, 1988.

———. *Friends or Strangers: The Impact of Immigrants on the U.S. Economy*. New York: Basic Books, Inc., 1990.

Bouvier, Leon F. "Early 1990 Census Numbers Suggest Higher Immigration and Fertility." *Scope* 7 (Spring 1991): 10–11.

———. *Fifty Million Californians*? Washington, D.C.: Center for Immigration Studies, 1991.

———, and Robert W. Gardner. "Immigration to the U.S.: The Unfinished Story." *Population Bulletin* 41 (November 1986), Population Reference Bureau, Inc.

Burns, Patrick. *Two Essays on Immigration*. The 21st Century Series, An American Issues Forum. University of Denver, 1990.

Campbell, Elizabeth, and Mary Jo Blain. "Community Education and Multiculturalism. Immigrant/Refugee Needs and Cultural Awareness." Washington: United States Conference of Mayors, 1982.

Carlson, Robert A. *The Americanization Syndrome: A Quest for Conformity*. London: Croom Helm, 1987.

Carnegie Foundation for the Advancement of Teaching. *Campus Life: In Search of Community*. Princeton, N.J.: The Carnegie Foundation for the Advancement of Teaching, 1990.

Carrera, John Willshire, Esq. *Immigrant Students: Their Legal Right of Access to Public Schools*. Boston: National Coalition of Advocates for Students, 1989.

Center for Immigration Studies. "Estimated Direct Public Assistance and Education Costs: 1990 Immigrants and Refugees Initial 12 Months in U.S." Washington, D.C.: Center for Immigration Studies, Revised February 1990.

———. "Estimated First Year Public Assistance and Education Costs: 1991. Immigrants, Refugees and Other Settlers Projected Under House Immigration Reform Bill (H.R. 4300)." Washington, D.C.: Center for Immigration Studies, 7 September 1990.

———. "Estimated Annual Costs of Major Federal and State Services to Illegal Aliens." Washington, D.C.: Center for Immigration Studies, February 1991.

———. "United States." Fact sheet distributed at conference on "Responses of

Western Industrial Nations to High Immigration Demand." Washington, D.C.: 24 October 1991.

Chang, Hedy Nai-Lin. *Newcomer Programs: Innovative Efforts to Meet the Educational Challenges of Immigrant Students*. California Tomorrow Immigrant Students Project, 1990.

Chavez, Linda., *Out of the Barrio: Toward a New Politics of Hispanic Assimilation*. Basic Books, A Division of HarperCollins Publisher, 1991.

Chiswick, Barry R. *Illegal Aliens: Their Employment and Employers*. Kalamazoo, Mich.: W. E. Upjohn Institute for Employment Research, 1988.

Chuong, Chung Hoang. "Working with Vietnamese High School Students." Berkeley, Calif.: New Faces of Liberty.

Conant, James Bryant. *Slums and Schools: A Commentary on Schools in Metropolitan Areas*. New York: McGraw-Hill Book Company, Inc., 1961.

Cornelius, Wayne A. *The Future of Mexican Immigrants in California: A New Perspective for Public Policy*. Working Papers in U.S.–Mexican Studies, 6. Program in United States–Mexican Studies, University of California, San Diego, 1981.

Cortés, Carlos E. "E Pluribus Unum: Out of Many One." In *California Perspectives: An Anthology from the Immigrant Students Report*, JoAnn Cabello, ed. San Francisco: California Tomorrow (Winter 1990): 13–16.

Cose, Ellis. *A Nation of Strangers: Prejudice, Politics and the Populating of America*. New York: Wm. Morrow & Company, Inc., 1992.

Council of Chief State School Officers. *Recommendations for Improving the Assessment and Monitoring of Students with Limited English Proficiency*, 1992.

———. *School Success for Limited English Proficient Students: The Challenge and State Response*, February 1990.

Crawford, James. *Bilingual Education: History, Politics, Theory, and Practice*. Trenton, N.J.: Crane Publishing Co., Inc., 1989.

———."Educating Language Minority Children: Politics, Research, and Policy." Paper presented at conference of the American Speech-Language-Hearing Association, "Partnerships in Education: Toward a Literate America." Washington, D.C.: 21 September 1989.

Crewdson, John. *The Tarnished Door: The New Immigrants and the Transformation of America*. New York: Times Books, 1983.

The Cuban American National Council, Inc. *The Challenge of Education: No Time to Waste, No Room for Failure*. Miami: The Cuban American Policy Center, Spring 1990.

Cummings, Alban, Mildred K. Lee, and Clement London. "Children of the Caribbean: A Study in Diversity." *Journal of Black Studies*. 13 (June 1983): 489–95.

Cummins, J. *Empowering Minority Students*. Sacramento, Calif.: California Association for Bilingual Education, 1989.

Cutler, Blayne. "Welcome to the Borderlands." *American Demographics* (February 1991): 44–57.

Delgado-Gaitan, Concha, and Henry Trueba. *Crossing Cultural Borders: Education for Immigrant Families in America*. London: The Falmer Press, 1991.

Dewey, John. "Nationalizing Education." *Journal of Proceedings and Addresses of the National Education Association* (1916).

———. "The School as a Means of Developing a Social Consciousness and Social Ideals in Children." *The Journal of Social Forces*. 1 (September 1923): 515.

de la Puente, Manuel, and Marc Bendick, Jr. "Employment and Training Programs for Migrant and Refugee Youth: Lessons from the United States Experience." Project Report. Washington: Urban Institute (August 1983). ERIC Microfiche ED 236372.

Diáz-Lefebvre, René. "The Hispanic Adult Learner in a Rural Community College." In *Adult Education in a Multicultural Society*, edited by Beverly B. Cassara, 211–231. New York: Routledge, 1990.

Edmonston, Barry, and Jeffrey Passel. "The Future Immigrant Population of the United States." Paper presented at conference on "Immigration and Ethnicity" 17–18 June 1991. Washington, D.C.: The Urban Institute. (Also PRIP-UI-19, revised February 1991).

Ellingson Jo Ann. "Problems of the 1980s: The New Influx of Immigrants: Policy Questions for the 1980s." ERIC Microfiche ED 313050, 1989.

El Paso (Texas) Independent School District. Office for Research and Evaluation. *Bilingual Education Evaluation: The Fifth Year in a Longitudinal Study*. August 1989.

Esquivel, Giselle B., and Merle A. Keitel. "Counseling Immigrant Children in the Schools." *Elementary School Guidance and Counseling* 24 (February 1990): 213–21.

Fernandez, Elizabeth M., et al. *Directory of Languages Spoken by Students of Limited English Proficiency in New York State Programs*. Albany: New York State Education Department. Bureau of Bilingual Education, 1984.

Fillmore, Lily Wong. "Latino Families and the Schools." In *California Perspectives: An Anthology from the Immigrant Students' Report*. JoAnn Cabello, ed. San Francisco, California: Tomorrow (Winter 1990) 30–36.

———. "A Question for Early-Childhood Programs: English First or Families First?" *Education Week* (19 June 1991): 32.

Fineman, Carol A. "The Training and Use of Interpreter/Translators in the Evaluation of Language Minority Students." In *Perspectives in Immigrant and Minority Education*, Ronald J. Samuda and Sandra L. Woods, eds. Lanham, Md.: University Press of America, 1983, 201–9.

Fix, Michael, and Jeffrey S. Passel. "The Door Remains Open: Recent Immigration to the United States and a Preliminary Analysis of the Immigration Act of 1990." Program for Research on Immigration Policy. Washington, D.C.: The Urban Institute, January 1991.

Fletcher, Peri L., and J. Edward Taylor. "A Village Apart." *California Tomorrow*. 5 (Spring-Summer 1990): 9–17.

Fuchs, Laurence H. *The American Kaleidoscope: Race, Ethnicity, and the Civic Culture*. Hanover, N.H.: Wesleyan University Press, 1990.

Gardner, Robert W., Robey Bryant, and Peter C. Smith. "Asian Americans: Growth, Change, and Diversity." *Population Bulletin* 40 (October 1985) Population Reference Bureau, Inc.

Gibson, Margaret A., and John U. Ogbu. *Minority Status and Schooling: A Comparative Study of Immigrant and Involuntary Minorities*. New York: Garland Publishing Company, Inc., 1991.

Gilzow, Douglas F., and Donald A. Ranard. "The Amerasians: A 1990 Update." *In America* 9 (October 1990).

Golini, Antonio. Paper presented at seminar, "Responses of Western Industrial Nations to High Immigration Demand," 24 October 1991. Washington, D.C.: Center for Immigration Studies.

Gonzalez, Berta. "Schools and the Language Minority Parents: An Optimum Solution." *Catalyst for Change: Journal of the National School Development Council.* 16 (Fall 1986): 14–17.

Gordon, Milton. *Assimilation in American Life: The Role of Race, Religion, and National Origins.* New York: Oxford University Press, 1964.

Govan, Reginald C., and William L. Taylor, eds. *One Nation Indivisible: The Civil Rights Challenge for the 1990s.* Report of the Citizens Commission on Civil Rights.

Gozdziak, Elzbieta, and Susan Forbes Martin. *The Refugee Early Employment Project: An Evaluation.* Executive Summary. Refugee Policy Group, August 1989.

Grognet, Allene F. "The Winds of Change in Adult ESL." Keynote address at Virginia Association for Adult and Continuing Education. April 1989.

Guth, Gloria S.A., and Heide Spruck. "Executive Summary: Adult ESL Literacy Programs and Practices." A Report on a National Research Study. San Mateo, Calif.: Aguirre International, May 1992.

Hayakawa, S.I. "Make English Official: One Common Language Makes Our Nation Work." *The Executive Educator* 9 (January 1987): 36, 29.

Hesburgh, Theodore, with Jerry Reedy. *God, Country, Notre Dame.* New York: Doubleday, 1990.

Higham, John. *Strangers in the Land: Patterns of American Nativism 1860–1925.* New Brunswick, N.J.: Ritgers University Press, 1988.

Hirschman, Charles, and Morrison G. Wong. "Immigration, Education, and Asian-Americans." Paper presented at Annual Meeting of the American Sociological Association, Detroit, August 31-September 4, 1983. ERIC Microfiche ED 236091.

"Hispanic America." *American Demographics Desk Reference* (July 1991): 14–15.

Imhoff, Gary. "The Position of U.S. English on Bilingual Education." *Annals of the American Academy of Political and Social Science.* "English Plus" edited by Courtney Cazden (March 1990).

Institute of International Education. *Open Doors: Report on International Educational Exchange,* 1985–86 - 1990–92.

Irwin, Paul M. "National Literacy Act of 1991: Major Provisions of P.L. 102–73." Congressional Research Service, The Library of Congress, 8 November 1991.

James, Daniel. *Illegal Immigration: An Unfolding Crisis.* Lanham, Md.: University Press of America, Inc. (Copublished by arrangement with the Mexico–United States Institute) 1991.

Kane, Parsons, and Associates, Inc. *A Survey of Public Attitudes Toward Refugees and Immigrants: A Report of Findings.* New York: Rockefeller Foundation, April 1984.

Kiang, Peter Nien-Chu. "Southeast Asian Parent Empowerments: The Challenge of

Changing Demographics in Lowell, Massachusetts." Jamaica Plain, Mass.: Massachusetts Association for Bilingual Education, 1990.

Kirschten, Dick. "Speaking English." *National Journal* 4 (17 June 1989): 1556–61.

Kutner, Mark, et al. *Study of ABE/ESL Instructor Training Approaches*. State Profiles Report. Prepared for U.S. Office of Education, Office of Vocational and Adult Education, by Pelavin Associates, February 1991.

Lee, Yongsook. "Koreans in Japan and the United States." In Gibson Margaret A., and John U. Ogbu. *Minority Status and Schooling: A Comparative Study of Immigrant and Involuntary Minorities*. New York: Garland Publishing Company, 1991.

Leon (Florida) County Schools, Department of Adult and Community Education. "Immigration Stress: Families in Crisis." 1989/90.

Levine, Arthur, and Jeanette Cureton. "The Quiet Revolution: Eleven Facts about Multiculturalism and the Curriculum." *Change* (January/February 1992): 25–29.

Lieberman, Janet E., et al. "After Three Years: A Status Report on the International High School at LaGuardia Community College." January 1989. ERIC Microfiche ED 303216.

Lopez-Valadez, Jeanne, ed. *Immigrant Workers and the American Workplace: The Role of Voc Ed. Information Series No. 302*. Columbus, Ohio: National Center for Research in Vocational Education, 1985. ERIC Microfiche ED 260304.

Lyons, James J. "The Past and Future Directions of Federal Bilingual-Education Policy." *Annals, American Association of Political and Social Science* 508 (March 1990): 66–80.

MacDonald, Jeff. "Adult Refugee Education in Portland, Oregon, U.S.A." *Convergence* 23 (3:1990): 71–82.

Marshall, F. Ray, and Leon Bouvier. "Population Change and the Future of Texas." Washington, D.C.: Population Reference Bureau, 1986.

McCarthy, Martha. "The Right to an Education: Illegal Aliens." *Journal of Educational Equity and Leadership* 2 (Summer 1982): 282–87.

McCarthy, Kevin F., and R. Burciaga Valdez. "Current and Future Effects of Mexican Immigration in California." Executive Summary. RAND Corp., November 1985.

Melville, Keith, ed. *Immigration: What We Promised, Where To Draw the Line*. National Issues Forum Series. Dayton, Ohio: Domestic Policy Association; New York: Public Agenda Foundation, 1986. ERIC Microfiche ED 287761.

Minicucci, Catherine, and Laurie Olsen. "Programs for Secondary Limited English Proficient Students: A California Study." Occasional Papers in Bilingual Education.

Mostek, Karlene. "Exploring the Definition of Culture Shock and Second Language Learning in Elementary Schools—Grades 4–8." Paper presented at the Annual Meeting of the Midwest Teachers of English to Speakers of Other Languages, Milwaukee, 17–19 October 1985. ERIC Microfiche ED 270975.

Muller, Thomas, and Thomas J. Espenshade with Donald Manson, et al. *The Fourth Wave: California's Newest Immigrants*. Washington, D.C.: Urban Institute Press, 1985.

"Myth #13: English Is Going Out of Style." *The Literacy Beat*. 4 (August 1990).

Nadelstern, Eric. "The International High School at LaGuardia Community College: Bridging the Gap." Paper presented at the Annual Meeting of Teachers of English to Speakers of Other Languages, Anaheim, Calif., 3–8 March 1986. ERIC Microfiche ED 270983.

National Association of Latino Elected and Appointed Officials Educational Fund. *Legalization's Second Step: The Availability of English/Civics Classes in the Chicago, Houston, Miami and New York City Metropolitan Areas.* Washington, D.C.: NALEO Educational Fund, 1989.

National Adult Education Professional Development Consortium. *The Adult Education Programs Annual Report, Program Year 1990.* Washington, D.C.: NAEPDC, 1992.

National Association of State Boards of Education. *The American Tapestry: Educating a Nation* (undated).

National Center for Education Statistics. "Are Hispanic Dropout Rates Related to Migration?" Issue Brief, NCES 92–098, August 1992.

National Coalition of Advocates for Students. *New Voices: Immigrant Students in U.S. Public Schools.* An NCAS Research and Policy Report, 1988.

"New Faces at School: How Changing Demographics Reshape American Education." Special Supplement, *Education Daily* 24 (18 October 1991).

New York State Education Department. *State Legalization Assistance Grants for Amnesty Education Programs.* Status Report for period 1 October 1989, 30 September 1990, 30 June 1991.

Nielson, Lynn E. "An Evaluation of the United States Government Immigration Materials [and] Investigation of United States Immigration Education Correspondence Courses." Paper presented at the Annual Meeting of the National Council for the Social Studies, Washington, D.C., 16–19 November 1984. ERIC Microfiche ED 253487.

North, David S. "The Missing Tallies in Julian Simon's Work." *Scope*, Center for Immigration Studies, 11 (Summer 1992): 13–15.

———, and Julia V. Taft. "Factors Affecting the Integration of Immigrants and Refugees in the United States." Paper prepared for the OECD Conference on "The Future of Migration" and for the Bureau of International Labor Affairs. U.S. Department of Labor, 13–15 May 1986.

———, and Anna Mary Portz. *The U.S. Alien Legalization Program.* Washington, D.C.: Trans Century Development Associates, June 1989.

Olivas, Michael A. "'Plyler v. Doe.' 'Toll v. Moreno,' and Postsecondary Admissions: Undocumented Adults and 'Enduring Disability.'" *Journal of Law and Education* 15 (Winter 1986): 19–55.

Olsen, Laurie. *Crossing the Schoolhouse Border: Immigrant Students and the California Public Schools.* A California Tomorrow Policy Research Report, 1988. ERIC Microfiche ED 295779.

———, and Carol Dowell. *Bridges: Promising Programs for the Education of Immigrant Children.* California Tomorrow Immigrant Students Project, 1989.

———, and Nina A. Mullen. *Embracing Diversity.* California Tomorrow Immigrant Students Project Research Report, 1990.

Ong, Paul M., Lucie Chang, and Leslie Evans. "Brain Drain Boomerang: The

Migration of Highly Education Asians." *International Education* (Fall 1991): 26–29.

Ontario Ministry of Citizenship. *Access! Task Force on Access to Professions and Trades in Ontario*, 1989.

Orum, Lori S. *The New Immigration Act: What Educators Ought to Know*. National Council of La Raza, March 1987. ERIC Microfiche ED 283633.

Ovando, Carlos J. Review of *Bilingual Education: History, Politics, Theory, and Practice*, by James Crawford. *Harvard Education Review* 60 (August 1990): 341–56.

Ovando, Carlos J., and Virginia Collier. *Bilingual and ESL Classrooms: Teaching in Multicultural Context*. New York: McGraw-Hill, 1985.

Padilla, Amado M., Kathryn J. Lindholm, Andrew Chen, Richard Duran, Kenji Hakuta, Wallace Lambert, and G. Richard Tucker. "The English-Only Movement: Myths, Reality, and Implications for Psychology." *American Psychologist* 46 (February 1991): 120–30.

Passel, Jeffrey S., and Barry Edmonston. *Immigration and Race in the United States: The 20th and 21st Centuries*. PRIP-UI-20. Washington, D.C.: The Urban Institute, January 1992.

———. *Recent Trends in Immigration to the United States*. PRIP-UI-22. Washington, D.C.: The Urban Institute, May 1992.

Patrick, John J. "Immigration in the Curriculum." *Social Education 50 (*March 1986): 172–76.

Pelavin Associates, Inc. *A Revised Analysis of the Supply of Bilingual and ESL Teachers*. Prepared for Division of Elementary, Secondary and Vocational Education; Office of Planning Budget and Evaluation, U.S. Department of Education, September 1991.

Pereira, Carolyn. "The Education of Juan Abdul Tipsuda. A Case Study of the New Immigrant in Chicago." Paper presented at Annual Meeting of the National Council for the Social Studies, November 1984. ERIC Microfiche ED 255436.

Population Crisis Committee. *Population Pressures Abroad and Immigration Pressures at Home*. United States Impact Series. Washington, D.C.: Population Crisis Committee, December 1989.

Porter, Rosalie Pedalino. *Forked Tongue: The Politics of Bilingual Education*. New York: Basic Books, Inc., 1990.

Ranard, Donald A. "The Hmong." *In America: Perspectives on Refugee Resettlement* No. 1 (1988), Center for Applied Linguistics.

———. "From There to Here: Views and Advice from Former Staff." *In America: Perspectives on Refugee Resettlement* No. 5 (August 1989), Center for Applied Linguistics.

———. "Family Literacy: Trends and Practices." *In America: Perspectives on Refugee Resettlement* No. 7 (December 1989), Center for Applied Linguistics.

———, and Douglas F. Gilzow. "Comments on James W. Tollefson's *Alien Winds: The Reeducation of America's Indochinese Refugees* and Elsa Auerbach's Review." *TESOL Quarterly* (Autumn 1990): 529–42.

Ravitch, Diane. "Diversity and Democracy: Multicultural Education in America." *American Educator* (Spring 1990): 16–20, 46–48.

———. *The Great School Wars: A History of the New York City Public Schools*. New York: Basic Books, Inc., 1988.

Riche, Martha F. "We're All Minorities Now." *American Demographics* (October 1991): 26–34.

Rist, Marilee C. "This Immigrant Wave Will Test Your Schools as Never Before." *Executive Educator* 9 (17 January 1987): 14–17.

Rockett, Ian R.H. "American Immigration Policy and Ethnic Selection: An Overview." *Journal of Ethnic Studies* 10 (Winter 1983): 1–26.

Rodriguez, Richard. *Hunger of Memory: The Education of Richard Rodriguez.* Boston: David R. Godine, 1982.

Roop, Connie, and Peter Roop. *The Hmong in America: We Sought Refuge Here.* Appleton, Wis.: League of Women Voters, 1990.

Rossell, Christine H., and J. Michael Ross. "The Social Science Evidence on Bilingual Education." *Journal of Law and Education* 15 (Fall 1986): 385–419.

Rumbaut, Reuben G., "Immigrant Students in California Public Schools: A Summary of Current Knowledge." Report No. 11. Baltimore, Md.: Center for Research on Effective Schooling for Disadvantaged Students, August 1990.

Schieffer, Kevin J. "Mapping the Migration of Talent." *International Education* (Fall 1991): 18–22.

Schlesinger, Arthur M., Jr. *The Disuniting of America: Reflections on a Multicultural Society.* The Largest Agenda Series. Whittle Direct Books, 1991.

School District of LaCrosse (Wisconsin). "Facility Needs Analysis." January 1989.

Simon, Julian. *The Economic Consequences of Immigration.* London: Basil Blackwell, Published in association with the Cato Institute, 1989.

———. "What Immigrants Take From, and Give To, the Public Coffers," *U.S. Immigration Policy and the National Interest.* Appendix D to the Staff Report of the Select Commission on Immigration and Refugee Policy—Papers on Legal Immigration To the United States. Washington, D.C., 30 April 1981.

Simpson, Alan K. "The Politics of U.S. Immigration Reform." *International Migration Review.* 18 (Fall 1984): 486–504.

———. "The Politics of U.S. Immigration Reform." *International Migration Review* 18 (Fall 1984): 486–504.

Skerry, Peter. "Borders and Quotas: Immigration and the Affirmative-Action State." *The Public Interest* (Summer 1989): 86–102.

Snow, Marguerite Ann. *Common Terms in Second Language Education.* Los Angeles: Center for Language Education and Research, University of California, Los Angeles, 1987.

Stein, Barry. "Understanding the Refugee Experience: Foundations for a Better Resettlement System." *Journal of Refugee Resettlement.* 1 (No. 4: 1981).

Stewart, David W. *Adult Learning in America: Eduard Lindeman and His Agenda for Lifelong Education.* Malabar, Fl.: Robert E. Krieger Publishing Co., Inc., 1987.

Sue, Derald Wing. "The Challenge of Multiculturalism: The Road Less Traveled." *American Counselor* (Winter 1992): 6–14.

Swinerton, E. Nelson. *Philippine Higher Education: Toward the Twenty-First Century.* New York: Praeger, 1991.

Terdy, Dennis, and David Spener. *English Language Literacy and Other Requirements of the Amnesty Program.* ERIC National Clearinghouse on Literacy Education, June 1990.

Texas. *Governor's Task Force on Immigration: Final Report.* June 1984.

Texas Education Agency. *A Case Study of the Impact of Students from Mexico upon a Typical Texas Border School District.* February 1977. ERIC Microfiche ED 254382.

Thompson, Frank Victor. *Schooling of the Immigrant.* Montclair, N.J.: Patterson Smith, 1971 (Republished edition edited by William S. Bernard).

Tollefson, James W. *Alien Winds: The Reeducation of America's Indochinese Refugees.* New York: Praeger, 1989.

———. "The Economics and Ideology of Overseas Refugee Education." *Response to Ranard and Gilzow, TESOL Quarterly* (Autumn 1990): 543–554.

U.S. Commission on Civil Rights. *Civil Rights Issues Facing Asian Americans in the 1990s.* February 1992.

U.S. Committee for Refugees. *World Refugee Survey.* 1992.

U.S. Congress. House. Committee on Education and Labor. *Hearing to Review Issues Relating to Immigration and Education.* 100th Cong., 1st sess., Los Angeles, 28 September 1987, Serial No. 100-54. ERIC Microfiche ED 296030.

U.S. Congress. House. *Immigration Reform and Control Act [IRCA].* Hearing before the Committee on Education and Labor. 100th Cong., 2nd sess., Los Angeles, 30 November 1988, Serial No. 100-111.

U.S. Congress. House. Committee on the Judiciary. Subcommittee on Immigration, Refugees, and International Law, Committee on the Judiciary; Immigration Task Force, Committee on Education and Labor. *Immigration Act of 1989 (Part 3).* Joint Hearings on S. 358, H.R. 672, H.R. 2448, H.R. 2646, and H.R. 4165, Immigration Act of 1989. 101st Cong., 2nd sess., 21 February, 1, 7, 13, 14 March 1990. Serial No. 21, Committee on the Judiciary; Serial No. 101-74, Committee on Education and Labor.

U.S. Congress. House. Committee on the Judiciary. *Immigration and Nationality Act (as Amended through January 1, 1989) with Notes and Related Laws.* 101st Cong., 1st sess., 8th edition, April 1989, Serial No. 2.

U.S. Congress. House. Committee on the Judiciary. *Family Unity and Employment Opportunity Act of 1990: Report Together with Dissenting Views to Accompany H.R. 4300.* 101st Cong., 2nd sess., 19 September 1990,. H. Rept. 101-723, pt. 1.

U.S. Congress. House. *Immigration Act of 1990.* Conference Report to accompany S-358. 101st Cong., 2nd sess., 20 October 1990, Report No. 101-955.

U.S. Congress. Senate. Hearing before the Committee on the Judiciary, Subcommittee on Immigration and Refugee Affairs. *Central American Migration to the United States.* 100th Cong., 1st sess., 21 June 1989, Serial No. J-101-26.

U.S. Congress. Senate. Hearing before the Committee on the Judiciary, Subcommittee on Immigration and Refugee Policy. *Immigration Emergency Legislation. Hearing on S. 1725 and S. 1983.* 90th Cong., 1st sess., Miami, 28 October 1983. ERIC Microfiche ED 263267.

U.S. Congress. Senate. Hearing before the Committee on the Judiciary, Subcommittee on Immigration and Refugee Affairs. *Immigration Reform. Hearing on S.358 and S.488.* 101st Cong., 1st sess., 3 March 1989, Serial No. J-101-3.

U.S. Congress. Senate. Hearing before the Committee on the Judiciary, Subcommittee on Immigration and Refugee Affairs. *Implementation of Immigration Reform.* 100th Cong., 2nd sess., 14 April 1988, Serial No. J-100-60.

U.S. Congress. Senate. Hearings before the Committee on the Judiciary, Subcommittee on Immigration and Refugee Affairs. *Legal Immigration Reforms, S.1611.* 100th Cong., 1st sess., 23 October and 11 December 1987, Serial No. J-100-41.

U.S. Congress. Senate. Hearing before the Committee on the Judiciary, Subcommittee on Immigration and Refugee Affairs. *Naturalization Procedures.* 101st Cong., 1st sess., 15 June 1989, Serial No. J-101-23.

U.S. Department of Commerce, Bureau of the Census, Economic and Statistics Division. *Studies in American Fertility,* Current population Reports, Special Studies, Series p-23, No. 176.

U.S. Department of Education, Division of Adult Education and Literacy. Clearinghouse on Adult Education. "Adult Education for People of Limited English Proficiency." Fact Sheet #3. Revised June 1989.

U.S. Department of Education. Division of Adult Education and Literacy. Adult Learning and Literacy Clearinghouse. *Basic Data on Literacy: Definitions and Costs.* January 1990.

U.S. Department of Education. Office for Bilingual Education and Minority Languages Affairs. *Teaching Adults with Limited English Skills.* October 1991.

U.S. Department of Education. Office for Bilingual Education and Minority Languages Affairs. *Final Report: Descriptive Study of the Family English Literacy Program.* 30 September 1991.

U.S. Department of Education. Office for Bilingual Education and Minority Languages Affairs. *Program Profiles Fiscal Year 1991.*

U.S. Department of Education. Office of the Secretary. *The Condition of Bilingual Education in the Nation: A Report to the Congress and the President.* 30 June 1991.

U.S. Department of Education. Office of the Secretary. *Biennial Report to Congress on the Emergency Immigrant Education Program.* 29 June 1992.

U.S. Department of Education. *America 2000: An Education Strategy.* Sourcebook. 18 April 1991.

U.S. Department of Health and Human Services. Family Support Administration, Office of Refugee Resettlement. *The Adaptation of Southeast Asian Refugee Youth: A Comparative Study.*" Final Report, January 1988.

U.S. Department of Health and Human Services. Family Support Administration. Office of Refugee Resettlement. *Refugee Resettlement Program.*" Report to the Congress, 31 January 1989.

U.S. Department of Health and Human Services. Family Support Administration. Office of Refugee Resettlement. *Guidelines for ELT Programs.* MELT Work Group, December 1988.

U.S. Department of Health and Human Services. Social Security Administration. Office of Refugee Resettlement. *Southeast Asian Refugee Self-Sufficiency Study.* Final Report, January 1985.

U.S. Department of Justice. Immigration and Naturalization Service. *Citizenship Education and Naturalization Information.* M-287, 1987.

U.S. Department of Justice, Immigration and Naturalization Service. *Immigration Reform and Control Act: Report on the Legalized Alien Population.* March 1992.

U.S. Department of Justice. Immigration and Naturalization Service. Office of Plans and Analysis. Statistics Division. *Provisional Legalization Application Statistics.* 23 December 1990.

U.S. Department of Justice, Immigration and Naturalization Service, El Paso District Office. "Citizenship Awareness Program."

U.S. Department of Labor. Bureau of International Labor Affairs. *The Effects of Immigration on the U.S. Economy and Labor Market.* Immigration Policy and Research Report 1, 1989.

U.S. General Accounting Office. Program Evaluation and Methodology Division. *Bilingual Education: A New Look at the Research Evidence.* Briefing Report to the Chairman, Committee on Education and Labor, House of Representatives, March 1987 (GAO/PEMD-87-12BR).

U.S. General Accounting Office. Human Resources Division. *Health and Human Services, Funding for State Legalization Impact Assistance Grants Program.* Report to Congressional Requesters, May 1991 (GAO/HRO-91-109).

U.S. General Accounting Office. *Immigrant Education: Information on the Emergency Immigrant Education Act Program.* Report to Congressional Committee, March 1991 (GAO/HRD-91-50).

U.S. General Accounting Office. *Political Asylum Applicants. Financial Effect on Local Services in the Miami Area.* Fact Sheet for the Honorable Bob Graham and the Honorable Connie Mack, U.S. Senate. (GAO/GGD-89-54 FS, February 1989).

U.S. Postal Inspection Service, *Law Enforcement Report* (Summer 1991).

Vargas, Arturo. *Literacy in the Hispanic Community.* National Council of La Raza, July 1988.

Veltman, Calvin. "Modelling the Language Shift Process of Hispanic Immigrants." *International Migration Review* 4 (Winter 1988): 545–62.

Vernez, Georges, and David Ronfeldt. "The Current Situation in Mexican Immigration." *Science* 251 (8 March 1991): 1189–1193.

Vialet, Joyce C., and Larry M. Eig. *Immigration Act of 1990 (P.L. 101-649).* Congressional Research Service, Library of Congress, 14 December 1990.

Waggoner, Dorothy. "Adults with Difficulty in English in the United States in the Eighties." April 1989.

West, Betsy E. "The New Arrivals from Southeast Asia: Getting To Know Them." *Childhood Education* 60 (November-December 1983): 84–89.

Wolfgang, Aaron. "Intercultural Counseling and Nonverbal Behavior." In *Perspectives in Immigrant and Minority Education*, Ronald J. Samuda and Sandra L. Woods, eds. Lanham, Md.: University Press of America, 1983, 210–27.

Wong, Frank F. "Diversity and Community: Right Objectives and Wrong Arguments." *Change* (July/August 1991): 48–54.

Woodrow, Karen A., Jeffrey S. Passel, and Robert Warren. "Recent Immigration to the United States—Legal and Undocumented: Analysis of Data from the June 1986 Current Population Survey." Paper presented at Annual Meeting of the Population Institute of America, Chicago, 29 April–2 May 1987.

Yale-Loehr, Stephen, ed. *Understanding the Immigration Act of 1990.* Washington, D.C: Federal Publications, Inc., 1990.

Yao, Esther Lee. "Working Effectively with Asian Immigrant Parents," *Phi Delta Kappan* (November 1988): 223–25.

Index